RESPONSE

Additional praise for

RESPONSE

The Complete Guide to Profitable Direct Marketing

"Finally, a Direct Marketing book with a benefit headline. It got your attention. Now read the book and find out how you can grab the attention of *your* customers."

> Karen Quinn, Vice President/Direct Marketing
> Education & Development, American Express

"Here's a real world approach to the art of Direct Marketing. This book will be viewed as a milestone work as American industry moves toward 'relationship marketing.' No one has done more than Lois Geller to define Direct Marketing from a practical perspective."

> Jack Clissold, Executive Vice President
> Ford Motor Credit Company

"Each month, over 4,000 women write directly to our company telling us of their positive experiences with Blast, our Sausalito-based women's sportswear company. Lois Geller's direct marketing savvy identified the fact that Blast had transcended a product-only relationship with these consumers. We learned from Lois that brands are defined by consumers, not marketers. Because of her coaching we have embarked on creating a "Have a Blast Club," which will correspond directly to over 500,000 known Blast consumers."

> Tony Marterie, President & CEO
> BLAST

"This is one bright lady, who has built a DM agency that does good stuff. Lois also writes articles that say something and books that say more. This is one of her books, *RESPONSE: The Complete Guide To Profitable Direct Marketing*. This book is a winner! I know . . . I've read it cover to cover."

> "Rocket" Ray Jutkins
> Marketing Consultant

Revised and Expanded

RESPONSE

The Complete Guide to
Profitable Direct Marketing

LOIS K. GELLER

OXFORD
UNIVERSITY PRESS
2002

OXFORD
UNIVERSITY PRESS

Auckland   Bangkok   Buenos Aires   Cape Town
Chennai   Dar es Salaam   Delhi   Hong Kong   Istanbul   Karachi
Kolkata   Kuala Lumpur   Madrid   Melbourne   Mexico City   Mumbai
Nairobi   São Paulo   Shanghai   Singapore   Taipei   Tokyo   Toronto

And an associated company in Berlin

Published by Oxford University Press, Inc.
198 Madison Avenue, New York, New York

Library of Congress Cataloging-in-Publication Data

Geller, Lois K., 1944–
Response : the complete guide to profitable direct marketing / by Lois
K. Geller.— Rev. and expanded ed.
p. cm.
Includes index.
ISBN 0-19-515869-5 (cloth : alk. paper)
1. Direct marketing. I. Title.
HF5415.126 .G45 2002
658.8´4—dc21
2002006543

1 3 5 7 9 8 6 4 2

Printed in the United States on acid-free paper

Credits

We appreciate permission granted to us to reprint the following materials:

Figure

2.2	Ron Dodds, Ford cars
2.3	Ron Dodds, Ford cars
2.4	Brian O'Neil, Lens Express
2.5	Joe England
2.6	Dr. Jan Teitlebaum, Smith-Teitlebaum Chiropractic
2.7	Dr. Jan Teitlebaum, Smith-Teitlebaum Chiropractic
3.1	Peter Canzone, Brylane LP
3.2	Ann Peters, The Statler Brothers
3.3	Brian O'Neil, Lens Express
5.1	Maura Pezzutto: Ontario, Canada Tourism
5.2	Maura Pezzutto: Ontario, Canada Tourism
5.3	Maura Pezzutto: Ontario, Canada Tourism
5.4	Andrea Nemetz: © Copyright 1995 by Girls incorporated. All rights reserved. Reprinted with permission from Girls Incorporated, 30 East 33rd Street, New York, NY 10016.
5.5	Scott Lapkoff: Courtesy of Scott E. Lapkoff, Scott Lawrence Direct Response, 14227 Arctic Avenue, Rockville, MD 20853
5.6	Scott Lapkoff: Courtesy of Scott E. Lapkoff, Scott Lawrence Direct Response, 14227 Arctic Avenue, Rockville, MD 20853
5.7	Scott Lapkoff: Courtesy of Scott E. Lapkoff, Scott Lawrence Direct Response, 14227 Arctic Avenue, Rockville, MD 20853
5.8	Scott Lapkoff: Courtesy of Scott E. Lapkoff, Scott Lawrence Direct Response, 14227 Arctic Avenue, Rockville, MD 20853
6.1	Joe England
6.2	Fergus O'Daly: The Olympic Commemorative Coin program for the 1984 Olympics was handled by Poppe Tyson Advertising as AOR.
6.4	Bernie Lozea, GMG Classics NY
7.1	Steve Leveen, Levenger
7.2	Stephanie Spanos, Pleasant Company
7.3	John Peterman: The J. Peterman Company, Lexington, KY
7.5	Peter Canzone, Brylane LP
7.6	Rich Harney: Used with Permission © Lands' End, Inc.
11.1	Stuart A. Heinecke: Courtesy of Stu Heinecke Creative Services, Inc. Seattle, WA
11.2	Stuart A. Heinecke: Courtesy of Stu Heinecke Creative Services, Inc. Seattle, WA
11.3	Carole Ziter, Sweet Energy
11.4	Carole Ziter, Sweet Energy
11.5	Carole Ziter, Sweet Energy
11.6	Carole Ziter, Sweet Energy
11.7	Susannah G. Smith: Ringling Bros. And Barnum & Bailey Combined Shows, Inc.
13.1	Geoff Wolf, Back in the Saddle, Inc.
13.2	Geoff Wolf, Back in the Saddle, Inc.
14.1	Dan McCormick, PhotographyTips.com
14.2	Peter Cobb, eBags.com
14.3	John Cadoux, Stonyfield Farm
14.6	Steve Boisden, OfficeMax
16.1	Jo Von Tucker: Clambake Celebrations material courtesy of direct marketer, owner
16.2	Jo Von Tucker: Clambake Celebrations material courtesy of direct marketer, owner

Dedication

It is said that if you do one great thing in your life . . . you are a success.

My "great" thing is having my son, Paul Geller. Paul is my teacher. He has taught me more lessons than I can write in an entire book . . . about perpetual optimism and how it energizes people and yourself.

How giving to people is gratifying . . . by itself.

And about how learning is exciting in every stage of life.

His wife Joan teaches us too . . . about balance and minimalism, and true love.

So this new edition is dedicated to them.

Contents

Foreword

I'm going to tell you the secret of Direct Marketing. It's not very complicated, so it's okay if you're busy—it won't take long.

The secret is this:

Do what works.

That's all. Just three words. And it's precisely the opposite of what most marketers do. Marketers want to be original or cutting edge or new or fresh. Direct marketers want to be rich.

I'm unbelievably flattered to be asked by Lois Geller to write the foreword for this new edition. Why? Because she was one of the people who taught me what works. The first edition of this book is on my bookshelf, within reach at all times. I moved five times in four years and this book came with me each time.

The essential thing to understand about Direct Marketing (you always capitalize it, by the way, in homage to Lester Wunderman, who invented the phrase, but that's another story for another day) is that *it doesn't make sense*. Why do long letters work better than short, coupons work better than no coupons, san serif headlines work better than serif? I have no idea. None. It doesn't matter.

What matters is that this is a science. You can test and measure. You can take someone else's results, repeat the test on a similar audience and get a similar result. How cool is that?

Of course, you can't (won't) get anywhere in Direct Marketing unless you know what works. There are two ways to do that, it seems to me. The first is to spend ten years and ten million dollars making a ton of mistakes, and then you'll be a wise and grizzled veteran. The second is to buy this book and steal, steal, steal.

I vote for the second.

Seth Godin
Author
Permission Marketing and
Unleashing the Ideavirus

Acknowledgments

In writing this page of the book, I looked back at the acknowledgements I had made in previous books.

Funny thing—friends, my supporters, stay the same . . .

My Mom, my son Paul and Joan (his wife) are my reason for being and provide the balance for my life.

Andrea Nierenberg is always my dearest friend. And though fame has come to her, she always has time to give me advice, an idea, and a positive thought. Jon Lambert is a real bonus. Michael McCormick is my Creative Director at the agency. He also creatively directs my life; because he is funny and has a quirky way of looking at life . . . that makes everything more interesting. Pepper Huff wandered into the Lois Geller Co. years ago, and has walked by my side through many changes. I cherish his loyalty and friendship. Dwain Jeworski has become a great source of energy, a real leader. Afrodite Boyiantzis, Bruce Wlach, and Lori Holden, all work together to accomplish great work at Mason & Geller—they are a real team. Thank you Charlie Mason for your support. Mary Battista, who typed chapter after chapter *perfectly,* I appreciate your work. And then there are my "super supporters": Renee Harris and Debbie Saccoccio from NYU, Murray Miller and Liz Bieler at American Express, Tom Amoriello from ARGI, and Anne McCall at Fairmont Hotels.

SPECIAL THANKS . . . to Jennifer Praeger, who helped me get the new material for this book in record time and with a twinkle in her eye . . . thought of great case studies and ideas to make *RESPONSE* better. She also fed me protein bars, gum and candy to help me keep focused.

Special Acknowledgment

To Dino Battista

I met Dino seven years ago when he was a Marketing Director at the Free Press, division of Simon & Schuster. He is a rare publishing person, who is actually kind to his authors, follows up with them, and delivers more than he promises. He has become my friend, and I've followed him to Oxford University Press with this new edition of my book.

Introduction

Treating Different Customers Differently

Don Peppers and Martha Rogers, Ph.D.

These days, everyone talks about the virtues of interactive marketing and building long-term relationships with customers by relying on websites, call centers, and bricks-and-clicks integration. We all know there is a compelling case for treating different customers differently and focusing on "share of customer" as a metric of success. We might not agree on all the details, but nevertheless one thing has now become accepted wisdom: Any forward-looking company should by now have deployed, or should at least be engaged in the process of creating and implementing a customer relationship management ("CRM") program of some sort, designed to zero in on the different values and needs of the company's individual customers, one customer at a time. To some of us now, it might seem that this new world of competition was created from the whole cloth of a newly available Internet technology, or that it was simply imagined out of the thin air of entrepreneurial drive and business guru creativity.

If this is how you think about it, then it may come as a shock to read a comprehensive book on the strategy and tactics of Direct Marketing, as written by someone whose credentials as an authority on the subject pre-date the Internet revolution. You will discover in this book that the rules and principles of one-to-one marketing have a time-honored and well-proven ancestry in the direct-mail business. Back when Direct Marketing was virtually synonymous with direct mail, long before the main worry of marketers was the development of broadband Internet access, there were smart, relationship-oriented companies trying to address their customers' individual needs, using conversational-like interactions with compelling, immediate offers. And they were employing mail. Snail mail.

Direct Marketing is a measurable, precise, competitive science—one that serves equally well as a vehicle for experimentation and learning, or for obtaining statistically predictable business results. Because the postal mail is an addressable medium, it can easily facilitate marketing strategies that require treating different customers differently. And because the postal mail has been available for many years to those businesses that sought out such marketing strategies, the science of Direct Marketing is an advanced science. It is not a "new" discipline still being explored and validated.

Moreover, the postal mail is still as vital and useful a tool as it ever has been. More vital, even—not only as a result of advances in information processing technology, but also because the very idea of treating different customers differently has suddenly become even more compelling. If anything, the rapid adoption of Internet technology has fueled an accelerating need for postal mail executions. Customers order catalogues from websites, browse the catalogues, and then go back online to order. Postcards are as likely to drive Web traffic as store traffic. Personalized email offers get printed and taken to the bank or the store or the movie theatre. At one point or another, nearly every company that puts up a website for the benefit of its customers, or prospective customers, must use traditional postal mail to fulfill offers, communicate details, or deliver products.

As companies continue to improve their websites, and as they rely more and more on electronic interactions with their customers to facilitate their marketing, sales, and customer service activities, what they sooner or later realize is that they need a completely different model for understanding the competitive dynamics of their business. Managing a series of ongoing, interactive dialogues with individual customers—treating different customers differently—requires a company to think carefully about its business objectives and strategies in a customer-specific manner. That is, simply by individually differentiating the treatment accorded to customers, a business is inherently acknowledging that its intermediate business objectives should be customer-specific, rather than simply product-specific or program-specific. That is, the business will necessarily have different objectives (and different strategies for achieving those objectives) for different customers.

The strongest, most elemental basis for customer-specific objectives is to focus on the overall value of the customer base. But the overall value of the customer base is nothing more or less complicated than the sum total of the individual customer lifetime values ("LTV's") contained within it. Whenever a company seriously begins to think through the question of what it ought to try to achieve by engaging a customer in a connected series of individual interactions, the most obvious central objective should be to increase the LTV of the customer. The customer, in the end, can be thought of as a financial asset, with a certain predisposition to continue providing profit to the company. The company's objectives for that customer—and by extension, for all its customers—should be simply to increase the value of the asset the customer represents, by getting the customer to buy more and more things, over longer and longer periods of time, in a manner that requires lower and lower servicing costs. But while thinking of customers as individual financial assets with lifetime values might require a total shift in perspective for a traditional business entering the Interactive Age, it wouldn't change a good direct marketer's perspective one iota.

One good look through Lois Geller's newly updated version of her Direct Marketing classic, *RESPONSE*, should easily convince you that the principles of Direct Marketing she documents are in no way outdated by technology. Nor have these principles been overtaken by "modern" marketing thinking. Rather, Geller's rules and suggestions, her tips and tactics, represent the very foundation of what some today would call "interactive marketing," thinking that they were defining a whole new genre.

This is a book of timeless marketing wisdom.

March 2002

Don Peppers and Martha Rogers, Ph.D., Peppers and Rogers Group, Norwalk, CT, have written a series of books on managing customer relationships, including *Enterprise One to One* and *One to One B2B*.

1

How I Got Started

Thank My Lucky Stars

There I was, a single mother, raising a young son. I had a full-time marketing job, running a book club for a New York publishing firm. But there was orthodontic work to pay for, heating bills were piling up, and there was no way around it—I needed extra income. Then one day I walked into Macy's and was window shopping at the jewelry counter. I saw a necklace I just loved. It had seven gold and silver stars hanging from a delicate chain, and I had an idea. If Direct Marketing works so well for publishing, I thought, why wouldn't it work for me?

I asked who the manufacturer of the necklace was. The lovely blond saleslady said she was not allowed to give out that information. The next day I went back to Macy's and asked the brunette saleslady the same question. She went to the stock drawer and came back to me with the name. Lucky for me, it was a local company—just two blocks from my office.

I called the manufacturer and told him I was interested in offering the hanging star necklace through direct mail, and he was delighted to sell them to me. I bought 144 pieces. To give the necklace extra appeal, I created a story around it. I said that from this necklace hung seven lucky stars; one for each day of the week. It was a good story and an appealing product, but I had no money for marketing.

Then I noticed that several magazines I read had new-product columns. I called the magazines and asked how I could get my product mentioned. They told me I needed to send a photo and a press release. I knew I could write the press release, but where to get a photograph? My photographer friend Bob and I made a deal (a signed agreement in fact): he would take the photo, which normally cost $150 for free—but as soon as I made any money from the necklace, I would pay him double his usual fee.

I sent my photo and press release, which included the post office box to which buyers could respond to several magazines. On my lunch break, I made follow-up calls to all the editors. The release and photo ran in *Family Circle*, and within the first week I had 350 orders.

All told, I sold several thousands of necklaces through direct marketing. Bob got paid back many times over, because I still use him in my business today. I made the extra money I needed and more—a lot more. I have never been so excited in my life—not even when I opened my own business—as when I opened the door of that little post office box and checks came pouring out.

That was the first time I realized that the Direct Marketing principles that were working so successfully for big business could work just as well for a small entrepreneur. Through the years, Direct Marketing has grown into a $1.86 trillion business. My conviction that these techniques are appropriate for all types of business has grown with it.

Catch the Luck Yourself

Everyone I know orders through Direct Marketing. Whether it is the contact lenses they get through the mail from Lens Express, or the bouquets they order from 1-800-FLOWERS, the books from Amazon.com, the subscriptions they purchase through *Time* Inc., or the products they buy through the dozens of catalogs they get in the mail or websites they visit.

Friends are always telling me they should have gotten into Direct Marketing before all these great companies became established or when response rates where higher, or when all the great mentors were in the business. To them I say: you can always make excuses. You can always find reasons *not* to take a chance. But if you really want to do this, if you believe in your product or service, there is plenty of room left in this industry, for anyone willing to put in the work and make the commitment. If you want proof, look in your mailbox, go online, turn on the TV, listen to the radio, open up the newspaper. These companies wouldn't be spending close to two trillion dollars on Direct Marketing if it weren't profitable.

Then there are people who say they never respond to Direct Marketing. I say that's fine. With direct mail, usually 98 percent of the people I mail to *don't* respond—and I'm as happy as can be. Why? Because that means 2 percent did respond, and that makes for a very successful program.

After 30 years in the Direct Marketing business, I still get excited every single day as I begin work. I can't think of too many people who can say that about their business. Not every day is perfect, but it is always interesting.

That's why I decided to write this book. I love this industry, and I want it to thrive and flourish. I want companies to expand through Direct Marketing. I want entrepreneurs to grow their businesses into major success stories. I want you who are now reading my book to get excited about this business too, and to apply the concepts you learn here to your own situation with competence and confidence.

Then I want you to tell me about it.

There is a form at the end of the book that you can fill in and let me know how you intend to use Direct Marketing in your work, what questions you have, or any specific challenges in business you are facing. Just place it in an envelope, put a stamp on it, and mail it to me. Or, send me an email at loisgeller@masongeller.com—I'll be delighted to answer any questions.

You see, I'm interested in you and your progress. So, read on, and don't forget to drop me a line. Good luck to you!

Lois K. Geller

2

Why Go Direct?

Every semester for the past twelve years, students have been crowding into a small, overheated classroom at New York University. These are not your ordinary degree-seeking students—these are innovators, inventors, importers, advertising account managers, catalog publishers, entrepreneurs, and small-business owners. They've all come to my class on Direct Marketing to learn what this industry's insiders already know: that Direct Marketing is the fastest growing, most cost-effective method of selling products and services in our country today.

Direct Marketing—a measurable, tested marketing method whereby products or services are offered to a targeted audience and a direct response is solicited—is nearly a $1.9 trillion business. Through 2005, sales are estimated to grow by 9.6 percent annually to reach $2.7 trillion. Every time you receive a subscription letter, fund-raising solicitation, or catalog in the mail, or reply to an advertisement in print, on radio or on television, you are a participant in a Direct Marketing campaign.

The people who come to class at NYU (like the woman who makes children's toys and clothes at home and wants to start a mail order business, and the building contractor whose only previous advertising success has been his ad in the Yellow Pages) don't have billions of dollars to spend. On the other hand, we also have students who are high-level executives at IBM, AT&T, and other large corporations who want to build loyalty among their customers, who want to build name recognition, and who want to venture into new areas of marketing.

This book is addressed to all those students, to small business owners and entrepreneurs, and to marketers at larger companies who want to branch out using Direct Marketing methods—to anyone who would like to get in on the successful strategies and concepts of the Fortune 500. What this book will tell you is how you can use the same Direct Marketing tactics the experts are using—within your own budget.

This book will:

- Provide you with step-by-step, scientifically planned, tested, and proven Direct Marketing tools and techniques that can be used in any type of business;
- Include case studies and illustrations that demonstrate how these tools and techniques have been used successfully by businesses (including examples of direct mail letters, reply envelopes, flyers, coupons, ads, and television and radio campaigns, as well as online programs);
- Describe how these same tactics can be scaled down to fit smaller budgets without losing their impact and effectiveness;
- Feature interviews with industry professionals in all areas of Direct Marketing, including creative directors, computer specialists, copywriters, fulfillment experts, printers, and, most importantly, entrepreneurs, business owners, and marketers who have successfully started and grown their own Direct Marketing enterprises. These stories from experienced professionals will prove the effectiveness of the tips and techniques offered in this book, and will help you understand how to implement these ideas in your own situation.

The Advantages of Direct Marketing

Although it seems as if Direct Marketing is a recent phenomenon, it's been around since the '90s—the 1490s! According to Nat Ross's *A History of Direct Marketing* (published by the Direct Marketing Association), catalogs have been traced back to the Middle Ages, soon after Gutenberg's invention of movable type. The oldest catalog on record was dated 1498, when Aldus Manutius of Venice offered fifteen books he had published by Greek and Latin authors.

The first form of a "customer satisfaction guarantee," a staple of Direct Marketing today, came from none other than Benjamin Franklin, who printed in a catalog (featuring more than 600 books) with the following statement: "Those persons who live remote, by sending their orders and money to said B. Franklin, may depend on the same justice as if present."

It was in 1872 that Aaron Montgomery Ward produced his first catalog, and the era of mail order as we know it was born. It was his idea to purchase large quantities of merchandise and sell this merchandise to farmers through the mail. By 1904, however, Richard Warren Sears and Alvah Curtis Roebuck had taken over as mail order leaders, when their catalog circulation reached over one million. Pioneers in the Old West relied on the Sears & Roebuck catalog for all their needs: clothes, farm equipment, household appliances, toys, dishes, pots and pans. Everything you could think of was available from the one source. Over the years, Direct Marketing expanded from catalogs to include direct mail campaigns, direct response print advertising, TV, radio, and the Internet.

Today, you may have to go to a variety of sources, but you can still buy almost anything through catalogs, personalized mailings, and direct response advertising. Here are just a *few* of the usual—and unusual— items you can now get through Direct Marketing, right from your home (not to mention your home itself, which you can get direct from the real estate cable channel, as well as websites featuring real estate). Some of these items are marketed by huge corporations. Many are from tiny companies that specialize in one type of product or even one single product:

Computers, software, vinyl siding, spices, insurance, septic tank cleaner, CD-ROMs, checks, furniture, food, jewelry, Fruit of the Month, Beer of the Month, Coffee of the Month, Potato of the Month, Vidalia onions, telephone services, credit cards, magazines, *Urology and You Newsletter*, mutual funds, time shares, insurance, books, vacations, music, tea, discontinued silver patterns, hazelnuts, apricots, mattresses, dinosaur bones, exercise equipment, steak, pet products, art, carbide canons (ammunition extra), teddy bears, furniture, gargoyles.

What's obvious from this list is that almost any product can be sold using Direct Marketing techniques. It is the most effective method of making a product or service visible and available to those people who are most likely to buy. Some of the reasons for its effectiveness are:

★ *Measurability*. Carole Ziter, Founder and President of Sweet Energy, a Vermont-based company that specializes in selling apricots, dried fruits, nuts, and chocolates through the mail, started her company out of her home with a $200 expenditure. Now that it's a $2 million business, Ziter says, "I love Direct Marketing because it's such a controllable situation. I wouldn't want to go retail. With Direct Marketing, I know if I put something in the mail, I get a response. If I don't put something in the mail, I don't get a response. I can control my business. Not only that, I can track everything so I know exactly how I'm spending my money."

Direct Marketing is the only form of advertising that is measurable. You know exactly how may responses you get, and where those responses are coming from. That information can be used to make decisions about continuing, expanding, or reworking your marketing plans.

★ *Testing*. The reason that big businesses are so successful with their Direct Marketing is that, as in scientific experimentation, each step is carefully tested, and its results analyzed, before another major step is taken. Large companies like L.L. Bean, Lands' End, and Victoria's Secret test different offer structures (an offer represents the terms under which a specific product or service is promoted, such as a particular price point, a discount, a premium incentive, or sale price). A Lands' End catalog on the East Coast, for instance, might contain one type of offer, and the same catalog on the West Coast have a different offer.

A small business can do tests as well. Many small-business owners and entrepreneurs will send out one letter or place one ad, get a disappointing result and give up. Perhaps if they sent out that same letter with a small change in the copy, they might have gotten great results. If you owned a restaurant, you could send one mailing in which you offered a free glass of wine with dinner. In another mailing, you could give a 10 percent discount on week-night dinners. Then you would continue using whichever offer drew the best response. The most effective methods of getting Direct Marketing to work for you is to create small tests of several versions, calculate which produces the best return, and then do a larger mailing using those results. Using the right tools, it is possible for a business of any size to do low-volume tests that will let them know which tactics have the best potential for success.

★ *Expanding customer base.* Lillian Vernon started out selling a few products from her garage. Banana Republic started out with a few Army & Navy surplus items. Sears Roebuck, Sharper Image, Domestications—there are literally thousands of examples of companies, both retail and mail order, that started out small and grew to amazing proportions through Direct Marketing. You might not expect or experience that kind of growth, but Direct Marketing can be the key to expanding your customer base and increasing your profitability.

★ *Long-term relationships.* As every sales and marketing book will tell you, it's much more expensive to get a new customer than it is to keep an old one. Once you lose communication with a customer, it's very hard to rekindle it. Direct Marketing is the perfect way to establish and maintain long-term customer relationships. I'm much more aware of this phenomenon since I opened my own business. We send out personalized cards to our customers every few months, even if they haven't done business with us in a while. That way, we know they'll keep us in mind if they do need us for a program. And we find that, even if they don't have any immediate business for us, they're constantly referring new customers our way.

Any small business can send out a flyer or postcard every few months announcing a sale, introducing a new product or a new staff member. This technique has been used for years. Recently, I was at an antique show looking through old postcards of New York City. I found one postmarked February 11, 1928 (Figure 2.1). This is an early example of Direct Marketing—Mrs. Fannie Goldberg, from Kirson's store in Waynesboro, Pennsylvania sent a postcard to one of her customers announcing her buying trip to New York City. I guarantee that Mrs. Goldberg's two-cent personalized mailing was as effective as any of today's million-dollar computerized marketing efforts.

Figure 2.1

A personalized Direct Marketing message on a postcard dated February 1928.

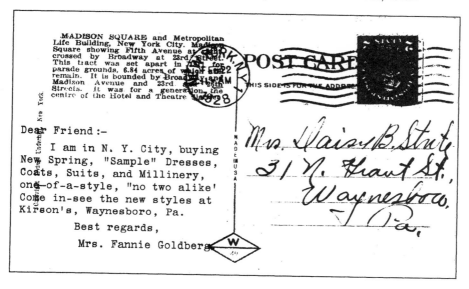

I'm usually a loyal shopper, but if I don't hear from a business for a long time, I start to wonder if they care about me as a customer. I imagine they've gone out of business. I look for a new place to shop. I'd be much more inclined to go in and shop at a store that sent me a personalized note, even one as simple as Mrs. Goldberg's, from time to time. When you work at establishing long-term relationships through Direct Marketing, you find that the money you lay out to keep a customer really pays off in the long run.

Dispelling Direct Marketing Myths

Those of us in Direct Marketing never use the "J" word when referring to the tons of mail we receive offering products and services for sale. We know that some people consider it "junk" and speak disparagingly about Direct Marketing. But that's only because they don't have the facts and figures at hand, nor have they had the more than 25 years of experience in the field that we have. Our experience in Direct Marketing enables us to dispel several myths:

Myth No. 1: "I never respond to Direct Marketing."

People tell me this all the time. They complain about all the "junk" mail they receive and say they simply throw it away. Yet when you actually get into a conversation, they tell you how many gifts they've ordered from catalogs, credit cards they've ordered from a telemarketer, and coupons they've clipped from magazines or newspapers. Or they tell you about a product they just ordered from a television infomercial or from the Internet. The truth is that these are all forms of Direct Marketing, and Direct Marketing is now part of the way we live. In a time when both spouses are usually working, people have less and less time to go out and shop. Almost all consumers use Direct Marketing at one time or another as an alternative to retail shopping.

Myth No. 2: "It's easier to sell retail."

It may seem that way. You put the product in the retail store, and it either sells or it doesn't. But you have no control over that sale. You may not have any input as to how your product is being marketed, where it's positioned in the store, or how long it stays out on the shelf. Another disadvantage is that for retail, all the products have to be manufactured up front. Then, whatever is not sold is returned to you. In Direct Marketing, you can produce the products as you need them. And what happens if the retailer you're dealing with goes out of business? Even if you use Direct Marketing as a secondary means of distributing your product, you have a much stronger base for future sales. If the retailer closes, or no longer wants your product, you'll still have your own direct mail list of customers to whom you can continue to sell.

Myth No. 3: "My advertisement in the local paper does very well. I don't need Direct Marketing."

How do you know that your ad is attracting customers? How do you know how many people came into your store because of the ad, or how many were just passing by, or how many heard of you through a friend? With Direct Marketing, you do know. Send out a mailing, or put an ad in the paper that includes a coupon that says, "Bring this coupon into the store and get a 20 percent discount," and you'll know how many people responded by the number of coupons you receive. You have an immediate method of calculating the results of your marketing dollars.

Myth No. 4: "I tried Direct Marketing and it didn't work for me."

We're back to the concept of testing again (which we'll go into in detail in Chapter 3). It's possible that you may have sent your offer to the wrong people. Or the wrong offer to the right people. There are a number of variables, and just because one try didn't work out, doesn't mean the next one won't. While you are reading this book, you will discover how to choose the right target audience, and you will make them an offer they won't refuse.

A Direct Marketing Success Story

As you read this book, you'll find profiles of Direct Marketing campaigns that were actually, and successfully, used by large and small businesses across the U.S. and Canada. These will illustrate how the tools and techniques described in each chapter work in the real world. To give you an overview of an extremely successful campaign, we'll start with what came to be known as the Ford Women's Campaign.

In 1986 I was working at Vickers & Benson Direct in Canada. Ken Harrigan, who was at the time chairman of Ford of Canada, called about a problem Ford was having getting women into the Ford dealerships across Canada. They had no effective sales training for selling cars to women, and they were losing market share to General Motors, who had implemented a successful training program. Ford of Canada found itself behind the times.

Ford had already tried a few programs, including one offering a cut-glass dish to women who came into the showroom. The women double-parked outside, came in, asked for the dish, and left! So just offering a premium was obviously not the way to go.

Our research showed that most women hated going to car dealerships. Not only were they treated poorly, or completely ignored, but they also felt cars were something they knew nothing about. The funny thing is that, through the same research, we found that men didn't know anything about cars either—they just wouldn't admit it. But buying a car often produced a lot of anxiety for women, who are very cautious car buyers. They do a lot of homework, and often visit several dealerships before making a purchase.

And the Survey Says...

We realized that the way to woo women customers was to begin a dialogue with them, and to continue to talk with them until they were ready to buy a car. Then, at the exact time they were ready to buy, we would invite them to the dealership. But how would we know when they were ready? We asked them. We decided to send out a survey, and we mailed it to 200,000 women across Canada. At the time, there were few lists available in Canada (see Chapter 4 for a full explanation of lists), so we used Canadian subscribers to *Money Magazine* and *Working Woman*, to women who were on investment lists, and to career women. We also mailed to women who had recently made large purchases, such as major appliances and Craftmatic beds.

We asked these women what kind of car they were currently driving, their income level, what they looked for in a new car, and when they next intended to buy. Enclosed was a letter from Ken Harrigan, telling them how interested he was in their response. As a gift for filling out the survey, we offered a book called *Car and Light Truck Buying Made Easier*.

In Direct Marketing, a response rate of 2 percent is considered highly successful. We got about 30 percent. The campaign had worked not only as an information-gathering process, but as the beginning of a relationship-building program. Women sent back the surveys accompanied by pictures of themselves, their families, and their cars, with cards that read, "It was so nice of you to ask. This is what our car looks like." We knew we had a good start, but we now had to translate these results into customers buying cars.

The $200 Hot Buyer Incentive

From the survey, we tabulated and databased three basic pieces of information: customers' names and addresses, the kind of car they currently drove, and when they intended to buy their next car. We divided these into hot, warm, and cold categories. "Hot" meant they would be buying a car within 0 to 3 months, "warm" mean between 3 to 6 months, and "cold" meant 6 months to a year.

We sent the women on the hot list an incentive in the form of a $200 check from Ken Harrigan, to thank them again for filling out the survey (Figure 2.2). We told them to go into the dealership, make the best deal they could with the salesperson, and then hand them the $200 check. We got another great response, and further strengthened our customer

Figure 2.2

Respondents to Ford's Car and Truck Driver's Survey received more than just a letter of thanks—they also received $200 toward the purchase of their next Ford vehicle.

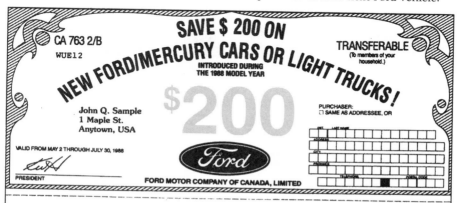

Dear

    Last fall you completed our 1987 Car and Truck Driver's Survey. Thank you again for taking the time to tell us your views on the vehicle you drive now, and what you'd like to see in the cars and trucks of the future.

    You also indicated that you might be considering the purchase of a new vehicle at just this time of year. And that means you'll find the attached $200 certificate handy. You, or any member of your household, may use it toward the purchase of your new Ford or Mercury vehicle.

    I have already notified all Ford and Mercury dealerships in Canada that your certificate is as good as cash toward the purchase of any new and unused Ford or Mercury car or light truck introduced during the 1988 model year. This is a special certificate for you to use in addition to any other available consumer offer from Ford of Canada. Please accept it as my thank you for helping us out with the survey.

    You have $200 that very few others will receive.

(over please)

relationships. Almost 50 percent of the people who received checks wrote us thank you notes. And more than 8 percent of those women actually became Ford car buyers!

Then we had to decide what to do with the warm and cold lists. We knew they weren't quite ready to buy a car, but we didn't want to lose them. So we sent them a newsletter, the Ford *Canadian Driver's News*,

Figure 2.2 (continued)

PLEASE SELECT ONE OF THE OPTIONS LISTED BELOW AND SIGN THE APPROPRIATE CHOICE.

CUSTOMER CASH-BACK FORM
USE THIS SECTION TO OBTAIN PAYMENT DIRECT FROM FORD
I certify that I have taken delivery of the vehicle identified under the terms of Ford of Canada's program. Please issue payment direct to me.

I have read and understand the program rules and provisions and agree to comply with the requirements described therein. I certify that the above customer qualifies for the program rebate. Records supporting the validity of this claim are available in this dealership for examination by Ford of Canada or its authorized representative.

DEALERSHIP ASSIGNMENT FORM
USE THIS SECTION TO ASSIGN PAYMENT TO SELLING DEALER.
I certify that I have taken delivery of the vehicle identified under the terms of Ford of Canada's program.
I hereby assign payment of the Cash-Back Allowance to the selling dealer.

I have read and understand the program rules and provisions and agree to comply with the requirements described therein. I certify that the above customer qualifies for the program rebate. Customer has assigned the rebate to this dealership. Records supporting the validity of this claim are available in this dealership for examination by Ford of Canada or its authorized representative.

DCP CLAIM FORM

Use it to save money! You can apply it any way you like: to your own down payment, to a lease, to an option package, or you may elect to receive a cheque for $200 from Ford of Canada.

It's up to you. All you need do is purchase or lease a new Ford or Mercury car or light truck and take delivery by July 30, 1988 to save your extra $200.

Thank you once again for your responses and the valuable information which we have shared with our corporate engineers and designers.

Sincerely,

Kenneth W. Harrigan
President

P.S.   This $200 is transferable to members of your household so, if you can't use it yourself, feel free to give it as a gift. It's sure to be appreciated.

The editor-in-chief was Lyn St. James, an American race-car driver and garage owner (Figure 2.3). The newsletter contained articles such as "How to Get Your Car Started on a Cold Canadian Day" and "What to Do When You're Stuck on an Ice Patch." This was our way of continu-

Figure 2.3

Ford maintained its relationship with prospective customers through an informative newsletter.

ing our relationship with the women who had responded to our survey until they were ready to buy.

As the months went by, we rotated the database: after three months, we sent the $200 hot buyers' incentive to women who had originally been on the warm list. We did the same thing six months later, when the cold list became hot.

There was another interesting fact that came out of this program. Our own bias had made us think that women were going to be buying Ford Escorts and less expensive cars. We were wrong. A large percentage of them bought trucks and the more expensive cars. So not only did we get a huge response and conversion-to-buy rate, we also sold the most expensive items.

Adapt the Concepts to Fit Your Business

If you're a small to midsize business owner or entrepreneur, you probably won't want to do a 200,000 piece mailing. But you can do a similar program, on a much smaller scale, to bring customers into your store. For instance, suppose you owned a small gift and hobby shop called the Gift Gallery, and you wanted to attract more male customers. You could rent a mailing list of 5,000 names (the usual minimum) of men in your vicinity who were subscribers to various hobby magazines, who belonged to certain clubs or sports teams, or whatever criteria fit your needs. You wouldn't have to mail to all 5,000 names at once, you could send several smaller mailings.

You might want to try a survey the way Ford did. Lens Express, a company that sells contact lenses via Direct Marketing, includes the survey shown in Figure 2.4 when it ships our orders. People love to be asked for their opinion. So you could send a letter or card saying, "We at the Gift Gallery are thinking about expanding our hobby department, and we'd like to know what you look for when you shop for your hobby." You could ask questions like, "What are your present hobbies?" Where do you currently shop for your supplies?" Are there any supplies that are difficult to find?" What items would you like to see our hobby department carry?" Then you could offer an inexpensive premium or a special discount for anyone who filled out the survey form.

To take this one step further, you can break your responses into various categories. Your survey gave you specific information about your

Figure 2.4

Lens Express uses this survey card, included with customers' orders, to continually improve service and keep communication lines open.

Serving You Better!

Your acceptance and comfort with our products and service are of the utmost importance to us. Please take a brief moment to complete the questionnaire below so that we can continue to provide you with the best products and services.

1. How often do you replace your lenses?
   - ❑ 1-2 weeks ❑ 2-4 months
   - ❑ 5-6 months ❑ 7-12 months
2. Was this your first order with Lens Express?
   - ❑ Yes ❑ No
3. Were your contact lenses delivered on time?
   - ❑ Yes ❑ No
4. Did you find our salespeople helpful and courteous?
   - ❑ Yes ❑ No
5. The best benefit you receive by ordering with Lens Express is:
   - ❑ Convenience ❑ Reduced Prices
   - ❑ Fast Service ❑ Other_____

6. Prior to this order, who did you purchase your lenses from?
   - ❑ Doctor ❑ Retail Store
   - ❑ Mail Order ❑ Other_____
7. Will you continue to use Lens Express as your replacement lens service?
   - ❑ Yes ❑ No
8. If not a club member, would you like to become a member of the "Club"?
   - ❑ Yes ❑ No
9. If not already, would you like to enroll in the New 'N Fresh Automatic Replacement Program?
   - ❑ Yes ❑ No

Comments:_____

Return to: Lens Express
350 S.W. 12th Avenue
Deerfield Beach, FL 33442

LENS EXPRESS
America's #1 Vision Care Service

Thank You!

customers' hobbies; therefore you might want to build separate lists such as dollhouse builders, military figurine collectors, and model train buffs. Then, if you were having a sale on dollhouse miniatures, you could send a focused, targeted mailing to the people on the list who fall into that category.

So the responses you get will help you in two ways: first, you'll be able to make more informed decisions about how to stock and market your new hobby department; second, you'll build your mailing list with names of people who have shown a definite interest in what you have to sell. From this list, you can build ongoing relationships. Ford created a newsletter to continue relationships with prospects. Instead of a newsletter, you could send postcards announcing a new product, a special sale for survey responders, or a simple reminder that hobby supplies are now available at the Gift Gallery.

Choosing a Product to Sell

Some people use Direct Marketing to increase sales of a service or product they're already marketing. Others use Direct Marketing to break into sales, and must decide what they want to sell, and to whom.

How do you find a product to sell? Some people who hope they'll make a fortune in direct response seem to think that any product will do. I've had potential clients come to my office and say, "I found a fantastic product at the merchandise show and I think it will sell like hotcakes!" But they don't really know anything about the product. They don't know its value. They don't know who will want to buy it, nor do they know how much competition there is out there.

Joseph England, veteran Direct Marketing entrepreneur and creator of hundreds of successful direct response ads, advises, "If someone has an existing business, they would be smart not to stray too far from home. They know their products, they know their markets, and they may be able to find something special that will appeal to their customers. If a person wants to advertise a product they don't know a lot about, to a market about which they are uncertain…the seeds for disaster are sown."

One of the most profitable direct response campaigns I ever worked on took place at the time of the marriage of Lady Diana and Prince Charles. A very knowledgeable stamp collector had access to some exquisite stamps issued by the Isle of Guernsey, featuring the royal newlyweds. Because this collector knew the value and appeal of these stamps, and knew who the market was, we sold several thousand stamps from small space ads in the back of some consumer and philatelist magazines.

You must know your market thoroughly for a Direct Marketing campaign to succeed. Visualize your target audience. Who is most likely to buy your product? Who, for instance, might buy the Littlest Reindeer pendant, another Joe England creation and a perennial bestseller (Figure 2.5)? This product is a perfect inexpensive stocking stuffer. Use your imagination to create a portrait of an ideal prospect. Make a list of their characteristics. The Littlest Reindeer buyer's portrait might include:

- Young mother with several children
- Middle to low income
- Drives a Ford or a Chevrolet (as opposed to a foreign car)
- Lives in a suburban or rural area

TIP In evaluating a product you're thinking of marketing, ask yourself these questions:

- Is this product unique?
- If it's similar to other products, is it better than they are? More attractive? Higher quality?
- Does it fill a need people have?
- Does it solve a common problem?
- If it doesn't solve a problem or fill a need, is it aesthetically pleasing? Entertaining? Fun?
- Does it have an interesting story behind it? (e.g., "each figurine is hand-painted with authentic Native-American symbols representing spirits of the earth and sky.")
- Is it something I would buy for myself, my friends, or my family?

Once you have completed your first portrait, your next step is to broaden your potential customer base and think about who else might buy your product. For instance, the Littlest Reindeer might also appeal to grandparents, especially since there is a discount offer for buying more

Figure 2.5

Figuring out the ideal prospect for the Littlest Reindeer Pendant helps to determine where to place this direct response ad.

than one. You would keep going with your list until you have exhausted the possibilities of potential buyers for your product.

You can use the survey tactics of Ford and Lens Express, but on a smaller scale. Ask people you know what they think about your product, and how much they might be willing to pay for it. Once you get to know your potential customers, you can design a Direct Marketing campaign directed specifically to them.

The Small-Firm Advantage

It might seem that a company like Ford has all the advantages when it comes to designing and implementing a Direct Marketing campaign. But that's not necessarily true. In large companies, office politics often gets in the way of cohesive marketing plans.

The people who allocate marketing funds disagree over how to spend them; departments fight over specific marketing tactics. There can be turf battles among the people responsible for each marketing function: advertising, promotion, public relations, and Direct Marketing. Each of these specialties has its own purpose and function:

★ Advertising's function is to position a product or company, to build an image that will stay in a customer's mind.

★ Promotion's job is to find unusual ways to get people into your store or to try your product. Promotion includes free sampling, contests, sweepstakes, and point-of-sale programs.

★ Public relations exists to get free exposure for your product. That means getting a story in newspapers or magazines, and/or making a guest appearance on radio and television talk shows. When I worked on the Olympic coin campaign, we arranged to have one of our coins tossed at the Super Bowl. When the announcers talked about the fact than an Olympic coin was being tossed, we got about $2 million worth of free publicity.

★ Direct Marketing's job is to get an immediate order—to get you to go right over to the phone and place an order, or to send in a coupon or order form with your money enclosed.

Each of the marketing specialties has a place in a unified marketing campaign. Yet in large companies, it's often more difficult to get all the interested parties to cooperate. In fact, they often try to compete with each other and end up accomplishing less than the best results.

I truly believe that the small entrepreneur has the best opportunity to put together a cohesive, integrated marketing program. A small business owner with a clear vision can often do a lot more with a small amount of money than many major companies can do with their big budgets and internal political challenges.

Play Up Your Personality

The greatest strength any company has is its own unique personality. Although small companies may do this more easily, Frank Purdue, Orville Redenbacher, and Ben and Jerry work hard to give their large companies small business personalities. Direct Marketing gives you an opportunity to let your customers know exactly who you are, and to build your business on the strength of that image.

When you send out a mailing that represents your company, it's as if you were employing a force of hundreds of salespeople going directly to your customers' homes to sell your product or service. And these salespeople reflect your company's image, whether it's country charm or chic sophistication, strict professionalism or down-home hospitality.

Dr. Jan Teitelbaum and Dr. Siri Smith (a husband and wife team) run a neighborhood chiropractic office in New York City. They are warm, caring people in person, and their mailings (see Figures 2.6 and 2.7) reflect that very well. In December, they sponsor a toy drive for children who are HIV positive or have AIDS. Their mailer focuses on the toy drive, but (because the doctors are smart marketers) it also includes an offer for a free visit for new patients, and some information about pinched nerves.

The doctors do no other advertising. They rely on referrals for their new business, which frequently come as a result of the mailings they do four to six times a year. Dr. Jan (as his patients call him) sends out two types of mailings. The first type is what he calls the "Hello, I'm still alive, informational" mailing. The purpose of this is to educate his patients, and keep his name in patients' minds. The second type is a mailing

Figure 2.6
A direct mailer announces a toy drive and a free visit offer.

**Smith-Teitelbaum
Chiropractic Center, P.C.**

Dr. Jan Teitelbaum
Dr. Siri Smith

140 West 79th Street • New York, NY 10024
(212) 873-6004

CELEBRATE THE HOLIDAYS IN A VERY SPECIAL WAY

Invite your friends and family to join us for our Third Annual

TOY DRIVE
Monday - Saturday December 5th - 10th

All new patients will receive a free first visit (including exam, x-rays and report of x-ray findings) when they bring in a new toy to donate to charity.*

Help us to spread good health and good cheer during the holidays!

*All toys will be donated to Northern Lights, an organization that provides care and support to children who are HIV Positive or have Aids.

Figure 2.7
This mailer also contains information of interest to patients.

Dear Friends,

Thanks to your generosity, last year's toy drive was a terrific success! We met a lot of new friends and collected enough toys to donate to four separate orginizations.

Once again, with your help, we want to spread the message of Chiropractic. At the same time we can make the holidays a little brighter for these special children.

All Our Love,
Drs. Jan & Siri,
Cindy, Leigh
and Jennifer

PINCHED NERVES
May Be The Cause Of Your Health Problems

1. **Headaches,** Migraines, Nervousness and Tension.
2. **Neck Pains,** Torticollis, Bursitis, and arm pains.
3. **Muscular Aches** of upper and middle back, shoulders and arms.
4. **Sciatica,** disc problems and lower back pains.
5. **Sacro-iliac pain** and menstrual problems
6. **Digestive disorders.**
7. **Dance and Sports** injuries

Smith-Teitelbaum Chiropractic Center, P.C.
140 West 79th Street
New York, NY 10024
(212) 873-6004

OFFICE HOURS
Monday, Wednesday, Friday
8:00 AM - 1:00 PM / 3:30 PM - 7:00 PM

Tuesday   Thursday
3:30 PM - 7:00 PM / 3:30 PM - 6:00 PM

Saturday
10:00 AM - 12 NOON

TOY DRIVE
December 5th - 10th

PAIN RELIEF TODAY. . . HEALTH FOR A LIFETIME

which combines a toy or food drive for the needy with a promotional offer. This mailing not only reminds his patients of Dr Jan's services, it reinforces his image as a kind, caring individual—qualities you often look for in a health professional.

Dr. Jan is living proof that Direct Marketing doesn't have to be complicated, ultrasophisticated, or high-tech to be effective. "I keep a folder of flyers and newsletters friends have sent me over the years, and they get recycled. I pick out the ones I like best and try to make mine look like that. We do it right on the computer. In the last year or so, we started doing email newsletters, as well."

Even the actual mailing is done the old-fashioned way. Dr. Jan keeps his 2,000-name mailing list on a computerized program (one designed specifically for chiropractors), but the labels and stamps are attached by hand by the office staff. "Everyone here picks up a pile, takes some home at night, and sticks and stamps," the doctor says.

Dr. Jan feels it's important that his mailings reflect the atmosphere and philosophy of his office. "There are several companies that offer predesigned mailers with four-color graphics I could purchase," he says. "But they're very general, and they're not me. I'd rather do it myself. I do the mailing because I think it's the right thing to do for my patients and for my business. Everyone in the world knows the name Coca-Cola, yet they still have commercials on TV every five minutes. I think repetition is important, especially because chiropractic isn't necessarily part of everyone's natural train of thought. One of my jobs is to disseminate information. That's really why I do this, and I think it works."

With Direct Marketing, no matter what the size of your business, you can form personal relationships with your customers. And in today's impersonal world, making that connection is what will keep customers coming back again and again.

The DM Questionnaire

Since it has been proven that surveys and questionnaires are an effective involvement device, here's one for you. Fill it out before you go on to read the rest of the book. Keep your answers in mind as you read the following chapters; you'll want to add to them as you learn about the specifics of Direct Marketing.

What are some of the offers you've responded to recently in direct mail, magazine or newspaper advertising, or on television offers?

_____

_____

_____

_____

What made you respond to these offers? What was the "closer" that made you go for your checkbook or credit card?

_____

_____

_____

_____

What kind of personality would you like to convey for your business? Sophisticated? Down-home country? Politically concerned? Next-door neighbor? Strictly business?

_____

_____

_____

_____

If you currently have a retail store, how could you put your store in the mail? How could you get the feeling and flair of your store across in a direct mail piece? How could you do it online? For example, would you use humor, your expertise in the industry, the quality of your merchandise?

_____

_____

_____

_____

Visualize your typical customers. Are they male or female? With children? Homeowners? Renters? Income?

_____

_____

_____

_____

What is the main reason your customers buy your product or use your service?

_____

_____

_____

_____

What kind of a test could you run using direct mail you're currently sending? Could you test the offer (e.g., a free sample, or 20 percent off your first order), or how the piece is worded, or the list of people to whom it is sent? If you market online, could you test different offers on your website and in your email communications?

_____

_____

_____

_____

How can you make your current advertising work harder for you? What special offers might attract people into your store or get them to use your services?

_____

_____

_____

_____

If you were to survey your customers to learn more about them, what would you ask?

_____

_____

_____

_____

If you've tried Direct Marketing in the past, how could you improve your ad, your mailing piece or your online presence? What would you do differently now?

_____

_____

_____

_____

3
CHAPTER

Elements of an Effective Offer

Clients come to my office all the time with a new product or service they want to market. "Here's my new Wonderful Widget," they say, "and it's going to sell for $19.95." When I ask them what their offer is going to be, they look at me in surprise. "I don't need an offer," they say. "My Widget stands on its own!"

My answer to that is, "If you're in Direct Marketing, there has to be an offer. Without an offer, it's just retail selling in the mail." The offer, or the terms under which a specific product or service is promoted, answers the customer's question: "What's in it for me?" It is what closes the sale.

Think about it. When customers visit a retail store, they're probably there to make a specific purchase, something they either need or desire at that particular moment. Even if they don't know exactly what they want, they're predisposed to making a purchase. With Direct Marketing, that's not the case. When customers get a Direct Marketing piece in the mail, come across a direct response ad in a magazine or newspaper, or open up an email, they're not automatically in a buying mode. They may not have an immediate need or desire for a Wonderful Widget, no matter how wonderful it is—unless there is some compelling reason, some incentive that will overcome their sitting-at-home-minding-their-own-business inertia and get them to buy immediately.

What Makes a Good Offer?

There are three characteristics to an offer that works. If you want people to sit up and take notice (and take out their credit cards), your offer must have at least one, and preferably all three, of these qualities:

★ Believability
★ Involvement
★ Creativity

Believability

Above all else, your offer has to be believable. If you're selling computer paper, no one will believe an offer that says, "Buy $50 worth of paper and we'll throw in a free computer." We've become a nation of savvy shoppers. We've heard it all, and we won't believe someone (or some company) that tells us we are going to receive something very expensive for FREE. On the other hand, if you're selling computers, and your offer says, "Buy a computer today and we'll throw in $50 worth of paper," we just may take you up on it. Any offer you make has to make sense to the customer. We will accept a 70 percent off sale at the end of the season, because we know stores want to make room for the new spring lines. But if we see a sale of 70 percent off at any other time, we'll wonder what's wrong with the merchandise.

Involvement

As savvy shoppers, most of us suffer from what I call the "glaze-over effect." Some offers are so common, we simply glaze over when we see them. The product or service may evoke a modest amount of interest, but if there is no special reason for a customer to buy, that modest amount of interest can evaporate rapidly. You want your offer to get prospective customers involved, to visualize themselves already using your product or service. Most of the time, an offer of a 10 percent discount is not very exciting. A coupon for $10 off the next purchase is a little more appealing. However, if we see "Buy one and get one at half price," our interest is beginning to get piqued. We immediately start to calculate how much we can save, particularly if the offer is on an expensive item. Once we've started calculating, we're already picturing ourselves as proud owners of not one, but two, Wonderful Widgets.

Creativity

Offers that get the highest response are just a little different. They're involving, but they're also specific to the product or service being offered, and they're human in their approach. Here's an offer that's almost irresistible:

> *The recipe for these brownies has been in our family for one hundred years. For over a century, taste buds (and their owners) have been swooning with delight at just the smell of these delicate delights. Buy one box of these brownies, and we'll throw in Grandma's special recipe for Toll House Cookies with a Twist. You can't find this recipe in any cookbook. We reserve it only as a special gift to our own customers. Enjoy!*

TIP   An exclusive offer is very appealing. If your item is in limited supply, is not available in stores, or exclusive to your company, feature this prominently in your offer.

Offer Options

There are many different types of offers you can make, and many can be combined to make your product or service even more enticing. No matter what type of offer you choose to make, keep the three elements outlined above in mind. Here are some suggestions which you can adapt to fit your unique product or service.

Price Incentives

This is probably the most common, though not always the most effective offer. A price offer means that the customer is going to get some discount off the regular purchase price. There are many ways to use price offers: You can offer a discount of a specific dollar amount ("a $25 value for only $19.95") or a percentage discount ("take 20 percent off the purchase price"). The bright red and yellow cover of the Roaman's

Figure 3.1
A 63 percent discount is a very attractive offer and an effective incentive for Roaman's customers.

catalog in Figure 3.1 screams out "SALE! Savings to 63% on must-have fashions!" The use of the 63 percent, as opposed to the more standard 20 percent, 30 percent, or 50 percent offers, makes the offer more intriguing.

Even price offers need to be inventive. A few years ago I developed a campaign for Marshalls Department Stores to get people interested in their Thanks Account. Customers could save up receipts until they'd reached certain dollar amounts, at which time they were entitled to gift certificates worth 10 percent of the amount they'd purchased. To give the offer an extra lift, we also announced a special Buyers' Sale. We told customers that the buyers for each department had gone shopping in New York City and made great deals on certain items—which we were passing on to our customers, with the *added* 10 percent gift they would get for participating in the Thanks Account. The numerical figure of 10 percent didn't bring in the customers, but the perception of added value (the buyers' special deals) made the campaign a success.

Payment Options

The easier you make it for your customers to buy from you, the better the chances they will. The Direct Marketing industry exploded when credit cards made purchasing even the most expensive items easier. Installment payment plans are always attractive, and can sometimes make a product seem less expensive than it really is. Some offers don't even include the full price of the item. For instance, the order form included in a direct mail package for a book of natural home remedies might state:

> **YES! I'd like to order THE BIG BOOK OF NATURAL HOME REMEDIES for only four installments of $6.99 each plus postage and handling.**

When home shopping networks began offering "easy pay" plans (payments in two or three installments on credit cards), their sales went way up. Other types of payment options might include:

No money down
No interest payments until...
Order now, pay later

"You Have Been Specially Chosen"

Studies have shown that recognition is the number one motivating factor for human beings. We all want to be appreciated, to feel special. If you are marketing a product for fishermen, for example, you're more likely to make a sale by stating, "This is a special offer for those people who enjoy the sport of fishing." Let them know they have been specially selected, because of their interest in this particular sport, to receive this offer.

Another way to make people feel special is to invite them to join an exclusive club. For instance, you might want to offer wine from special vineyards every month. You could rent a list of people who have subscribed to wine magazines, purchased wine books, or frequented wine tasting parties. Your offer might then be:

You are cordially invited to become a charter member of the American Vineyard Society, an organization devoted to the best wines from around the United States. Our board of directors includes owners of some of the country's most highly regarded vineyards, and every month they are going to select the finest wines to offer to you at unbeatable prices. Since you are a lover of fine wines, we are inviting you and a small group of others to become charter members of AVS.

You want your targeted customers to feel that they have been specially selected for the very special honor of spending money for your product.

A third variation on this offer is to recognize your best regular customers and do something special for them. You can form your own club for customers who spend over a certain dollar amount, and offer them specific privileges, such as preview sales and special discounts.

TIP It costs you more to get a new customer than to keep an old one. Doing something to retain your best customers makes smart business sense.

Premiums

A premium is an item usually free or at a nominal fee offered as an incentive to purchase a particular product or service. The magazine industry uses premiums quite often; some of them have been quite popular, such as the *Sports Illustrated* cordless phone, or *Money* magazine's tax guide. In a recent mailing for the Statler Brothers 30th Anniversary Celebration, a simple postcard was mailed out to music lovers with the offer of 62 Statler Brothers hits, PLUS a free Statler Brothers career scrapbook PLUS a free CD or cassette of a Statler Brothers comedy album (Figure 3.2).

A premium need not be expensive, but it must have some perceived value for the customer. The most effective, and usually least expensive premium is free information. If you were offering children's casual clothing, for example, you might also include a free booklet called "Outdoor Activities for Children Ages One to Five." If you're offering vitamins in the mail, you might give your customers a vitamin guide which tells the benefits of each vitamin and its recommended dosages. If you're offering a food product, you might give away an entertainment guide or recipe book. A dry cleaner might offer a small booklet on how to store and hang clothes, and rinse out small stains before they become major problems. This information need not be complicated, nor costly. If you're on a limited budget, even three or four photocopied pages can enhance your offer, as long as the material is seen as valuable to your customers.

When I worked at Meredith Corporation, we offered a series of *Better Homes and Gardens* Recipe Cards for sale. As a premium, we offered the first set of recipe cards free, along with an attractive box in which to store the cards. Usually, we don't want to give away free what we're later trying to sell. The exception to this rule is when you're selling a continuity program (one where many similar items are sold to a customer over time). Once customers received the first set of recipe cards, they wanted to continue to fill the box. Magazines often offer a free issue to entice readers to subscribe. With both the recipe cards and the magazines offers, the premium is an example of what they will later receive.

The premium you offer should be related to your product or service. Offering a free tax guide along with recipe cards, for instance, doesn't make sense, nor does it enhance the product in any way. A few years ago, Club Med sent potential customers a letter saying, "Your next vacation should offer sunny days, dazzling beaches, round-the-clock fun and great holiday pictures." They then offered a free Olympus 35mm color flash camera to vacationers who booked their trips by a certain

Figure 3.2

Two free premiums gave added value to this Statler Brothers direct mail offer.

Dear Friend,

It's here! Brand new and hot off the press!

The 30th Anniversary Celebration box set from The Statler Brothers, the best-loved group in the history of country music.

It's got everything: Their 62 greatest hits on 3-CD's or 3-Cassettes plus The Statlers' career scrapbook with 52 rare photographs. And there's more!

If you order now, you will also receive a FREE CD or Cassette of *The Complete Lester "Roadhog" Moran & The Cadillac Cowboys,* The Statler Brothers' hilarious comedy album.

To order by credit card, just call 1-800-434-2344. $34.95 for 3 Cassettes, $49.95 for 3 CD's. Please add $3.95 for shipping and handling.

This is a great offer...The Statlers' greatest hits, their career scrapbook and the *"Roadhog"* comedy album. Why not order now before this postcard goes astray?

Call now...toll-free!

1-800-434-2344

Or send check or money order to the address below.

The Statler Brothers
Mercury Nashville Records
P.O. Box 8873, Red Bank, NJ
07701

Presorted
First Class Mail
U.S. Postage Paid
West Caldwell, N.J.
Permit 67

You will also receive the complete list of all available Statler Brothers' Cassettes and CD's.

date. Vacations and photographs are a natural tie-in, so the Club Med offer and premium were a perfect match.

Of course, you have to factor in the cost of the premium when you calculate your costs per mailing and potential profit. If your Wonderful Widget makes you a profit of $5 for each sale, offering a premium that costs you $10 is obviously not the way to go. If, however, you offer a premium that costs you $1, but increases your sales by 20 percent, you have increased your overall profit.

If you're a manufacturer, you can make premiums yourself. But most people purchase gift items in bulk in order to get the best price. To find out what kinds of premiums are available and how much they cost, you can attend premium and incentive shows, which are held in major cities at least once a year. There are companies devoted to premiums and incentives, which you can usually find in the Yellow Pages or online. These companies also advertise frequently in Direct Marketing industry publications such as *Target Marketing* and *DM News*.

Always keep your eyes open for gift ideas. If you see something you like in a store, find out who the manufacturer is, and call them directly. Tell them you are considering using the item as a premium (which means you want to buy in bulk) and ask for the best price they can give you.

Samples

There are some products that are difficult to describe. When Post-its were invented by Art Fry, they were a big hit around the 3M offices where he worked. For over ten years, the company tried various advertising campaigns, but the product just didn't take off. Then someone decided that if people would only try the product, they'd love it. So 3M sent out samples to the secretaries of the CEOs of Fortune 500 companies. The samples were accompanied by a letter signed by the secretary of the CEO of 3M. Almost immediately, Post-its became an office staple.

Recently, my office took on a client who's trying to market a new shaving cream. It's a terrific product, but its advantage over other brands are hard to describe. Yet everyone who's tried the product loves it. So we decided the best way to launch this particular product was to allow people to send away for free samples. We took out small ads in *The New York Times* and *The Wall Street Journal*, booked some inexpensive radio time to talk about the benefits of the product, and gave people an address to write to for their samples. Once they sent for a sample, we had their name and address on file, and could follow up with a direct mail offer.

Anything that appeals to one of the five senses is a good candidate for sampling. Cosmetics and perfume manufacturers do this all the time. Walk into a department store or open any magazine, and you get the "scents" of what they're offering. Food products may be delicious, but are often indescribable; therefore restaurants, catering halls, and gourmet catalogs can use sampling to good effect. If you were opening a new restaurant, and wanted to introduce yourself to the community, you might participate in a street fair, where you could give away bite-size samples of some of your featured dishes.

If you're providing a service, rather than selling a product, you can still use the free sample concept. You might offer potential customers a free consultation or evaluation. I had a student in one of my classes at New York University whose business was to go into hospitals and update their bookkeeping and budgeting procedures. She was having difficulty getting new clients, because resistance to change is so high. I suggested that she offer potential clients a free evaluation of their current system, so that even if they didn't end up hiring her, they would have gained something of value for their time spent. Of course, once people spent the time with her, witnessed her expertise, and listened to her suggestions, many of them hired her and her business picked up dramatically.

Free Trial

There are any number of ways to say, "If you don't like what you've bought, send it back." One of the best ways to turn this into a positive statement is to state it as a 30-day (or 60-day or 90-day) free trial period. The free trial offer has a fun aspect to it; it makes us think we can take the product home, try it out, play with it, enjoy it, and then if we don't like it, we can always return it. Of course, chances are we won't return it. Return rates for Direct Marketing are very small. According to the 2002 Direct Marketing Association's State of the Catalog/Interactive Industry Report, only slightly higher than 5 percent of cataloguers' shipments are returned for credit (this figure is higher for clothing items). Even if we're not absolutely sure we want to keep an item, it's often easier to keep it than to repack it and take it to the post office or shipping facility.

Some companies make it easy to return items—they give you pre-addressed labels and forms to fill out. Other times it's not so easy. I recently responded to an offer for a trial subscription to a magazine, (that also came with a free gift). The offer was that if I didn't like the magazine, I could cancel the subscription after the first issue, and keep the gift. I didn't like the magazine. But when I got the bill for the subscription, there were boxes to mark as to how I wanted to pay for it, but nowhere to indicate I wanted to cancel. My only option was to write a note on the form saying I didn't want the magazine after all. The point of the free trial is not to be underhanded or try to trick people, of course. The point is that your product will stand up to scrutiny, and that after trying it out, customers will be more than happy to accept your offer.

Automatic Shipment, Negative Option Offers

Most book and record clubs run on negative option offers. This means that they keep sending out merchandise until you tell them differently. Once you send in the initial order, you will be shipped two books every four weeks, until you cancel the membership.

We associate this type of offer most often with publishing companies; however, it could be an effective offer for any company that sells products that get "used up" regularly, such as disposable contact lenses, diaper products, pet food and pet products, and pantyhose. If your product is one that people order over and over again, you might want to consider this option.

Member Get a Member

In all likelihood, your best customers know other people who could use your product. Therefore, one effective method of getting new customers is by offering your regular customers gift or dollar incentives to introduce others to your product or service. Lens Express offers customers credits toward a free pair of contact lenses if they bring in other paying customers (Figure 3.3). Probably the most well-known example of this was MCI's

Figure 3.3
Lens Express uses a Member Get a Member offer to get the names and addresses of prospective customers.

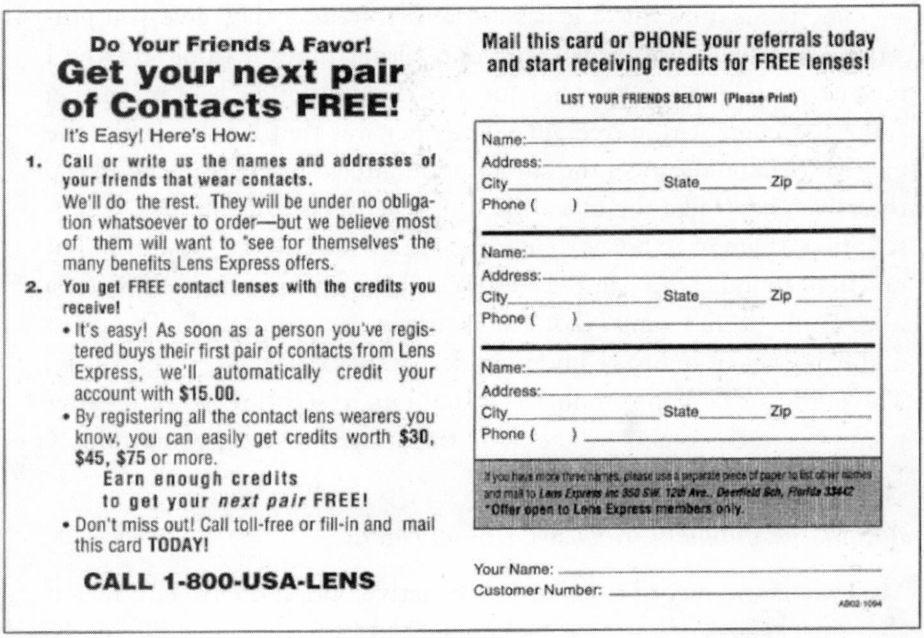
Do Your Friends A Favor!

Get your next pair of Contacts FREE!

It's Easy! Here's How:

1. **Call or write us the names and addresses of your friends that wear contacts.**
   We'll do the rest. They will be under no obligation whatsoever to order—but we believe most of them will want to "see for themselves" the many benefits Lens Express offers.
2. **You get FREE contact lenses with the credits you receive!**
   - It's easy! As soon as a person you've registered buys their first pair of contacts from Lens Express, we'll automatically credit your account with **$15.00.**
   - By registering all the contact lens wearers you know, you can easily get credits worth **$30, $45, $75** or more.
     Earn enough credits to get your *next pair* FREE!
   - Don't miss out! Call toll-free or fill-in and mail this card **TODAY!**

CALL 1-800-USA-LENS

Mail this card or PHONE your referrals today and start receiving credits for FREE lenses!

LIST YOUR FRIENDS BELOW! (Please Print)

Name:
Address:
City State Zip
Phone ( )

Name:
Address:
City State Zip
Phone ( )

Name:
Address:
City State Zip
Phone ( )

If you have more three names, please use a separate piece of paper to list other names and mail to *Lens Express inc 350 SW. 12th Ave., Deerfield Bch, Florida 33442*
*Offer open to Lens Express members only.

Your Name:
Customer Number:

A802-1094

Friends and Family program, where customers got a discount for every member they brought into their calling circle. AOL offers members $25 when they refer a friend and that person then signs on for the service.

Early Bird Offers

The gist of this offer is that if you buy before the deadline, you will pay a special low price. Restaurants use early bird offers all the time to bring in customers during what would normally be off hours. Seminars and conferences almost always use early bird offers. If you register before a particular date, the fee is often far less than if you wait and pay later. If

> TIP **The early-bird offer is known as a "call to action." It gets people to make an immediate decision and then act on it. It can be an effective incentive, and can be used for any type of product or service.**

you have a product or service that is seasonal in nature, you can often increase profits during your slow time by offering discounted rates during a limited time period.

Contests and Sweepstakes

Everybody loves the chance of winning. And the perception—usually not necessarily true—is that if you buy something, you have a better chance of winning. Many people have purchased magazine subscriptions with the added hope of winning the publishers' sweepstakes. Skill tests can be fun as well. Kodak has had great results with photo contests. If you have a food product, you could run a recipe contest. Some companies create contests where people have to qualify to enter: answer a trivia question, fill out a crossword puzzle, or solve an anagram. Once you get people involved with you in these kinds of contests, they're almost certain to consider buying from you.

You must be sure, however, that any contest or sweepstakes meets with Federal Trade Commission standards. Check with your lawyer before sending out any contest mailings. Also be sure that your prizes are in line with your product or service. If you're offering a serious product, such as a professional tax guide for accountants, a trip to Disneyland may not be a compelling incentive to enter. However, a trip to Harvard Business School for a special professional seminar could be received better by your target audience.

Multiple Discount Offers

Customers who spend a lot of money with you want to know that they are getting special treatment. One bonus that you can offer is a discount on volume purchases. This can mean that if you order one item at $19.95, you can get a second for $14.95; or that you can get one for $19.95 or three for $54; or it can mean you get free shipping and handling if your order is over a certain dollar amount.

Multiple Product Offer

Remember the old Ginsu knife ads? One reason they were so effective is that they kept compounding the offer until it became almost irresistible.

First, the offer was one knife for $19.95. Then they said they would throw in an additional knife for the same price. This was followed by two more knives, and not only that, it was followed by six more knives . . . The offer just kept getting better and better. If you can group related products under one price, you can often entice customers to go for the whole package.

Of course, you don't want to diminish the value of your product by adding on too many products. You do want to sweeten the deal as much as possible to increase your response rate. Ginsu knives were probably inexpensive to produce, so the company could afford to offer several of them. Ginsu knives also work—they *can* cut through cans as well as tomatoes. Once customers used the knives, they would probably be responsive to other offers from the same company. So the seemingly outrageous offer for the Ginsu knives was used to get as many people as possible to respond, thereby building a mailing list (database) for future sales.

Direct response television ads or infomercials are most successful using multiple product offers because they're trying to capture the undecided buyers before the commercial ends. Print offers usually contain only one or two add-ons.

Deluxe Edition

In this type of offer, you make your regular product available at a specific price, and then you also offer a "deluxe" edition, or enhanced version, of the product at a slightly higher cost. For example, if you're selling a hardcover book, you may offer it at $29.95. In the same direct mail piece you might also offer a leather-bound copy with etched lettering on the cover for $49.95. Or if you're selling a box of Valentine chocolates for $9.95, you might offer the deluxe box, with 20 percent more chocolates and a keepsake bracelet, for $16.95. Once you've got customers filling out your order form, it's not such a great leap to go for the special edition.

Bounce-back

Studies have shown that the customers who have bought from you most recently are the most likely to purchase from you again. These customers, usually those who have purchased from you within the last six months, are known as "hotline" buyers. If you were renting a company's mailing list, you would pay a premium for the hotline buyers because they have the greater propensity to purchase again.

Once a customer has bought something from you, you want to make another offer right away. The easiest, least expensive way to do that is with the bounce-back offer. So you would include another offer to the customer, along with the product that's already ordered. For instance, if I order name and address labels from a catalog, chances are when I get my order I'll find an offer for more name and address labels, along with offers for related items such as stationery or stamp dispensers. The shipping and handling (which the customer has paid for) has been taken care of, so essentially you're mailing a new offer for free.

The Money-Back Guarantee

According to the Federal Trade Commission, a guarantee or warranty is an oral or written promise by a manufacturer or retailer that they will stand behind a product or service. A guarantee is not required by law, but this is an offer that should be included in every Direct Marketing campaign. Although this a common offer, and suffers from the glaze-over effect, people still have the need to be reassured that if they make a mistake in ordering, they have the option to change their minds. One way to counter the glaze-over effect is to make the offer tangible—send a real guarantee certificate. When I worked on the Olympic coin campaign, we sent each recipient an 8"x10" paper certificate, ornately designed, with our guarantee printed on it. Although the guarantee was perfectly good without the certificate, it made people feel more secure about their purchase decision.

Including a guarantee establishes credibility for your company. If you do include a guarantee or warranty, I suggest you visit www.ftc.gov to be sure you follow the guidelines established by the Federal Trade Commission.

TIP   There are times when people are not quite ready to buy, even though they like your product and your offer. One way to take advantage of this indecision is to include a check-off box option that reads: "I'm not interested in accepting your offer at this time, but please keep me on your list." If people take the time to fill in the order blank and send it back to you, it's a good indication they will be future buyers.

Testing: The Ultimate Opinion Poll

With such a wealth of alternatives, how do you know which offer you should use? Which will draw a better response for you, a discounted price or a free trial? A premium or a sweepstakes? The best way to find out would be to take a poll, to ask each of your customers and potential customers which offer would make them buy. Since that's not a very efficient method of gathering this information, your alternative is to try one offer, try another, and yet another until you find one that works best for you.

Testing is an integral part of Direct Marketing. When large companies test, they use charts and probability tables to track the return percentage of each offer. If you have that in-house capability, you may want to do the same. However, even businesses with limited mailing lists and databases can make testing simpler and more efficient by following these procedures:

- *Test only one feature at a time.* In other words, you can change the offer, and you can change the package, but not at the same time. If you were to change more than one element, you wouldn't know which change buyers were responding to. Test like against like—test an offer of a discounted price against a free trial offer, for example.

- *Code your tests so you can measure results.* Each version of a promotion must have its own code so that you will know exactly which ones garner the best responses. Suppose you run the same direct response ad in two different magazines. For testing purposes, the only difference should be the code printed on the coupon, so that when you receive the orders you'll know which magazine delivered more buyers.

- *Keep accurate records.* Coding doesn't mean anything if you don't keep track of the results. In the example above, if you receive 500 responses from magazine A, and 75 from magazine B (assuming they both cost the same and have similar circulation), you would obviously choose to continue advertising in magazine A. If your offer of 20 percent off draws twice as many responses as your offer of a free egg timer, you'll want to discontinue offering the premium. So whether you tally responses in a computerized database or write them in a ledger book, be sure to keep an accurate count of which tests produced the best results.

- *Analyze test results and take action.* When the testing is completed ask yourself this simple question: "What did we learn from this test?" If you have kept accurate records, your testing should clearly indicate the actions you need to take to capitalize on those results. If your 20 percent discount is producing the greatest responses, that is the offer that should be repeated.

Checklist

DOES YOUR OFFER HAVE
- ☑ Believability
- ☑ Involvement
- ☑ Creativity

HAVE YOU TRIED THESE OFFER OPTIONS
- ☑ Price incentives
- ☑ Payment options
- ☑ "You have been specially chosen"
- ☑ Premiums
- ☑ Samples
- ☑ Free trial
- ☑ Automatic shipping, or negative option
- ☑ Member get a member
- ☑ Early bird
- ☑ Contests and sweepstakes
- ☑ Multiple discounts
- ☑ Multiple products
- ☑ Deluxe edition
- ☑ Bounce-back
- ☑ Money-back guarantee

WHEN TESTING, DID YOU
- ☑ Test only one feature at a time
- ☑ Code your testing to measure results
- ☑ Keep accurate records
- ☑ Analyze test results and take action

4

Identifying Your Customers

Suppose you created a brilliantly written, beautifully designed direct mail campaign for Fabulous Fakery, costume jewelry that looks so much like the real thing it could sit in Tiffany's picture window. You have an irresistible offer. Now all you need is to get this direct mail package into the right hands.

Some Direct Marketing specialists say that 40 percent of the success of a campaign comes from marketing to the right list of names. That percentage can be even higher. If you send your offer of Fabulous Fakery to fishermen, for example, you won't get much of a response. So sending your mailing to the right lists of people can be the most important element of your Direct Marketing effort.

Many marketers make the mistake of waiting until all the other steps in creating a campaign are completed before they start to think about exactly whom they will be mailing to. Choosing your potential customers first can influence decisions about your product or products and the design of your entire campaign, enabling you to target a select group of people who are ready, willing, and able to buy what you have to sell.

The way to get your message into the hands of targeted prospects is through your mailing list. According to the Direct Marketing Association, a mailing list is made up of names and addresses of individuals and/or companies who share a common specific interest, characteristic, or activity. There are three basic types of mailing lists: the in-house list, the compiled list, and the direct response list.

An in-house list, usually called a house file, is most often comprised of your own customers—people who have bought from you (or made inquiries about your products or services) before. These are the people most likely to buy from you again. If you could generate enough business from mailing repeatedly to these same customers, you wouldn't need any other lists. However, due to natural attrition rates, all lists shrink in time. Some people will move away. Some people won't need your products anymore—if you're selling children's clothes, for instance, and the children have grown. Some people won't want your products anymore. People go through buying phases, and their buying habits change as their lives do. Some unhappy customers may move over to your competitor. There are hundreds of reasons your house file might shrink. Therefore, to keep your business going and growing, you need to look outside your own customers for more prospects, or potential buyers.

You could try to put together such a list yourself, but it would be extremely difficult and time-consuming. The most efficient way to gather a usable list of prospects is to rent one. There are thousands of such lists available for rent, divided into the two major categories of compiled and direct response lists.

Compiled Lists

A compiled list is made up of names and addresses—derived from telephone books, business and association directories, newspapers, public records, and car and voter registrations—of people who have one basic interest or characteristic in common. Those interests or characteristics might include geographical area, a particular occupation, an alma mater, purchase of a particular brand of automobile, or membership in an association. Some examples of compiled lists might be: all pediatricians in the United States; all people living in zip code 90210; all families with children attending school in the state of Connecticut.

Many business-to-business marketers use compiled lists. For instance, if you were marketing a service or product for dentists, you might want to mail to every dentist who has opened a practice within the last year. A compiled list will give you those names. For a book offer, you might want to mail to all high schools and libraries in a particular geographical area.

While compiled lists are less expensive than direct response lists, and are good for gathering large quantities of names, they're not always the best lists for gathering large responses. There's no way of telling if the people on a compiled list have ever responded to Direct Marketing offers—and those are the people you're trying to reach.

Direct Response Lists

A direct response list is made up of people who have previously purchased items through Direct Marketing from some company other than your own. Essentially, these are other people's house lists. The people on these lists were solicited to buy something through direct mail or direct response advertising, and they responded. Direct response lists generally perform much better than compiled lists, because people who have a track record of buying through the mail are the most likely to make such a purchase again.

How to Choose a List

Doug Flynn, President of Flynn Direct Response with offices in the United States and Canada, and one of the country's leading authorities on mailing lists, suggests that if you wanted to choose *the* list that would garner you more customers than any other, the one you would choose would be your own. If you wanted to expand your customer base, the next best list would be your direct competitor's. However, in many cases your direct competitor will not rent you their list. Therefore, you'll have to go to the third best list—people with similar characteristics to the ones you presently have in your own customer file. In other words, customers who come as close as possible to your own buyers.

The first requirement before looking for such a list is that you know your own customer in as much detail as possible. Are your customers of both genders, or do you sell more to one than the other? Do they own homes? Cars? What is their age range? Their income level? You may need to take the time to find out who your typical customer is. Conduct a survey if necessary. Call your customers, or write them a letter explaining that you're trying to improve your service and would like to know more about them. Or send them a postcard, similar to the Lens Express survey card in Chapter 2.

Besides asking them facts about themselves, you might want to ask what kinds of things they presently buy in the mail, besides your merchandise. For instance, if you sell women's apparel, and you discover most of your customers also buy linens and bedding though the mail, you might want to rent lists from companies who sell those particular items. You might also ask your customers about their general interest. If it turns out that a number of your customer are skiers, for instance, you might want to rent lists from companies who sell sporting equipment through the mail, as well as those who offer winter vacation packages.

Creative List Planning

Sometimes it pays to be creative when you're looking for new customers. If you're selling cameras, you might immediately consider lists from companies who sell film and film processing through direct mail. But these companies will also have been considered by everyone else selling photographic equipment, so the competition is likely to be high and the people on these lists are probably getting several mailings similar to yours.

One of the hidden benefits of creating a list plan is that it forces you to analyze your customer base. What do your customers have in common besides the fact that they purchase photographic equipment? If you let your mind go and try a little free association, and allow yourself to be creative and playful, you might come up with some unusual—but effective—sources for new prospects. Subscribers to *Photography* magazine would be an obvious choice. But what about subscribers to *National Geographic*, a magazine known for its high-quality photos? People who read that magazine are interested in exotic locales, probably travel a lot, and probably buy cameras. And since cameras are related to the visual arts, you might also focus in on people who buy prints and artwork through the mail, or who have ordered from museum catalogs.

What you're trying to do is build a bridge between your product and someone else's when there's nothing obviously similar about them. A campaign for the Nintendo Power Club was targeted to the obvious— young boys interested in computer games. But marketing surveys revealed that grown men also enjoy Nintendo products, and subscribers to *Field & Stream* turned out to be an effective list. When Club Med was looking to expand its customer base, it had to look beyond the obvious as well. Lists that came from sports clubs, health-oriented magazines, and sport equipment catalogs were moderately successful. But one of the lists that produced the best results was to people who had ordered chocolates and expensive candies through the mail, because these were people who indulged themselves—something they had in common with Club Med vacationers.

To flesh out your customer profile, it often helps to think of a specific individual who matches your customer target. A few years ago, I worked on a campaign for Old Fort Williams, a historical site in Canada. Our original focus was families with young children, who made up a large segment of the Fort's visitors. Then I began to think about who else likes to visit historical sites, and I pictured an old friend of mine, a single gentleman, who often visited similar places. I thought about what else he liked to do, and remembered that he was an avid biker. So we created a very successful campaign targeted to hikers and bikers.

Using a List Broker

Considering the huge number of lists from which to choose, making a decision can be very difficult. That's why list brokers are a valuable asset to the Direct Marketing industry. A list broker is a specialist whose business is to match Direct Marketers with list owners. A list broker will make recommendations to you based on information you supply about your product or service and your typical customers. Once you've decided which lists are best for you, the broker will then order the list from a list manager or list owner.

Choose your list broker carefully. Ask other direct mailers you know whom they use. Call your local chapter of the Direct Marketing Association for recommendations. Comparison-shop between two or three different brokers. Ask each broker for client references you can call, and ask each to submit proposals to you on what lists they would recommend. Most will be willing to do that for you.

Look over the proposals and make sure the selections make sense to you. You want to know why the broker has suggested these particular lists. If you're offering a pet newsletter, for instance, a broker will probably suggest lists of pet-supply buyers and lists of subscribers to pet-oriented magazines. You might also find a suggestion for a list of new-home buyers. When you ask why, the broker may tell you that, through his experience, he's found that new-home buyers often buy pets as well. An experienced list broker, with knowledge of the thousands of available lists and what has worked well for companies similar to yours, can be invaluable in helping you find and target prospects.

You may not want to use any list brokers your competitors are using, because you might end up with a list plan that is too similar to theirs. Every list broker can find out who has been using a list and what the past usage was, and using a different broker might be a way to give you a fresh look at the market. On the other hand, that list broker now has experience researching products similar to yours, so a lot of the testing has already been done. You might want to come right out and ask them, "Since you've worked for my competitor, how would your strategy be different from theirs? How would it be similar?"

Once you've decided on a broker, he or she will send you list cards for each company recommended (these used to be printed on actual cards; now they're usually on 8" x 10" sheets of paper). Figure 4.1 is a typical list card you might receive (this one is for a fictional company called Acme Coin Collectors) which contains the following pieces of information:

1. *Number of buyers and cost per thousand*: This tells you how many names are under a particular category, usually divided into years or months (i.e., people who bought during the last year, the last quarter, the last month), and how much it costs, per thousand names, to rent this list. Typical base costs for renting a list range from $75 to $125 per thousand names. Hotline buyers are the ones who bought most recently, and there is generally an added charge for these names, because it has been proven that people who have *just* purchased something have a propensity to buy again.

2. *Description of buyers*: Here you are provided with general information about the products this company sells, sometimes including a short description of their typical customers.

3. *Restrictions*: Mailing list owners who care about their customers often set rules about who can and cannot rent their lists. They

Figure 4.1
A typical mailing list data card.

ACME Coin Collectors

1	123,455 **2001-2003 Buyers** $100.00M 51,648 **Last 12 Month Buyers** +10.00M 26,839 **Last 6 Months Hotline** +10.00M	**11/02** **7** ---------------------- ***AVG Unit of Sale*** **8** $80.00
2	Direct Response purchasers of United States coins ranging from Mercury dimes to Susan B. Anthony dollars. High quality proof sets. Respondents have above average income. Average age is 40+	---------------------- ***GENDER*** 73% Male **9** 27% Female (Selectable)
3	**Restrictions:** No direct competition; no contests or sweepstakes; no telemarketing	---------------------- ***ADDRESSING*** 4-Up Cheshire P/S Labels $5.00M 9T 1600/6250 BPI **10** $25.00 Flat fee Non-refundable
4	**Source:** Direct Mail & Space	---------------------- ***KEY CODING*** $1.50M **11** Up to 6 Digits
5	**Selections:** State, Zip Code, Multi-buyers, Gender, $5.00M; Hotline Buyers $10.00M	---------------------- ***MINIMUM ORDER*** 5,000 **12**
6	**Notes:** **1.** Cancellation of order after mail date will require payment in full. **2.** Cancellation prior to mail date will require a $100.00 flat fee plus any applicable running and shipping costs.	---------------------- ***NET NAME*** 85% + $5.00M Running Charge **13** 5,000 Minimum ---------------------- ***UPDATE SCHEDULE*** **14** Bi-Annually ---------------------- ***REQUIREMENTS*** Sample Mailing **15** Piece Required For all orders

want to make sure their customers do not get offered products that are not the same quality as their own. Many companies don't rent to their direct competitors. Some companies don't want their customers inundated with contest or sweepstakes offers, or solicited by telemarketers. If a list card specifically states no telemarketers, the company won't supply you with phone numbers and you are not allowed to purchase the names and then look up corresponding phone numbers. However, there are companies that will rent you lists which include phone numbers.

Lists are rented for one-time-only usage. You can't rent a list and continue to use these names over and over for your mailings. Companies always include "decoys" on their list—people who are on the list to check that the mailing they receive is the one you represented to the company prior to renting the list, and that they receive only one mailing from you per rented list.

4. *Source*: One of the things you want to know before you rent a list is where the company got these names. Acme Coin Collectors' list came from people who either purchased directly from a catalog or mailer that was sent to them, or responded to a direct response advertisement in a newspaper or magazine (also called a space ad). Some cards also include people who purchased from the Internet. People who have a history of responding to direct mail are likely to respond to other direct mail offers, so they are usually a better choice than people who have responded to space ads.

5. *Selections*: These are the categories from which you can choose in order to focus on your target audience. You may be interested in a particular geographical area, which you can narrow down into zip codes. You may also be interested in knowing when customers last bought, and how many times they made purchases from the company. Buyers who have ordered frequently from the company are called multi-buyers. For instance, out of the 123,455 2001–2003 buyers names available, you may be interested only in male hotline buyers in the state of California. You pay an additional fee for each selection you choose. The base cost of this list is $100 per thousand names. If you want a list of male hotline buyers from California, it will cost you $120 per thousand, or $20 over the base cost ($5 per thousand for selecting a particular state, $5 for selecting the gender, and $10 for selecting hotline buyers).

6. *Notes*: There are rules about canceling your order. When you rent a list, you must tell the company when you plan to do your mailing. If you rent the list and, after your planned mail date, decide

not to go ahead, you must pay for the whole price anyway. If you cancel your mailing prior to your planned date, you must pay a cancellation fee plus a computer running charge.

7. *Date:* This tells you when this list card was compiled. This is important, because you want to rent lists that include the most recent buyers. So if it's now February of 2003, and this list card was compiled in November of 2002, you want to get a later update.

8. *Average unit of sale:* It's also important for you to know how much the typical Acme Coin Collectors customer spends on an order. If your typical customer spends only $20 per order, this list may be too upscale for you. If your typical customer spends $120 per order, Acme Coin is probably offering lower end merchandise than yours.

TIP   When choosing a mailing list, you want to find prospective customers who can afford your products, so you want to look for a unit sale that is equal to or above your own.

---

9. *Gender:* Most of Acme's customers are men. If you wish, you can choose to mail to only one gender or the other. If your customers are also mostly men, you might choose to mail to Acme's male population. If most of your customers are women, you may not want to use this list.

10. *Addressing:* This tells you the types of labels available. Cheshire labels are printed out on ordinary computer paper and then mechanically glued onto mailing envelopes. P/S stands for pressure-sensitive, or peel-off, labels, which are self-adhesive and can be removed from the envelope and attached to an order blank or card. "9T 1600/6250 BPI" represents the format used for a list stored on magnetic tape, which will cost you a $25 nonrefundable flat fee. Using magnetic tape allows you to personalize direct mail letters at the same time you're printing the labels. If you're going to be using a lettershop to do your mailing, consult with them to find out which format is best for you to use.

11. *Key coding*: If you want each label to contain an identifying code to let you know it came from the Acme list, it will cost you an additional $1.50 per thousand.

12. *Minimum order*: Most direct response lists have a 5,000 name minimum.

13. *Net name*: This is a discount arrangement for large-volume orders (usually a minimum of 50,000 names). Suppose you rent 10 different lists from companies engaged in selling to a special-interest group, such as gardeners. There are bound to be duplications on these lists. You would then go through a process called merge/purge to remove those duplications. The net name arrangement allows you to pay only for the names you use (with a minimum of 85 percent), plus a running charge.

14. *Update schedule*: If you are interested in buying hotline names, you need to know just how "hot" they are. Lists can be updated annually, biannually, quarterly, or monthly. Acme's list is updated biannually. So if you were looking for lists in May, and you know that Acme updates its list in June, you might want to wait the extra month to get their most recent buyers.

15. *Requirements*: Most companies ask to see a sample of your mailing piece before they will agree to rent you their list. If you don't have your mailer printed yet, you can send them a simulated version which includes the written copy and an artist's rendering of how the finished piece will look. You'll also be required to let them know your intended mailing date. This is so that list owners and brokers are not renting lists to companies with similar products who want to mail at the same time.

There is one other thing you should ask your list broker before you make your final decision: Who has used the list in the past? If a company's list proved to be successful for a product or service similar to yours, it will probably be successful for you as well. Recently, we were asked to do a direct mail campaign for a CD/tape offer. Through a list broker, we located several lists that had been successfully tested and rolled out by other music companies, including Columbia House and BMG (companies usually test a list by renting only a portion of the list first; then, if the test is successful, they do a rollout, which is a large-scale mailing to the bulk of the names on the list). Since the people on these lists had a history of responding to this kind of offer, we knew they were likely to respond again. The high response rate our campaign received showed us to be correct in this assumption.

You don't have to use a list broker; you can usually rent a list directly from a company or an association itself. You can find out what lists are available by going to the library and researching *Standard Rate and Data Direct Mail Lists*. If you're renting only a few lists, this might be the simplest way to do it. However, lists brokers get a commission from the list owner, which means that, although you send your money to the list broker (who then pays the list owner), you are not paying anything for the broker's services. So going directly to the list owner doesn't save you any money, and if you're looking at multiple lists, an experienced broker can help you make effective choices and track down any problems should something go amiss. They'll keep track of when your list needs to arrive at the lettershop (a company equipped with machines necessary for inserting, addressing, postage application, and sorting of mail for delivery to the post office), make sure you're billed properly, and oversee the running of the whole operation.

List Maintenance and Computer Service Bureaus

The link between renting your lists and sending your mailing out through a lettershop is most often a computer service bureau. These are companies that build and maintain databases. Service bureaus can perform a variety of functions. Some specialize in one or two, and others are full-service houses. According to Hank Garcia, Executive Vice President of Automated Resources Group Inc., a New Jersey-based computer service bureau, those who specialize in Direct Marketing applications perform four main functions:

1. *List maintenance*: When you're developing a database, your names may come from many different sources. The first function of the

service is to standardize the lists—to make sure that all the names are in the same format so that separate lists can be merged into one large database.

2. *List preparation*: Suppose you've rented lists from 10 different companies. John Doe, of 1400 Lilly Lane, Columbus, Ohio, may be on four or five of those lists. The service bureau will perform a merge/purge operation, which eliminates duplicates from the various lists.

Merge/purge operations are done democratically, so that all testing can be analyzed on an equal basis. For instance, suppose you are testing five lists. Four of those lists consist of 5,000 names each, and the last one contains 10,000 names. If you were to take all the duplicates out of the first two lists, you might end up with two lists of 2,000 names, two lists of 5,000 names, and one list of 10,000 names. That would skew the testing results. Therefore some duplicates are taken off the first list, some off the second, some off the third, and so on, to keep the lists as close to the same size as possible.

3. *Validating address information*: The service bureau will then run the database through software developed by the post office called the Certified Accuracy Support System, which validates that the names on the list are being sent to deliverable addresses.

4. *Postal sortation*: The post office requires that large volumes of mail be sorted into various categories, such as nine-digit zip codes and carrier routes. The more categories into which you can sort the mail, the bigger the discount you get on your postage costs.

Once a database has been prepared for mailing, the next step is to generate output either on Cheshire or pressure-sensitive labels, or magnetic tape to be sent on to the lettershop.

Your list broker will usually be able to recommend a service bureau to you, or you can contact your local branch of the Direct Marketing Association. The best way to look for a service bureau, as with any vendor, is to talk to other people who use their services. Go out and inspect the facilities if possible. Is it well organized? Most of the errors that are made in service bureau functions are made by humans, not by the computer systems. So if the facilities are sloppy and disorganized, the work is likely to be that way too.

Service bureau charges are always based on a unit cost per thousand, with a minimum charge. Costs can run anywhere from $10 to $40 per thousand, with minimums of $50 to $100, depending on what particular services you want the bureau to perform.

Large companies such as American Express often have their own in-house computer service bureaus, which means they do their own list maintenance, address validation, and postal sortation. Sometimes they actually get so good at this end of the business that they start taking outside companies' work as well. Some companies have their own in-house facilities, and use computer service bureaus as well. However, it's difficult even for these large companies to rely on their own in-house facilities because the technology is changing so rapidly. An in-house facility can't always respond to these changes as quickly as a computer service bureau can. There comes a time when a company that is dong large mailings (millions of pieces at a time) has to make a cost comparison between creating an in-house facility or using an outside service.

Target Your Ideal Prospects with Database Marketing

The technical advances in computerizing mailing lists have fostered the growth of what is known as database marketing. Database marketing is a refinement of your house file and your prospect lists that allows you to customize your marketing efforts to those people who are most likely to buy your products.

The more specific the profile of your prospective customer, the more effective your mailing can be. Large companies often use computerized methods of discovering specifics about their existing customers. They use a system known as data appending, or overlay. For instance, the Marshalls Thanks Account described in the previous chapter offered a 10 percent discount to people who came into the store and spent over a certain dollar amount. The customers supplied the store with their name, address, and phone number. But that's all the information Marshalls had about this group of approximately 200,000 customers. So they sent their list to a computer service bureau, which did what is known as an overlay from huge compiled databases, and added information contained in those lists.

An overlay, or enhancement, of a database compares the names on your database with the names on the compiled list. There are several companies that offer such compiled lists, including Equifax, Experian, InfoUSA, Dun & Bradstreet Corporation and TRW. When the computer finds a match, the additional information found on the compiled list is added to the information you already have about the customer.

For instance, before they added the enhancements, Marshalls knew that their customer, Barbara Smith, who lived at One Main Street, had bought $200 worth of merchandise with her Thanks Account. After the overlay, they also knew Barbara Smith's annual income, and that she owned her own home, had two cars and three children. One purpose of this type of file enhancement is to be able to offer your customers specific products of interest to them. Once Marshalls was able to identify Barbara Smith as a mother of three, for instance, they could then be sure to include her in their direct mail campaign announcing an upcoming sale in the children's department.

Another purpose of doing an overlay is that it helps you build a profile of exactly who your customers are. Once you have that model, you can then look at lists which have customers who are most similar to yours.

In an article called "Closing the Loop," in *Catalog Age* magazine (February 1995), author Kathleen Kiley noted that, "Now, with new types of data technology using more powerful computers and sophisticated statistical techniques, [marketers] can key in on smaller and smaller niches—with the ultimate goals of marketing to the individual." Large companies use their database information to segment their own customer lists, so that they can target particular products to specific segments of their lists.

Database segmentation helped save independent grocer, Green Hills Farms in Syracuse, New York. When two major competitors opened up within five miles of the relatively small supermarket, management determined to use its information-rich customer database to focus on its Most Valuable Customers (MVCs). First, customers were ranked according to their profitability and then by the department they most frequently patronized. In doing so, management was able to tailor their products to better service MVCs and ultimately to increase retention. Retention efforts began with a personalized thank you letter including a coupon for a free gift basket, redeemable at the store. Later on, management wanted to re-connect with lapsed MVCs. However, it was quickly learned that the grocer's best customers hadn't lapsed but instead had simply left for Florida to escape the cold Syracuse winter. Management responded by offering products to their customers that were hard to find in Florida. Green Hills Farms' results speak for themselves: retention among MVCs exceeded 95 percent year after year, and 80 percent for all customers. Rather than succumbing to its larger rivals, the company netted $18 million in 2001.

Enhancing your list can be an expensive proposition. "However," says Hank Garcia of ARGI, "you end up with a much more targeted list. Therefore your response rate is higher, which makes it worth paying that extra money. After all, a marketer's main objective is to mail less and get a better response."

Prioritize Your List with RFM

A small or midsize business may not need to include such extensive—and expensive—information in the database. But there is some important information you should be able to gather from your own house list: Who are your best customers? When devising your own database, you should be able to pull out that information, which is usually determined by these three factors: recency, frequency, and monetary.

★ *Recency* answers the question: When was the last time this customer ordered from you? Last month? Six months ago? Last year? You want to know who your own hotline buyers are.

★ *Frequency* refers to the number of times this customer has ordered from you within a specified period of time. What is the average number of purchases the customer made during the past quarter, or the past year?

★ *Monetary* means the total dollar value from a customer within a given period, generally 12 months.

TIP   In business, there is what is called the "80/20 rule." That means that 20 percent of your customers bring you 80 percent of your business. Keeping track of your customers' RFM ratings will let you know exactly who these 20 percent are. They are your best customers, and should be treated as such.

When Your Business Grows...Consider a Database, Think CRM

In the simplest sense, a database is a kind of list that includes information from a variety of sources. The *Dictionary of Marketing Terms* defines a database as, "A collection of data stored on a computer storage medium in a common pool for access on an as-needed basis."

When I go to my dry cleaner, they know that I like my button down cotton shirts hanging with no starch because that's what I told them, and they put that information in their database. They also have my address, so they know where to deliver my things and they have my credit card on file and charge my dry cleaning each time I bring it in.

A database enables a company to organize customers into smaller groups that have similar demographics, buying behaviors, lifestyles. Any information that has been entered for customers in a database can be broken out. These elements help identify specific customer groups with similar attributes, so products, promotions, offers, and service can be targeted. They allow us to be more attuned to the customer and prospective customer's needs.

Databases become important when volume and details increase to such a degree that an organization can no longer personally keep track of what their customers are doing. In addition, these systems can also give marketers a powerful new way to communicate with existing customers and find more customers just like them.

The most important element is the accuracy of the data. That's what is meant by GIGO—or "Garbage In–Garbage Out." Even the most sophisticated "rich in features" applications can't give you accurate knowledge from inaccurate data.

Five years ago, we'd get these huge reports and it would literally take weeks to decipher the information. Now, in today's dynamic environment, data management has evolved to such a degree that you can get a really clear snapshot of what's going on, which allows you to react faster in the marketplace, with better and more targeted approaches.

For example, if you see that your direct mail programs are bringing in higher value customers, you can afford to offer higher value premiums. Or, if you have a product that has automatic shipment, and you see that customers who come in through your TV ads are dropping out of the program faster than other customers, you can put these customers on a customer retention program (offer them more incentive to stay), to try and hold on to them.

This kind of marketing intelligence is of enormous value and it's driven by something called CRM (Customer Relationship Management). The convergence of all information—profile data, behavior, transaction history—allows an organization new capabilities in terms of managing relationships. According to Alex Amoriello, President of ARGI, the result is, "You really see the 'DNA' of each customer. It's all in a common format: it's single, complete and eminently useful."

Checklist

BEFORE YOU CHOOSE YOUR LISTS

☑ Do you know your own customers? Have you found out about their:
  √ Gender
  √ Age
  √ Income
  √ Home ownership
  √ Type of car
  √ Number of children
  √ Level of Education
  √ General interests
  √ What types of items they presently buy through the mail

☑ Is a compiled list suitable to your purposes?

☑ Is a direct response list suitable to your purposes?

HAVE YOU TRIED CREATIVE LIST PLANNING

☑ What do your customers have in common besides the fact that they purchase your product?

☑ Envision your customers as real people, not just buyers

☑ Try free association and playful brainstorming

WHEN CHOOSING A LIST BROKER, DID YOU

☑ Ask other direct marketers whom they use

☑ Call your local chapter of the Direct Marketing Association

☑ Ask the list broker for references

☑ Ask each broker to submit a list proposal

WHEN YOU CHOOSE A LIST

☑ Do you know the important components of the list cards?
  ✓ Numbers of buyers and cost per thousand
  ✓ Description of buyers
  ✓ Restrictions
  ✓ Source
  ✓ Selections
  ✓ Policy regarding cancellation of orders
  ✓ Date the list was compiled
  ✓ Average unit of sale
  ✓ Gender of buyers
  ✓ Addressing or types of output available
  ✓ Key coding
  ✓ Minimum order
  ✓ Net name discounts
  ✓ Update schedule
  ✓ Requirements (sample and date you are mailing)

☑ Do you know who else is using the list? Who has used it successfully in the past?

COMPUTER SERVICE BUREAUS

☑ Four main functions for Direct Marketing:
  ✓ List maintenance and standardization
  ✓ List preparation and merge/purge
  ✓ Validating address information
  ✓ Postal sortation

☑ Output generation:
  ✓ Cheshire labels
  ✓ Pressure-sensitive labels
  ✓ Magnetic tapes

DATABASE MARKETING

☑ Two purposes of data appending:
  ✓ To segment your own customer list so that you can target focused mailings
  ✓ To build a model of your present customers so that you can target prospects who are most similar to your own buyers

☑ A Direct Marketer's main objective: to mail less and get a better response

☑ Prioritize your list using RFM:
  ✓ Recency
  ✓ Frequency
  ✓ Monetary

☑ Database and CRM

5
CHAPTER

Creative Techniques for
Successful Direct Mail Packages

I t's time for a survey. Keep track of your mail for one week. Then fill in
the number of pieces of each type of mail you received:

_____ Personal cards and letters
_____ Bills
_____ Magazines
_____ Catalogs
_____ Direct mail offers

Unless you picked a week that included your birthday or a major
holiday, it's a safe bet that your week's mail contained more catalogs
and direct mail packages than any other category. And chances are you're
responding to more and more of these direct mail offers. In fact, according to the Direct Marketing Association, in 2001 over 60 percent of the
adult U.S. population are Direct Marketing consumers, a number that is
growing every year.

The Direct Mail Advantage

Those marketers who know so well that direct mail works, also know its
downside: the cost. Direct mail is relatively expensive. In fact, it can

cost up to 15 or 20 times more to reach a person with a direct mail package than it does to reach him with a television commercial or a full-page ad in a newspaper.

Why then is direct mail chosen so often as an advertising medium? Because of its overriding advantages, which include:

- *Immediacy*: With direct mail, you're reaching prospect with the immediacy of a personalized letter. There is a certain "open me now" urgency to many a letter we receive in the mail, even if we know it's a solicitation—especially if the envelope grabs our attention (for instance, "Dated material, open immediately," or "Here is the information you requested," or You may have already won 10 million dollars!). Other forms of Direct Marketing have to work hard to produce the sense of immediacy inherent in direct mail.
- *Qualified prospects*: In sales, there are two kinds of prospects, or potential customers: qualified and unqualified. An unqualified prospect is someone you advertise to or call upon at random. A qualified prospect is someone who is known to have an interest in and the ability to purchase your product. A qualified prospect results in a sale five times more often than an unqualified prospect.

  In direct mail, you are going right to the people who have the highest likelihood of buying from you. When you place an ad in a newspaper or magazine, or on TV or radio, there's no way of knowing exactly who is reading, watching, or listening, Anyone can pick up a magazine or turn on the TV. But with direct mail, you know who's receiving your message, because you sent it directly to them! You can practice pinpoint marketing (for instance, you can send to families who have children between the ages of one and four, or to men who have purchased a car within the last six months). Your direct mail recipients have been carefully chosen (through list selection) to match your criteria; therefore they are qualified prospects and much more likely to buy from you.
- *Testability*: Since you have chosen specific lists of people to receive your mailing, you know exactly who is responding to you. If you send out different versions of your direct mail packages, you can determine exactly how many responses each one has produced, and use this information to determine your next actions. You can

test one mailing list against another, or one offer against another, and you can accurately measure the results. No other form of advertising or marketing gives you as much information or is as valuable in helping you plan future marketing strategies.

- *Repeat customers*: People who buy through the mail do so over and over again. Also, people who've purchased from you before, whether in your store on on your website are more likely to respond to your direct mail promotion. People who respond to direct mail often develop a loyalty to that product or company, and are more likely to become repeat customers than those who respond to commercials or print advertising.
- *Creative license*: There are times and space limitations involved in both the broadcast and print media that do not affect direct mail. You're not limited by a 60-second time allowance, or paying by the square inch. You can determine how long you want your message to be. You can print it on plain paper, or use another medium (e.g., cardboard, felt, balloons, a block of wood, a photograph, a CD). You can make it large or small, plain or fancy. You're limited only by your budget and your imagination.
- *Expandability*. If you've ever sent out applications for college, or resumes for a job, you know that direct mail campaigns can be managed from the smallest home office or marketing department. You can, quickly and inexpensively, send out a hundred letters tomorrow telling people about your product or service. As time goes on, and your budget increases, you can increase your mailings accordingly.

Your goal in putting together a direct mail package is to get your envelope opened, your letter read, and your product or service sold. The successful direct mail pieces described in this chapter will give you an idea of what works, and why. Some are elaborate, some are not. Some were costly to produce; others were done on a modest budget. But they have in common one or all of the elements of a typical direct mail package:

The outer envelope
The letter
The brochure
The order form
The business reply card or envelope

The Outer Envelope

There is no federal mandate that says an envelope has to be rectangular, or white, or must have the stamp in the upper right-hand corner and the address in the middle. Of course, the government does have certain regulations about how mail is to be sent. For instance, if you mail anything other than a standard size envelope you will be subject to a nonstandard surcharge. An envelope must be at least 3 1/2" x 5" to be mailed. The largest envelope that fits into the standard size category is 6 1/8" x 11 1/2." The minimum thickness must be .007 of an inch.

Mail is also divided into classes. First class is used for business and personal mail; second class is used for periodicals; third class is used for direct mail advertising; and fourth class is used for parcels. You can get a complete description of all postal regulations at www.usps.com. You can also ask your local post office for a free copy of the U.S. Postal Service publication *Third Class Mail Preparation*. As you will see, many of the post office guidelines are rather loose—which means you have a lot more leeway than you think when designing the outer envelope.

The outer envelope is often the most ignored part of the direct mail package. Even professional marketers or art directors tend to focus on the letter, the brochure, and the order form; the envelope is often treated like a third-class citizen (pun intended).

But in direct mail, the envelope can make or break your sale. Your envelope is the customer's first impression of your company and your product. It's been my experience, in my more than 25 years in the business, that an interesting, unusual envelope can increase a response rate by one percent or more. In direct mail terms, that constitutes an unqualified success!

Creating an Impression

Here are several ways you can get your envelope noticed—and opened:

- *USE BOLD HEADLINES!!!* Thousands of envelopes are sent every day with the phrase "Special offer. See inside," printed on the front. We've all seen it before, and we know the offer's not so special. Into the circular file it goes. Be brave! Be Bold! Why not say instead, "If you throw this letter away without opening it, you'll be missing something really special!" Or, if you've included a discount offer or a small gift, say so on the envelope. If your gift is a package of seeds, for example, you could say, "Inside this envelope is a beautiful bouquet of wildflowers, just for you!"

- *Amuse people.* Which would you open first, an envelope that read, "$20 coupon inside" or an envelope that says "Open this envelope and save yourself a fortune! Okay, maybe not a fortune, but isn't $20 good enough?" The other day, I received a letter addressed to "Cody Boy Geller"—my cat. It made me smile, and I opened the letter, which was from a new veterinarian in the area. Not every product or service lends itself to the humorous approach, but if you can add a lighter touch, you'll probably get better results.

- *Be a tease.* Asking a question is a great way to tease people into opening the envelope to find the answer. Some examples of teasers are: "Want to know where the 10-pound bass are biting this year? See inside." "Are you doing everything you can to ensure your child's safety?" "Can you ever be too rich or too thin? Wouldn't you like to find out?"

- *Be visually engaging.* Print graphics on both sides of the envelope. Use vibrant colors for the printing, or for the envelope itself. Draw a cartoon that starts on the front and continues on the back. Change the shape of the envelope—square, triangular, octagonal. Add a sticker or a die-cut piece of cardboard that can be moved from the envelope to the order form.

- *Use a live stamp.* If you're doing a major mailing, you may be thinking of using third-class bulk mail, with an indicia you print on the envelope after paying the post office or the mailing house. An indicia is an inked envelope marking substitute for a stamp. However, for some recipients, that automatically puts your letter into an undesirable category. Instead, check with your post office or mailing house about the possibility of putting a live stamp—an industry term meaning real stamp, as opposed to an indicia—on the envelope (even if you're not using a mailing house, you can always call and ask for advice). Most people won't look carefully enough to see that it's not a first-class stamp, so you increase the chances of your letter being opened.

Another way to create interest in your envelope is to use more than one stamp—for instance, instead of using one 34-cent stamp, use two or three stamps of varying denominations.

- *Leave off the return address.* Sometimes, when I get the 98th mailing from a company or charity, I think, "Oh, no, not them again." I usually chuck the letter, unopened. Or, if I see a return address from a company in which I have no interest, I might not open the envelope. Like most other people, I don't always give a Direct Marketer the chance to convince me that I might want their product after all. Hopefully, your mailings will never evoke such a response—but if you're a frequent mailer, or want to try something different, don't put your return address on the envelope. There's nothing as mysterious as a plain white envelope without any indication as to who might have sent it. It might be a bill, it might be something you need, it might be something you sent away for. There's only one way to find out, and that's to open the envelope.

- *Feature your offer on the front.* Featuring an enticing offer on the front of the envelope will often make recipients curious enough to want to open the envelope and read more about it. This is especially effective if you're offering something for free. For instance, if you've targeted a mailing to women who've previously bought lingerie through the mail, an envelope that states, "FREE pantyhose with your next purchase! See inside," is very likely to be opened.

- *Hand-address your envelopes.* If you're mailing out a small number of envelopes, you can actually address them by hand for that personal touch. But if you're a major mailer and you're mailing tens of thousands of pieces, there are now many script fonts available that closely resemble handwritten envelopes. We recently sent out invitations to a party. We addressed the envelopes in-house on our computer, and they looked like they had been done by a calligrapher. There are now some fonts available that look like sloppy handwriting. You should be careful when choosing this kind of font however; some American Express customers were offended when what they thought was a handwritten note turned out to be a business mailing.

- *Create a self-mailer—a flyer that folds and serves as its own envelope.* This can be an interesting piece of mail because of its simplicity. Recipients know that it will be short and to the point. They can take a quick glance at it and easily determine whether or not it is of interest to them. Of course, this means that it has to be designed effectively to catch attention and get your points across within a limited amount of space.

Envelope Success Stories

The Incredible Fish Story. How do you get American fishermen to test out their luck and skill in Canadian waters? The Ontario Ministry of Tourism and Recreation asked Creative Director Michael McCormick to help them do just that. They also gave him several restrictions along with the assignment: The word "incredible" has to be included, because that was their theme in promoting Ontario. The government didn't want to promise fishermen they would catch any specific size or type of fish in Canada, just that the fishing was really good. So the obvious idea of "You can catch really big fish in Ontario" had to be conveyed in a creative way (Figure 5.1).

"I couldn't *say* 'really big fish,'" says McCormick, "so I thought I would show a really big fish. A photograph wouldn't do, because then it would be a specific fish, and, since it couldn't be life-size anyway, it wouldn't get the big idea across. So I had an illustrator create a nonspecific fish. In order to show how big it is, I wrapped it around a longer-than-normal envelope. We put the tail and the nose on the back. The point being, this fish is so *big*, it doesn't even fit on the envelope." On the back of the envelope, along with the nose and tail of the fish, is the copy, "The only word for it is...INCREDIBLE." Of course, fishermen fell for this campaign, hook, line, and sinker.

The Only Thing Texas Hasn't Got... This tourism Canada campaign was based on the concept that since Texans are such fans of wide-open spaces and new frontiers, they would love what Canada has to offer. The only problem is that Texans often feel they already do, and have, everything that's bigger and better than anyone else. Tell a Texan about any aspect of your home state and he'll likely reply, "Oh yeah? We've got that in Texas—and bigger too!" Just about the only thing they don't have in Texas are moose. In order to appeal to Texans' love of size, McCormick pictured a moose on an oversized 9" x 12" envelope, with the headline "Got any of these in Texas?" (Figure 5.2). Who could resist the temptation to open this envelope?

Figure 5.1
This fish was so big…it had to be wrapped around the back of the envelope.

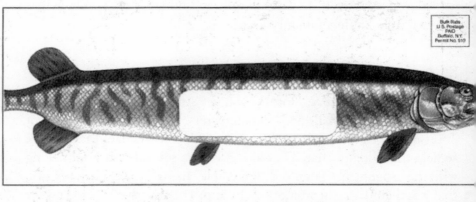

The only word for it is…
INCREDIBLE

"What's an envelope's job?" asks Michael McCormick. "To get opened? That's not quite true. *The real job of an envelope is to get opened by someone in the mood for what you have to say.*" As a Direct Marketer, it's your job to get your customers' attention, to get them in the mood to open your envelope (and eventually buy your product). As you can see from the preceding examples, there are many ways to go about this. Obviously, a sense of humor helps—and you don't need big bucks to have a sense of humor.

The Letter

The letter is probably the most important component in the direct mail package. If the envelope is like a window display to draw your customers in, the letter is your salesperson—it's your direct communication with

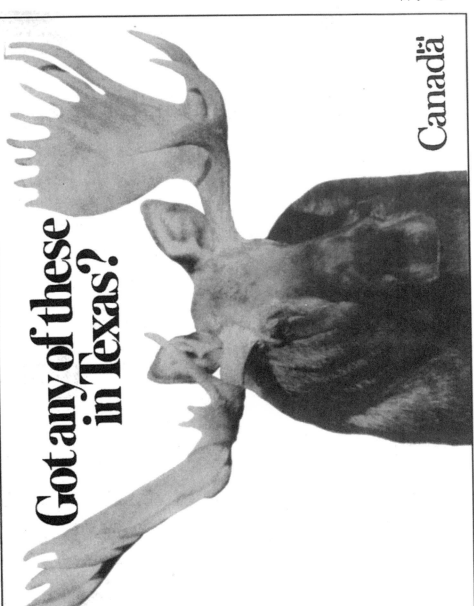

Figure 5.2
The true size of this envelope is 9" x 12".

your prospective customer. If you have the smallest budget in the world, and can only send out one element of the direct mail package, the one you'd use would be the letter.

A letter has two main functions. First, it has to position you as a credible company, so prospects will feel comfortable purchasing your product or service. Second, it has to explain why they should buy that product or service. There is no set length for such a letter. It can be one page or eight pages—it should be as long as it takes you to explain the benefits of your product to your customers.

My own new business letter is only one page, and it has been very effective. But some letters have to be much longer, perhaps because they appeal to several different audiences and you have to be sure you're addressing all of them. For instance, if you want to do a mailing to doctors—including cardiologists, oncologists, and internists—but it is not cost-efficient for you to print separate letters for each, you may want to make mention of how your product would benefit each of these specialties. You can appeal to different audiences within the same letter, as long as they're all in the same category of audience (in this case, they're all doctors). If there are enough names in each category, however, it probably makes sense to do separate mailings to each of the categories. That makes it more personalized and usually more effective.

Another reason to write a long letter is because you're selling a high-ticket or technically complicated item with a lot of benefits. Even if people don't read the entire letter, they usually skim through the various sections until they find something that interests them.

Long letters have proven to be successful. Not long ago I received a four-page letter introducing a vitamin regimen used by a particular health institute. The letter talks about the fact that this particular vitamin regimen is available only through the mail, it describes all the vitamins included in this regimen and the purity of their formulas, it explains how these vitamins will benefit your health, and it guarantees the product. This is a long letter that has been used successfully by this company for many years. Shorter letters have not worked as well.

The Elements of a Great Letter

Letters can be of any shape or size, but most have one or all of the following elements:

The opening attention-getter
The salutation
The body
The postscript

Before you sit down to compose your letter, make an outline of what information you need to include. The opening should be engaging and explain your reasons for writing. Then, describe your product or service, and list its benefits. Let your customers know what the offer is. Then go back and elaborate on the benefits, and repeat the offer. Include a call to action, which lets the customer know just what you want them to do (e.g., "Please order before December 30" or "Join our membership club today"). End with your signature, and a P.S. (people tend to look at the beginning and the end before reading the whole letter).

- *The opening, or attention-getter.* Many direct mail letters today begin with what is known as the "Johnson Box." It's positioned at the top of the letter to emphasize a particular benefit, introduce the special offer, or serve as a teaser to get readers interested in what's to come. When Scott E. Lapkoff, an award-winning Direct Marketer, was creating a membership letter for the Society of Naval Architects and Marine Engineers, he used a Johnson Box to excite potential members about advances in undersea technology. Directly beneath the society's letterhead, he wrote:

> The date is 1985. Using the very latest in sophisticated sonar imaging, Robert Ballard makes a final, last sweep over a confined area of the ocean floor, some six miles down. He is tired, it is late, and after months of searching for the wreckage of the Titanic, he is ready to pack it in...when all of a sudden, alarms go off all over the board. "We've found it!"

With a teaser like that, you can't resist reading on. A Johnson Box doesn't have to be that elaborate, however. It can be something as simple as:

> Read on and find out how to get your delicious candy sample— ABSOLUTELY FREE!

You don't have to have a box, either. You can use a Post-it, a few sentences printed in different color ink, a drawing or cartoon…Anything to get the customer's attention and entice him to read on.

- *The salutation.* The standard "Dear Ms. Geller" or "Dear Lois Geller" continues to be successful. But you may want to be more creative. If you don't know your customers personally, but you know his interest, you may want to address him by "Dear Classical Music Lover" or "Dear Gourmet Cook." The more ingenious, the better. But you have to be honest. We've all gotten direct mail letters that are addressed "Dear Friend." I know when I get such a letter, I usually think, "I don't know these people, I'm not their friend."
- *The body.* Sometimes, when you're creating a direct mail letter, you get carried away with trying to be clever; you're trying too hard to make the sale, or you're writing in a way that you think sounds professional. When that happens, the letter fails in its purposes: to convince people to have confidence in you and to buy your product.

  The body of the letter must contain all the information your customers need to know about the product. They need to know the benefits, the offer, the guarantee—everything you would tell them if you were selling in person. Also include the call to action (Order by December 31…). If possible, repeat the information at least twice so that someone skimming the letter gets it all. Then sign the letter, and let them know who it's from (the president, the vice president, the director of marketing). If possible, print the signature in a different color than the body of the letter, to make it appear more like a hand-signed letter.
- *The postscript.* Since people often read the end of the letter first, a P.S. is an essential item in a direct mail letter. It gives you an opportunity to reiterate your offer, to make an additional offer, to spell out your guarantee, and to repeat the call to action. An effective P.S. might look like this:

P.S. Remember, you'll receive 20 percent off every item you order before October 15. And, if your order totals $100 or more, we'll send you an exciting gift free! As always, you can return any item within 30 days, no questions asked. So let us hear from you today by return mail.

- *The lift letter.* This is also called the publisher's letter, because it started in the publishing industry. It's a separate, small insert in the direct mail package that says on the front flap, "Don't open this unless you've decided not to buy," or "A special note from our founder." Inside is a short message repeating the most important benefit, or telling subscribers that if they don't act now their subscription will lapse. A lift letter isn't necessary, but many marketers have found it gives the response rate a "lift" and gives some hesitant customers the gentle push they need to place an order.

Six Strategies for Winning Copy

Scott Lapkoff has been a professional copywriter for more than 20 years. To him, creating a direct mail letter is like stepping into a boxing ring. The ropes are the boundaries set up by the client and the product: the budget, the company image, the product or service itself. His job is to "step into that ring, and get creative. Start bouncing around, off all the ropes, until something clicks. It's not so much waiting for inspiration, but looking at everything you have and taking creative steps with it."

Customers, bombarded by your competition and the million other distractions of daily life, take about three seconds to make the decision as to whether or not to read your letter. Here are six success strategies for writing winning copy, which will help you get past the three-second mark:

Strategy No. 1: Humanize Your Letter

The best letters we receive are those endearing missives from family and friends who give us the latest gossip, tell us a story, bring us up to date on what's happening in their lives. The best direct mail letters do the same. They're sincere and honest, they give us a hint of what's going on behind the scenes, and they tell us the latest news about the company and the merchandise.

One example of how honesty really works in direct mail letters comes from my days at Greystone and Hearst Corporation. This is what happened: We had customers belonging to two different book clubs, one from *Good Housekeeping* and one from *Cosmopolitan.* By mistake, we sent our *Good Housekeeping* customers the *Cosmopolitan Love Book,* and we sent the *Cosmo* customers the *Good Housekeeping Cookbook for Calorie*

Watchers. Now, mistakes do sometimes happen, and we had form letters for this type of error. But we felt we needed a better apology. So we bought some stationery, and wrote a letter from my secretary explaining how terribly sorry she was for the mix-up, that it had been an error on her part, and that she hoped they would choose to keep the book sent in error or buy something else. As it turned out, this letter generated the highest response rate we ever received on anything. People were writing to my secretary for months saying they hoped she still had her job—and ordering books for themselves and their friends.

Although millions of people enjoy shopping by mail, most of them miss the old-time connection with real people that shopping used to afford. So when you let them know who you are and what your story is, you bring some of that old-time feeling back.

Creative Director Mike McCormick humanized the "Dear fishing friend" letter in Figure 5.3 by having it come from Babe Winkelman, the well-known host of a syndicated fishing program, who talked about his own personal reasons for fishing in Ontario. McCormick also emphasized the long, lean look of the "incredible fish" envelope by printing the letter on both sides of 10 1/3" x 4" sheet of paper.

Both McCormick and Lapkoff agree that the success of Direct Marketing copy is all in the story. L.L. Bean owes their success to the stories they add to their catalog. The same would apply to you if you were a mom-and-pop tie manufacturer. Do you get your silks direct from China? What's the story behind your ties? What would make an interesting read? If you send out a letter that says, "I've got 5,000 ties and one of them is for you"—big deal. But if you send a letter that says, "Deep in the Orient, along trails that most merchants don't get to, a single vendor makes the silk found in every tie bought at..." Now you've got your customers hooked!

You can do the same with any business, large or small. Tell your customers who you are, and what your business is all about. Use your sense of humor, and let your personality come through. One small business in New York used this idea to great effect. The owner would send out letters similar to the following:

Dear Ms. Geller,
    I have just been searching through the basement of my building and came across some wonderful pieces of African art that were some-

Figure 5.3

This odd-sized letter continues the "incredible fish" theme started on the outer envelope of this mailing package. The salutation addresses prospects' known interest: fishing; the P.S. includes a call to action, as well as a tease to get prospects to read the brochure.

ONTARIO
CANADA

Dear fishing friend,

I don't know when you started fishing — I've been doing it for 35 years, myself. And no matter where in the world I fish, I keep coming back to Canada's great fishing province, Ontario.

Let me tell you why.

First, it's because I think a big fishing experience is more than just a big fish, although Ontario has plenty of those. It's everything else that comes with it. And that's where Ontario is so incredible. Especially the Northern part of it.

Northern Ontario still is one of the greatest areas of unspoiled nature in the world. You don't have to travel far to find country that's still the way its Creator intended it to be.

It's a country with more lakes, streams and brooks than you could count in your lifetime. And it teems with wildlife — including fish that are fighting fools.

Ontario has great accommodations, too — from simple and rustic to plenty comfortable; near towns and people or so remote you have to fly in. (One of the few frontier experiences remaining in this crowded world is a fly-in fishing lodge in Ontario's North.)

continued on reverse

Ontario has nights so crisp they crackle — and a sky flickering with Northern Lights. It has guides both friendly and knowledgeable, and resort hotels run by people who know what you want and see that you get it. It's accessible, too: within about 8 hours drive (on good roads) or 2 hours flying time.

And above all, it's got FISH. All kinds of 'em, in all sizes and shapes, just waiting to match wits with you.

I hope you won't disappoint them. I hope you'll turn to the enclosed brochure now, open it, and find out how easy it is to have your Incredible Ontario fishing experience.

Be sure to request our Information Kit. It includes a brochure with Northern Ontario fishing and accommodation packages that will fill your head with dreams. BIG dreams!

See you there. Good fishin,

Babe Winkelman

P.S.: Send back the enclosed Reply Card before June 15, 1990 and you could be in line for a pretty terrific prize. See brochure for details.

how stored here and forgotten. I know that when I die (and in my last letter I told you about my terrible heart condition) my ne'er-do-well son-in-law will not know the great value of these pieces.

As one of my best customers, I know that you will appreciate these stunning artifacts. If you come in to the gallery, we can commiserate about health and family, and you can take 20 percent off the price of any of these pieces. I'd much rather you have them, than my son-in-law.

Of course, even if you weren't interested in African art, you would feel you had to go down to the store, buy one of the pieces, and help the owner out of his predicament!

In many ways, smaller businesses have the advantage when it comes to direct mail letters. When you receive a well-written letter from a small business, it's like getting mail from a distant cousin. Big business has a very difficult time establishing the same kind of personal relationships with customers.

I recently bought a new computer, and ever since then I've received dozens of direct mail letters from various computer-related companies. I have not responded to any of them. They seem to have forgotten that, although I run a business, I'm a person first. There is a fine line between sounding professional and being cold and impersonal. This is a special challenge for business-to-business Direct Marketing, but it applies to consumer marketing as well.

Smaller companies have often been successful in Direct Marketing by emphasizing the unique personalities of the people behind the products. Big business is often hampered by lawyers, style manuals, and executives who are afraid to associate themselves with a campaign in case it should turn out to be less successful than they anticipated. This mentality distances companies from their customers. When big business does talk to customers on a one-to-one basis it solidifies their relationships and humanizes the company for their customers.

I tried very hard to find a letter from a large organization that had successfully used this approach. I went through stacks and stacks of letters. Most of them were deadly dull. They were not warm welcoming, they were cold and impersonal. Many of the letters were so ineffective I never read past the first paragraph.

One successful letter I did find was from Girls Incorporated (formerly Girls Club of America). Figure 5.4 shows the first page of this two-page letter. It couldn't be more human or personal (even the "Dear Friend" salutation works in this case). It is a touching story of a woman who was taught to believe in herself and her abilities. As the letter states on the second page, it comes from Joan Greenfield, an award-winning writer

Figure 5.4

Here is the first page of a humanized letter used successfully by a large organization.

Hillary Rodham Clinton
Honorary Chair

Donna Brace Ogilvie
Chair of the Board

Alice Hilseweck Ball
President

Isabel Carter Stewart
National Executive Director

Regional Offices

*Atlanta
Boston
Indianapolis
New York
Santa Barbara*

Formerly
Girls Clubs of America

**girls
inc.**

Growing up is
serious business

GLTS

Dear Friend:

For as long as I can remember, my father told me I could be anything I wanted to be. Finally, I believed him.

He taught me to decide what I wanted and go after it...to get educated, to work hard, to stay focused. Above all, to believe in myself.

Not unusual things for a father to teach his son. But I was his daughter. All the girls I knew were planning to become secretaries or teachers until they got married and stopped working.

That wasn't my choice.

The day I was first made a vice president, I cried like a baby. My father had died two months earlier. I wanted so much to thank him.

I was lucky to have someone who wouldn't let me settle for second best, just because I was a girl.

                    Girls in Jeopardy

Many girls don't have someone like my father to propel them past the gender bias they face throughout their lives. For every lucky one with a supportive teacher, mother, father, minister or friend, there are hundreds of girls in jeopardy.

Without encouragement, guidance and inspiration, most will settle for less than they want, less than they deserve, less than they're capable of. And we're all too familiar with the results...

*   From a very early age, girls' self-esteem and curiosity about the world are seriously eroded.

*   More often than not, they're discouraged from choosing leadership roles and guided towards less demanding goals.

*   They're not getting a fair chance — and they don't even know it.

But, there is a solution, an answer, a way to empower hundreds of thousands of girls: to realize their potential...to make the right choices...to believe in themselves...to help them become strong, smart and bold instead of under-educated, under-paid and patronized.

That solution is offered by Girls Incorporated.

                    Strong, Smart and Bold

Girls Incorporated (formerly Girls Clubs of America) is a nonprofit national youth organization dedicated to helping girls become strong, smart

                                          (over, please)

who doesn't actually work for Girls Incorporated. However, she goes on to explain, "Because I'm so certain they're doing a job nobody else can do, I've volunteered my time to tell you their story." This has become the organization's control package (which means they test all other packages against this one, the winner) because of its continued success in acquiring new donors.

Here are some hints for creating effective direct mail letters, no matter what the type of business or the size of your company:

- *Personalize your letters.* If you have a computer program that can drop personalized information (such as recipient's name, the product he purchased, or the last time he used your service) into the letter, the less it seems like a form letter. If you know any of your customers personally, a handwritten P.S. at the bottom saying "Come on in! Love to see you again!" can be extremely effective.
- *Let people know what's going on in your business.* Nobody cares if a large department store puts down new carpet. But if you're remodeling your small business, adding a new line of merchandise, have hired a new assistant...let people know. They'll want to come in and check it out. You can also use personal tidbits—a birth announcement, an engagement or wedding in the family—to make your customers feel part of the family. This can be done by a large company as well. A newly appointed corporate executive could send out a letter of introduction, stating his goals and philosophy for the corporation, and how he plans to be personally involved in improving relationships with the company's customers.
- *Be sure your copy is clear and includes all necessary information.* Don't get so carried away with telling a story that you forget the purpose of the letter—to sell your product. Be sure to include all the information your customers need to know.
- *Sign each letter personally.* Even 500 letters can seem like a lot to sign by hand—but who says you have to do them all at once? Try signing 20 at a time; you'll be done before you know it. Make sure to sign them in a different color from the type, for example, if the type is black, write your signature in blue ink. Customers will notice, and appreciate the gesture. A large company, sending out millions of pieces, can use a script font that resembles a signature (printed also in a second color).
- *Get your customers to sell for you.* Get permission from some of your customers to use their names and their comments, and include their personal testimonials. Don't just include "John Smith says, 'This store is great!'" Ask John Smith to write about how you helped his family book their dream vacation, or how you came through for

him in a business crisis. Then include John Smith's name, a photograph (if possible), and the city and state where he lives. The more specific you are, the more credible your testimonial will be.

- *Use winning words.* Here are some words and phrases that are particularly appropriate for humanizing letters:

Handmade	Family-tested
Hand-crafted	Neighborhood
Hand-picked	Personally chosen
Home style	Family-owned
Personal service	Preferred customer

Strategy No. 2: Describe Benefits

Despite what you may think, people don't buy actual products. They buy those things the products can do for them. People don't buy vacuum cleaners; they buy a way to make cleaning the house quicker and easier. People don't buy an air conditioner because they want a big brown box sticking out of their window. They buy an air conditioner to be more comfortable during the hot summer months.

To sell a product, you must help people discover its benefits. All products and services have two components: features and benefits. Features describe what a product or service is. Suppose you wanted to sell a folding table. It has four legs, is 45" long and 31 1/2" wide when completely opened, 6" wide when both leaves are folded, is made of wood and topped with Formica. These are the table's features.

Would I buy this table? Not until I know how it will benefit me. I might be able to figure out some of the benefits myself, but if you want me to buy, you're going to have to make it easy for me. I'll buy the table if you tell me: "It's perfect for small spaces, since it folds down to only 6" wide. When folded out completely, it comfortably seats 6. The wooden construction makes it incredibly sturdy and the Formica top makes it extremely easy to clean." Knowing the benefits entices me to buy this product.

Strategy No. 3: Get As Much Feedback As Possible

Talk to people you know, your friends, your family, your present customers. Ask then why they buy your product. Or what makes them buy products similar to yours. They'll give you ideas on how to focus your letter. Once, while developing a Direct Marketing campaign for Marshalls Department Stores, a creative director spoke to several women about their experiences while shopping at the store. One frequent shopper said, "I know they get in new shipments every week. I don't know what bargains I might miss if I skip a week!" Out of that one conversation came a new, highly successful campaign theme for Marshalls: "When you miss a week, you miss a lot!"

Strategy No. 4: Immerse Yourself in the Product or Service

There are copywriters who get paid huge amounts of money to write about products they've never seen. Sometimes they're successful, but more often than not their copy seems stale and all too familiar. If you want to create an irresistible letter, you've got to know the product or service you're selling, inside and out. Use it yourself. Touch it, feel it, study it, give it to your kids or neighbors. Live with it for a while.

For instance, if you're selling children's toys, watch your own kids (or your sister's or your neighbor's) play with it. Do they like the colors? Do they find creative ways to play with it? Does it hold up after the kids have tried to tear it apart? In your letter, write about how your two-year-old squealed with delight when the toy came out of the box; about how your son left it out in the snow for two weeks and it was none the worse for wear when you brought it back inside; about how you gave it to your granddaughter for her birthday, and she looked up at you and said, "I love you, Grandma, up to the sky." Who wouldn't want to give that toy to a favorite child?

You have to truly understand who your target market is and why they would want to purchase your product. If you're selling technical equipment, you may not personally want or need that product. But you must understand and be enthusiastic about the benefits of this equipment to your potential customers. You have to learn to love the product from your customer's point of view.

When I was working in publishing, I marketed several worm-fishing and fly-tying books. I don't know anything (nor do I care) about these subjects. But I spoke to fly-tyers and worm fishermen and I asked them what they would like in these kinds of books. They wanted a lot of pictures. So even though these were not products I loved or needed, I knew how to make these books exciting to my audience.

Strategy No. 5: Change the Rhythm

Study some direct mail letters you receive, and analyze why they work. The most successful letters are not just straight prose, one paragraph after another. They're broken up by headlines, subheads, a different typeface, or a few sentences centered, bolded, or underlines. Bullets and lists can also be used effectively to break the monotony. If you can afford to have a letter printed in different color inks, use that for a change in the rhythm. Or you can break up your sales pitch with a statement like, "Excuse me for a minute. I have to stop this letter now because the new shipment of silk ties from China just arrived, and I can't wait to see them... I'm back, and I was right. These ties are spectacular..."

Some people are turned off by reading letters with a lot of bullets and underlining. They feel that they can find the important information without it being so blatantly shown. However, letters using these techniques have sold millions of dollars worth of products. Until people stop buying from such letters, Direct Marketers will continue to use them.

Strategy No. 6: Get the Prospect Involved

If a reader has to *do* something, he or she automatically pays more attention. This chapter began with a survey. Hopefully, it piqued your curiosity, and kept you reading. Your direct mail letters can do the same. Surveys are good, and so are questions. Include a quiz or a contest. Invite prospects to send away for a free sample, or a booklet of relevant information, even if they don't buy from you. Give them an 800 number hotline so they can ask questions if they have any. Chances are good, once they spend the time to do any of these things, they'll be more inclined to make a purchase.

More Winning Words

Even though we want to use copy that's humanized, creative, and benefit-oriented, we also need words that are going to attract attention. The following words have been used successfully time and time again, and appeal to a majority of people. Some people might say they're overused, but testing shows that they're effective nonetheless. If you want to write copy that sells—on your envelopes, order forms, or in your letters—

here are some words and phrases **guaranteed** to grab your customers' attention:

Free	Revolutionary
New	Yes
Confidential	First-time offer
Free trial period	Special invitation
Limited-time offer	Secrets
Early bird special	Act now
Guaranteed	Congratulations
Two-for-one	Save
Don't send money	Proven
Smart	Introducing
Success	At last

Typography and Design

The look of your letter can often make or break a sale. Earlier, we talked about using bold type, subheads, and underlining to change the rhythm of a letter. Don't go overboard, however. You don't need to use all these techniques in one letter to create a sense of rhythm. Copy is most effective when the typeface is appropriate to the product and the audience. Too many different typefaces can be confusing; avoid excessive use of capital letters, highlighting, and underlining. Typography should be both visually appealing and easily read.

The typeface you choose is an important design element. A study conducted by Colin Wheildon for the Newspaper Advertising Bureau of Australia demonstrated that 67 percent of those tested showed poor comprehension of articles set in sans serif body type (serifs are the little lines that appear at the upper and lower ends of letters). Comprehension improved immediately with the use of a serif body type.

This is a typeface with serifs.

This is a typeface without serifs.

Remember when you were first learning to read? You trailed your finger underneath the words as you read to help you keep your place. Serifs serve the same function, which is why a typeface with serifs is easier to read.

Letters should be single-spaced with indented paragraphs and wide margins to make them appear friendly and easy to read. Body copy should be set in 10-point minimum (anything smaller is difficult for many people to read). Type should be set not longer than 1 1/2 to 2 alphabets long (39 to 52 characters) per line, and long copy should be broken up by frequent paragraphs and subheads.

Don't end a page at the end of a paragraph. Make your customer read on by ending the page in the middle of a sentence.

Letter Success Stories

When Scott Lapkoff was asked to design a campaign to get people to renew their memberships in the Navy League (an organization for retired Navy men and women), he sent out a series of letters, signed by various officers of the organization. The response was good, but he wanted one more letter to go after those fence-sitters who just couldn't make up their minds. His fourth letter is a wonderful example of all the elements of a successful direct mail piece.

"One day I went down into the bowels of the Navy League offices," says Lapkoff, "and sitting there was an art director who's been with them for 38 years. Imagine Wilford Brimley with an attitude. I said to him, 'I'm having a hard time figuring out who should sign the fourth letter,' and he said, 'Why not have God sign it?'"

Lapkoff didn't think that was his solution, but it did get him thinking about who was the highest authority in the Navy League. That led him to Teddy Roosevelt, who founded the organization in 1902. Why not have Teddy Roosevelt write a letter? Lapkoff went up to the executive offices, researched Roosevelt's speeches, and, using the former president's own words, created a letter that was so successful it won the prestigious Maxi Award—the Academy Awards of direct mail (Figure 5.5). He sent the letter in a parchment envelope stamped "delayed mail" to further the impression that it had been mailed by Roosevelt himself (Figure 5.6).

Lapkoff also included a lift letter in this mailing (Figure 5.7). The "handwritten" message on the front, "A Special Note From the President," made you want to open it immediately. Once opened, you discovered this note was not from President Roosevelt, but from Evan S. Baker, national president of the Navy League. This was a clever play on the words and the concept of the overall mailing package.

Figure 5.5
What could be more convincing than a letter from a president—dead or alive?

From the Office of
Theodore Roosevelt

June 29, 1903

Dear Navy Leaguer:

When I first endorsed the idea of the Navy League—I had but one thought in mind:
The building and maintaining in proper shape of the sea services.

And the Navy League can't do that without your support.

You see, it seems to me that all good Americans interested in the growth of their country
and sensitive to its honor, should give hearty support to the policies for which the Navy League
is founded.

Your membership . . . your support of this broad and farsighted ideal, is perhaps the best
calling an individual can answer.

Only with your continued participation can the sea services of our great nation thrive and
survive to adequately defend American interests.

It is with heartfelt pride that I ask for your help in this most important endeavor. I am most
proud of our sea services and the place of honor they have in our nation's history. I am proud of
the job that they perform today—and will unswervingly do in the future.

Share with me this symbol of our collective patriotism, and begin anew your dedication to
the Navy League.

Sincerely,

Theodore Roosevelt

Theodore Roosevelt

Figure 5.6
The "delayed mail" stamp reinforced the impression that this letter had actually come from Teddy Roosevelt.

Theodore Roosevelt
Sagamore Hill
Oyster Bay, L.I., New York

DELAYED
MAIL

The Brochure

Some products and services require more visual representation than others. If you're an accountant marketing your services, a well-written letter will probably suffice. People will be interested in your professional qualifications and in the various services you offer; there's no real need for a photo of yourself or your offices. But for other types of products and services, the brochure is the component of the direct mail package best suited to show off your product.

If you're marketing your bed and breakfast, a written description by itself will probably not be enough. No matter how many times you say the surroundings are beautiful, people will want to see for themselves. They'll want to see the rooms, the grounds, perhaps even nearby sightseeing opportunities. The brochure can illustrate these features and also help you set the mood. If you're stressing that this would be a perfect honeymoon hideaway, you can show photos of couples enjoying a private candlelit dinner in their room, or taking a romantic walk in the woods.

If you were marketing your printing services, for instance, you might use the brochure to show your printing plant and the various presses you have. You might even want to show a photo of yourself, and of the people in your company. Better yet, you might want to include a few samples that show the quality of your printing.

Figure 5.7

The clever play on the word "President" makes this lift letter a very effective part of this mailing package.

A Special Note From the President

**EVAN S. BAKER
NATIONAL PRESIDENT**

Dear Navy Leaguer:

If our founder, Theodore Roosevelt, had written you a letter—it would have been precisely as you have just read.

One thing is for sure—I couldn't have said it any better than Mr. Roosevelt. Your continuing support is absolutely vital to our efforts to educate the American Public on the importance of maritime capability—and to support the sea services.

We don't want to lose you. Therefore, even though your membership lapsed last month, we want to offer you this last opportunity to renew now without any further loss of continuity or benefits. Don't wait. Return the enclosed renewal card today!

Sincerely,

Evan S. Baker

Evan S. Baker

Whether it is two-color or an elaborate four-color piece, a brochure is usually much more expensive to design and print than a letter or postcard. So be sure you really need one before you decide to include one in your package. A brochure is a good idea if:

1. The appearance of the product is a strong sales factor (such as furniture, giftware, fashion, real estate).

2. The product can be adapted for many different uses (such as a cleaner for carpets, upholstery, car seats, and other products made of fabric).

3. The product contains many different parts or features (such as a set of dishes or tools, or a computer that includes keyboard, monitor, hard drive, CD-ROM, and speakers).

4. You're selling a high-priced item. Most people don't want to spend a lot of money unless they can see what they're getting (e.g., audio equipment, vacation spots, fine jewelry).

5. The product or service has a "before-and-after" effect (such as a cleaning service, a landscaping service, a remodeling contractor).

6. You need to show a product in action (e.g., an exercise machine, adjustable furniture, sports equipment).

The brochure is the part of the direct mail package that's most dependent on good design. If you're including a brochure in your package, you probably want to have a professional designer put it together. If you're on a limited budget, look for an art school, or a college art department near you. You may be able to find a student who can do a good job for a reasonable fee. Study brochures you receive in the mail, decide what you like and don't like about them, and share these ideas with your designer.

TIP   In my experience, red brochures pull in more customers than any other color. Perhaps it's because red is a vibrant, exciting color, and tends to stand out from the rest of mail.

A brochure usually focuses on a single product or service. A brochure that tries to focus on too many products would only be confusing. If you are going to offer multiple products, you're probably better off going with a small catalog format.

The Brochure Copy

Brochures contain more than photographs. They contain copy as well. A brochure should start out with a tantalizing headline that announces the major point you want to get across to your customers. That could be the quality of your service, the low cost of your products, or the huge variety you offer. It has to tantalize readers so that they'll look through the entire brochure.

The copy in the brochure is not as extensive as the copy in the letter, although it must contain all the most important elements, including product description, the price, the offer, and the guarantee. The brochure has to include enough information to be able to sell the product on its own, if the letter should get lost or be ignored.

Sometimes brochures are sent without a letter. This is not a good idea. You're asking your customer to respond to an advertisement. Sending a brochure without a letter defeats the whole idea of direct mail, which is to establish a relationship with your customers, and talk to them on a one-to-one basis—and that can only be accomplished in a letter.

The only time you might send a brochure without a letter is when you use it as a statement stuffer. This is a brochure that is sent along with a bill or monthly statement. You often find them included with your credit card bill. A statement stuffer can be an effective mailing piece because you're not paying the postage for a solo mailing. It's a free ride, since you have to send out the statements anyway. A lot of large companies actually sell "space" in their statements to other companies. For instance, *Encyclopaedia Britannica* may pay a bank to include a stuffer in their credit card mailing.

When you include a brochure in your mailing piece, be sure that it matches the tone and feel of your letter. Your entire package should create a united front. If your letter is modest and homey, the brochure should be too. If your message is slick and urbane, the brochure should reflect a more sophisticated image. Each year when I am a judge for the

ECHO Awards, which are the Direct Marketing Association awards for the best Direct Marketing campaigns, hundreds and hundreds of direct mail packages are submitted for consideration. The most effective of these packages are the ones that present a unified theme throughout the envelope, the letter, and the brochure. Some use a distinctive message to tie the three together, and others use a unifying design element.

Brochures on a Budget

Many small businesses or marketing departments choose not to send a brochure because of the expense involved. That may be the right choice. But remember, limitations don't hurt creativity, they help it. Imaginative ways of presenting your product or service may stimulate more business than any standard, just-like-all-the-others brochure. Here are some ways you can create a brochure, or eliminate the need for one, on a small business budget:

★ Instead of a formal brochure, enclose one excellent photograph of your product.
★ Use an unusual fold to make a simple brochure unique.
★ Use an interesting typeface.
★ Print in two colors instead of four.
★ Use colored paper stock.

The Order Form

Not everyone will read your entire brochure, or the whole direct mail letter. They may just read the headline or look at the pictures. If you've piqued their interest, they may skip the rest of your copy and go directly to the order form to check out the price of your product. So your order form must be as inviting and as information-packed as the other pieces of your package. It should be more than just a space for people to fill in their name and address; it should be an effective selling tool. Here are some hints to help you accomplish that:

• *Reinforce your offer.* Suppose your letter stated that you were offering a special $129.95 price on an exercise bike that normally sells for $160. If your letter stressed the offer, your order form might start out with: "YES! I want to order the $160 Exercise Wiz at the one-time price of <u>$129.95</u>." You might even cross out the $160 for greater effect. Or if your letter stressed benefits, you might say "ABSOLUTELY! I want to start losing weight and living a healthier life today! Please send me the Exercise Wiz at the special one-time price of $129.95."

- *Include your guarantee.* Reassure your customers—when they're debating whether or not to fill out the order—that you stand behind your product: "Look this book over for ten days. If you're not completely satisfied, we'll refund your purchase price."
- *Use involvement devices.* This has become very popular in the "You may have already won $1 million" sweepstakes industry, where you find "yes," "no," or "maybe" stickers somewhere in the letter which you must "unstick" and move to the order form.

TIP Another effective involvement device is a little scissors "✂" and a "cut here" instruction on the order form.

- *Make the lines on your order form as long as possible.* My bookkeeper, Lucille Santoliquido, can never fit her entire name on an order form. If it's at all possible, design the form to that there's plenty of room for people to fill in their information. Underneath each of the blanks, write in "first name, last name," and other types of information that you want. When you're designing the order form, consult with the people who will be inputting the data into the computer. For instance, some database software requires a format of last name first, and some requires first name first. Whether it's Stella in the shipping department, your son who's home for college vacation, or a service bureau inputting your database, ask if your order form is compatible with their computer programs. You can save money by doing it their way.

List all the credit cards you accept, and include blanks for the credit card numbers and customer signature. Also include a place where people can mark "Enclosed is my check" and tell them to whom to make out the check. Believe it or not, if you don't include that, some people will think you don't accept checks. If possible, put in a blank for the phone number, so that you have a way of contacting the customer if there is any problem with the order or the credit card number. Also, ask for their email address, as you might need it for future promotions.

Give people ordering options. Include the address of your company so that they can mail the order to you (even if you've enclosed a reply envelope); include your telephone number; include the option of faxing in the order, and if you have a website, be sure to include the URL.

- *Get them on your mailing list.* Even if some do not order right away, you want to get them into your database. If you have room, include a place where they can check off, "I haven't decided to buy, but please keep me on your mailing list." If a person goes to the trouble of mailing back the order form without an order, he'll often respond very well to future offers. You might also include a statement such as "If you would like your name deleted from our mailing list, please check here." That way, you can eliminate customers who are definitely not interested. But you don't want to give customers too many options. Keep the form as simple and clear as possible.

- *Make it lively.* The order form is where the action is, and the duller it is, the fewer the responses you're going to get. Make it fun to order! If you're offering a cookbook series, design your order form in the shape of a cake. Print the form in vibrant colors, odd shapes, with huge arrows pointing to it—anything that makes ordering from you a memorable and pleasurable experience.

- *Provide an example of how you want people to fill in the order form.* This is especially useful if they have to include sizes, colors, or any information other than vital statistics. Fill out one line on the top of the form, and write "sample" next to it. Include a chart that calculates shipping and handling charges. Also include instructions about sales tax. If you have a business operation in a particular state, customers from that state must pay tax on your merchandise. For instance, if you have a distribution center in Ohio and a marketing organization in New York, you would have to include a statement that says, "New York and Ohio residents add appropriate sales tax."

- *Don't forget the source code.* Source codes allow you to track your incoming mail. With a code on every order form, you'll know exactly where each of your orders is coming from. So if you're using 20 lists, each order from each of the 20 lists has to have a different source code. If you're mailing out a large number of pieces from various lists, discuss the source code process with your printer. If you're doing a smaller mailing to a few lists, you may be able to do the coding yourself.

Order Form Success Story

Dear Mr. President. The Teddy Roosevelt theme for the Navy League renewal campaign was carried through right to the order form (Figure 5.8). Addressed to the president himself, it is otherwise a standard order form. Note the size—there's plenty of room for members to fill in the vital information.

An order form can be very simple, and still reaffirm your position and personal relationship with your customers and prospects. Here are some ways to make the order form work for a small or midsize business:

★ Use an inexpensive involvement device. Instead of a sticker that's been specially printed for your mailing, buy stickers from the store

Figure 5.8
The "President Roosevelt" theme is continued even into the order form. Also, notice the long lines, making it easy for anyone to fit his or her whole name.

Dear President Roosevelt:

I have pledged my renewed support for the policies and ideals of the Navy League of the United States and have enclosed my membership dues. Please renew my commitment for:
☐ One year, $30   ☐ Five years, $125   ☐ Life membership, $325
☐ My cheque is enclosed, made payable to: The Navy League.

☐ Please charge my: ☐ VISA   ☐ MasterCard

Account Number: _____ Signature: _____

Expiration Date: _____

(PLEASE PRINT)

Name _____

Address _____

City _____ State _____ Zip _____

Home Phone (____)_____ Work Phone (____)_____

that say "YES" on them, and have readers move them from one place to another. Or simply print a "yes," "no," or "maybe" on the order form, and have prospects check off the appropriate answer.

★ Make the order form part of your letter or brochure. Instead of going to the expense of printing a separate form, put yours on the bottom of your letter or the back of your brochure.

★ Eliminate the preprinted name and address that many big businesses use. On this type of order form, your name and address will have already been filled in by computer. This often gets a higher response rate; however it is an expensive process. To save money, stick to the simpler, fill-in-the-blank variety of order form.

★ If yours is a small business, make its size an asset. If you don't take credit cards, state: "We're still too small to accept credit cards, but we'll gladly take your check or money order. It will help us with our cash flow, and you won't have to worry about any interest charges…"

The Business Reply Envelope

It's amazingly easy for a customer to lose interest in your product between the time she reads your letter and the time it takes to hunt up her own envelope and stamp. If you want to make it as easy as possible for customers to place an order, include a preaddressed reply envelope. If you can afford it, pay the postage yourself. A prepaid envelope always lifts the response rate. If people have to stop the impulse to buy to look for a stamp, they may have second thoughts.

If you do use business reply mail you must obtain a permit and permit number from the United States Postal Service, and the number must be printed on your envelope. There are stringent postal regulations that apply to business reply mail concerning the location of the address, the bar code, the indicia, and other elements. Since these regulations change periodically, you should check with your post office or mailing house about them. However, there is also enough leeway to make your envelope an aid to your sale. You can add in an address line such as, "Best

Deal of the Century Department." On the back of the envelope or on the inside back flap, you might want to print a checklist for the customer with questions such as: "Have you signed and enclosed your check?" "Have you included the order form?"

If you can't afford to use preprinted reply envelopes, you can make your own envelopes, put first-class stamps on and print your address on the front. Let your customers know that you're so confident they will order from you, you've paid for first-class postage yourself.

In certain instances, you can use a business reply card instead of an envelope. They can be used for an inquiry ("Return this card for information on our exciting new product"), or for information gathering ("Please fill out this survey card so we may serve you better in the future"). But most of the time a business reply card isn't used for actual ordering. Prospective customers are worried about sending their credit card numbers through the mail where anyone can read them. You're better off including an order form which can be enclosed in envelope.

Keep Your Printing Costs in Mind

The purpose of your creative efforts is to grab prospective customers' attention and get them to order your product. However, this must be done in the most cost-effective way possible. A pop-up centerfold for your brochure may be a great idea in theory, but costs so much it makes it almost impossible for you to break-even on the campaign.

Before you (or your creative staff) begin designing the various pieces of your creative package, get estimates for printing costs. Find three or four printers, send them the details of your printing needs, and compare their estimates. If you're not familiar with the printers, ask to see samples of work they've done for other direct mailers.

If you don't know much about printing, ask your graphic designer for help with the specifications of the job. Be as specific as you can about each piece in your package. You'll need to give the printer information about the size of each piece, the type of paper you want to use, the number of colors you'll be using, whether you'll be using photographs or illustrations, and how you want each piece cut or folded. Factors that affect printing costs include:

★ *Paper stock*: These days, paper is very expensive, and the type of paper you choose can make a big difference in printing costs. Paper comes in two finishes: coated and uncoated. Uncoated paper is best for pieces that feature a lot of text. Letters and books are usually printed on uncoated stock (sometimes called matte finish). Coated stock, which usually has a high luster or shine, is good for reproduction of photographs, and is often used for magazines, catalogs, and for fine art books. Printing your letter or brochure on colored paper will also add to the cost.

★ *Paper weight*: Postage costs are determined by weight, so you may be able to save money by choosing a lighter weight paper. But keep in mind the message and image you want to portray; in some cases, a heavier paper will make a better impression and give you a better response.

★ *Size*: If your letter or brochure is an odd size, it may cost you more because it doesn't fit into standard press sizes. You may be able to save money using a technique called "ganging." This happens when you can print more than one piece on the same press at the same time. For instance, your odd-size brochure may leave extra room on the sides, which may enable you to print a small order form or package-stuffer coupon. Your printer should be able to tell you if it is possible to gang any of your pieces, which can save you considerable money.

★ *Ink color*: Color is another factor that affects printing costs. Obviously, the more colors you include, the more expensive the job will be. A straightforward letter, printed in one-color ink, will be less expensive than a letter that contains a second color for underlining and a signature. In some cases a two-color brochure may be effective. But if you want to reproduce full-color photographs, a four-color process is necessary.

★ *Time*: If you need rush delivery on your order, you'll pay extra for it. Plan far enough in advance so that you give the printer plenty of time to do your job without incurring extra rush charges.

★ *Size of the run*: Costs can vary according to how many pieces you have printed. Small runs are usually printed on a sheet-fed press, which rolls individual sheets of paper through each color press. Larger runs are printed on a web press, which runs huge continuous rolls of paper through the presses. Not all printers have both presses. Some printers may not be equipped for large runs. That's why it's important to shop around, not only for the best price, but the printer who is best equipped for the type of job you need.

Printing is a substantial part of the cost for any direct mail program. Finding a good printer is one of the most important aspects of your campaign. Take the time to shop around and find someone who will give you a good price, but who is also willing and able to give you advice and cost-saving ideas.

Below are some ballpark figures of printing costs for three different direct mail packages. This will give you an idea of what costs might be. These costs will vary from printer to printer. The cost of paper has been going up steadily and may continue to rise (or may begin to fall), which will affect your prices. The costs also vary depending on the area of the country. Prices in the Midwest are lower than on the East or West Coasts. We've used these examples just to give you an idea. Sometimes Canadian printers (due to the exchange rate) can offer better prices than U.S. printers. Of course, you then have to factor in shipping costs.

The first estimate is for a four-color self-mailer, 8" x 14", which folds down to 8" x 5". It contains one large color photo and four small ones. We have gotten estimates for printing 10,000, 50,000, 100,000, and 500,000. You'll notice a category called "Film" (from which the copies are actually printed) in each estimate. This cost remains the same no matter how many copies are being printed. The category called "Labeling/Lettershop" refers to the cost of putting the labels on the pieces, putting the pieces in postal code sequence, placing them in the proper types of bags, and delivering them to the post office.

Self-Mailer	10M	50M	100M	500M
Film	$ 800			
Printing	3,200	5,200	7,893	22,600
Labeling/Lettershop	600	1,200	1,935	8,820

The next estimate is for a traditional direct mail package, including:

- a 2-color No. 10 window OE (outer envelope)
- 2-page, 2-color letter, not personalized
- labeled order form, 2 colors
- 1-color No. 9 BRE (business reply envelope)
- 4-color brochure: 8" x 8" folded once to 8" x 4", with 1 large 4-color photo and 5 small ones
- a lift letter, 7" x 7", folded once to 3 1/2" x 7"

Traditional Package	10M	50M	100M	500M
OE Film	$ 195			
OE Printing	475	1,075	2,035	9,925
Letter Film	425			
Letter Printing	1,650	3,325	4,885	16,925
Order Form Film	45			
Order Form Printing	1,510	2,375	3,700	14,200
BRE Film	95			
BRE Printing	590	1,450	2,600	11,200
Brochure Film	1,060			
Brochure Printing	2,170	3,800	6,560	22,600
Lift Letter Film	95			
Lift Letter Printing	910	1,895	2,945	10,850
Labeling/Lettershop	1,050	2,350	3,640	17,910

The last estimate is for a 50,000, 100,000, and 500,000 mailing of a personalized direct mail package, where the recipient's name is printed on the letter, including:

- a 4-color 6" x 9" window OE
- 2-page, 2-color letter, with first page laser-personalized so address shows through the window. The first page is 14" long and perforated at 10 1/2", and the bottom 3 1/2" is a personalized order form.
- 1-color BRE, 5 1/2" x 8 1/2"
- 4-color brochure: 24 1/4" x 17" flat and folds down to 8 1/2" x 5 3/4", with 3 large photos and 8 small ones
- a lift letter, 7" x 7", folded once to 3 1/2" x 7"

Personalized Package	50M	100M	500M
OE Film	$ 830		
OE Printing	4,850	6,950	26,000
Letter Offset Film	185		
Letter Offset Printing	3,825	5,280	17,965
Laser Lettering	2,850	5,200	24,650
BRE Film	45		
BRE Printing	1,450	2,600	11,200
Brochure Film	1,880		
Brochure Printing	10,500	18,813	66,425
Labeling/Lettershop	2,350	3,640	17,910
Lift Letter Film	95		
Lift Letter Printing	1,895	2,945	10,850

Seasonality

Companies have done exhaustive studies about which products do well in which seasons of the year. Overall, the best months for mail order are late August, September, October, and—surprisingly—January. In August, September, and October, people are obviously shopping for Christmas. You would think that January would not be a good month. But studies have shown that most people don't get what they want for Christmas. Because many people also receive cash for Christmas, they treat themselves to the gifts they really wanted all along.

Obviously, what you're selling has great impact on when your best selling months will be. Many people buy books for summer reading, so May and June are good months. Home decorating and furniture suppliers do well in October and November, when people are spiffing up their homes for their holiday parties. Outdoor furniture sells best in April and May.

You may need to do your own testing to find out what months are best for you. One client of mine, who heard that January was a good month for mail order, insisted on sending out his direct mail piece January 1. But he was selling winter clothing, and people have already made their winter clothes purchases by January and were already perusing spring catalogs. So what's generally true for the industry may not hold true for your product. It may take you a few mailing cycles before you can determine which seasons produce the best response for your product or service.

Checklist

THE OUTER ENVELOPE

Did you:

- ☑ Use bold headlines
- ☑ Amuse people
- ☑ Create a teaser
- ☑ Make the envelope visually appealing
- ☑ Use a live stamp
- ☑ Use an unusual size envelope
- ☑ Feature your offer on the front
- ☑ Hand-address your envelopes
- ☑ Create a self-mailer

THE LETTER

Did you:

- ☑ Include a Johnson Box, or other attention-getter
- ☑ Choose an appropriate salutation
- ☑ Humanize your letter
- ☑ Speak about benefits
- ☑ Get as much feedback as possible
- ☑ Immerse yourself in the product or service
- ☑ Change the rhythm
- ☑ Get the prospect involved
- ☑ Include a postscript
- ☑ Include a lift letter
- ☑ Choose an appropriate typeface
- ☑ Indent paragraphs
- ☑ Break up long copy with paragraphs and subheads

THE BROCHURE

Did you:

☑ Determine that you really need a brochure

☑ Create a catchy headline

☑ Match the tone and feel of your letter

☑ Include product description, offer, and guarantee

☑ Make sure photographs are high-quality, not grainy and fuzzy

☑ Use an interesting typeface

THE ORDER FORM

Did you:

☑ Reinforce your offer

☑ Include your guarantee

☑ Use an involvement device

☑ Make blank lines as long as possible

☑ Ask for an email address

☑ Include a way for prospects to get on your mailing list

☑ Put in a key code

☑ Make it lively

☑ Provide an example of how to fill in the order form

THE BUSINESS REPLY ENVELOPE

Did you:

☑ Check with the post office to be sure you know all the regulations

☑ Include a questionnaire on the back, inquiring if customers have enclosed and signed the check

☑ Make sure you've included your address in the letter and/or on the order form, in case someone loses your envelope

KEEP YOUR PRINTING COSTS IN MIND

Remember the factors that influence printing costs:

- ☑ Paper stock
- ☑ Paper weight
- ☑ Size of your pieces
- ☑ Ink colors
- ☑ Time needed for printing
- ☑ The size of your run (the number of pieces you need)

SEASONALITY:

- ☑ Remember the best months for mail order:
  - √ August
  - √ September
  - √ October
  - √ January
- ☑ Do your own testing to find out which months are best for you

6

Distinctive Direct Response Advertising

Before Steven Spielberg produced *Jurassic Park*, before Barney's giant purple onslaught, there were:

Prehistoric Playthings Your Child Will Love
A Dozen DINOSAURS for $1.50

This extremely successful direct response ad (Figure 6.1) generated over 240,000 orders. That's 2,880,000 dinosaurs!

It's this type of response that hooks people into trying direct response advertising (advertising in any medium designed to generate an immediate response via mail or telephone). This is also the reason many people are disappointed with direct response: if they don't sell thousands of products their first time out, they walk away and don't try again.

Direct response ads have many of the same elements as direct mail packages. The difference is that in direct response advertising, you have much less space and time to make your sale. You have only a few square inches and the few seconds it takes to turn the page of a newspaper or magazine to hook your customers and grab their attention.

In a direct mail campaign, you can grab your customers with a teaser on the envelope, explain dozens of benefits in a letter, and reinforce

Figure 6.1

This extremely successful ad sold more than 2,880,000 dinosaurs.

your offer in a brochure or lift letter. In a direct response ad, you have only one shot to accomplish the same results. And that one shot is not only competing with the direct mail, catalogs, bills, and letters that may have come in your mailbox, it's competing with other ads on the page, with the editorial content of the publication, and even with the comics. Given the fact that most readers are not going through the newspaper or magazine with the intention of purchasing your product, your ad must convincingly promote an impulse buy.

There are, of course, advantages to direct response advertising. You can usually reach large numbers of people for less money than it takes to do a direct mail campaign or to produce a catalog, and there aren't as many steps involved in the process. Large full-page ads with tear-out coupons or bind-in business reply cards have been doing very well for companies like the Franklin Mint and Lands' End for years. But many small ads—from an eighth of a column in *The New Yorker* to a tiny classified in the back of *Adweek*—have proven to be successful as well.

Setting Clear Objectives

There are three possible objectives for direct response advertising:

1. To make money
2. To build your customer list
3. To learn something

Objective No. 1. If you're selling one item by itself—such as a new software program—with no plans to offer your customers any other products, your objective is purely to make money. You simply want a customer to buy your product, after which he or she has no further value for you.

Objective No. 2. The real reward from print advertising is being able to build a loyal customer base who will buy repeat products. If you have more than one item to offer, or you're offering a product that customers will want to purchase again and again, you may want to use direct response advertising to expand your database and create long-term relationships with customers. Since you can't possibly rent every list there is on the market, you might choose a direct response ad to reach a large number of people.

For instance, suppose you decide that readers of *Newsweek* magazine are an ideal target for your product. You could rent their list. If you place a direct response ad in the magazine, however, you also have the possibility of reaching people who are not subscribers, but buy the magazine at the newsstand, or read it at their doctor's office (these people may be direct response buyers of other products, but they might not have subscribed to *Newsweek*). The people who order from you then become part of your own database for future direct mailings.

If you were to advertise in *Newsweek*'s "Business Plus" segment, which is sent to approximately one million high-income professionals and managerial subscribers, it will cost you about $76,000 for a full-page, two-color ad. Additionally, the copywriting, design, and mechanics of ad production will cost about $4,000. Rounding it off, we might say the ad will cost you $80,000.

It might cost you as much as $1 million to reach the same number of *Newsweek* subscribers through direct mail. Of course, you'd never just mail to one million subscribers. You'd start out by mailing to 10,000, then if that was successful you'd mail to 25,000 and so on. So if you want to reach one million potential buyers all at the same time, with the object of converting them into loyal customers, you should consider a direct response ad.

Once someone orders from you, they've become a direct mail buyer. As any list broker will confirm, people who buy from direct mail offers are more likely to become loyal customers than those who buy through direct response ads. So if a customer buys a case of juicy oranges from your direct response ad, your next step should be to include an offer for ruby red grapefruits inside the case of oranges. Then follow up their purchase with a catalog of your full line of fresh-fruits-by-mail. That way you've converted a one-time responder to a customer who is likely to continue buying from you.

Some companies, such as those that offer collectible plates or dolls, place expensive full-page ads in national magazines knowing they will not get enough initial orders to pay for the ad. They also know, however, that once a customer buys one of their collectibles, they are likely to buy several more. Although they may not initially make money from these ads, they're worth the cost because of the long-term value of these buyers and the total dollars these customers will eventually spend.

If you're offering an expensive product, or one that is complicated to explain, you can use direct response ads as part of a two-step process. The first step is to get the name and address of an interested prospect, and the second step is to make a sale. Many two-step ads offer something for free to draw prospects in. This could be a booklet, a brochure, a catalog, or a free sample. For instance, an ad to promote tourism in a particular state might offer a free guide to the state's most exciting attractions. A company that sells window treatments might offer a booklet explaining how to measure your windows for curtains, shades, or blinds. You need to think of your offer from your prospects' point of view. You need to figure out what you can give them to help solve their particular problem.

TIP Sometimes your objective is to gather as many leads as possible. If you place an ad that includes a bind-in reply card, test cards with prepaid postage and cards that require the prospect to pay the postage, you may find that prospects who are willing to invest the 21¢ are more likely to be qualified leads.

The second step in the process is to convert the lead into a sale. The vacation guide might include discount coupons for some of the state's attractions and special vacation package deals. After the company that sells window treatments sends out its free booklet, the next step would be a telemarketing call saying, "Since you recently sent away for our free booklet, we'd like you to know that we're having a sale of 20 percent off all our merchandise. Would you like our experts to come measure your windows and give you an estimate for blinds, shades, or curtains?"

Objective No. 3. The third objective of direct response advertising is to learn something. For instance, a large company launching a new product might place ads in both *Woman's Day* and *Mademoiselle*. If most of the responses they get come from *Mademoiselle*, they know that their target audience is more upscale than the typical *Woman's Day* readers. Now they can change their vision of who their target market is and start renting lists that are more upscale.

Other lessons can be learned from testing in newspapers and magazines. Many publications offer A-B splits, which means that half the print run will contain one ad, and the other half a different ad. Suppose you're selling a book on interior design and you visualize two separate target markets. One is the novice, perhaps a recent college graduate or newlywed, who needs help in decorating his or her first home. The second target is the person who's slightly older, has the home in place, and is trying to decorate on a budget. With the two targets in mind, you create two separate marketing strategies and two different ads.

The first ad has a headline that reads "Need help decorating your home? Learn the secrets the pros use!" The headline for the second ad reads "Discover how to decorate your home on a budget." You can then run an A-B split in one geographical area. Every other issue of the newspaper or magazine in that area will run a different ad. That means your results won't be skewed by zip code or neighborhood.

You can find out the costs of running A-B splits by reading *Standard Rate and Data*, or by calling the specific publication in which you want to advertise, and asking for a rate card. Once you discover which ad produces the best results, you can roll it out to the publication's total circulation, or use it as the basis for a more targeted direct mail campaign.

Location, Location, Location

They say that success in retailing is due to three things: location, location, location. The same is essentially true for direct response advertising. Where your ad is placed can make a difference of thousands of orders. Placing a well-written, well-conceived ad for a software program in *Gourmet* or in *Travel & Leisure* would not do as well as placing it in *PC Magazine*.

The best way to decide where to place your ad is to talk to some people who fit the profile you've developed by visualizing your ideal prospect. Ask them if they'd be interested in your product. And most importantly, ask them what they read. Talk to as many people as possible when developing your list of ideal prospects. They often give you marketing ideas you never would have thought of yourself.

If you're unsure about what publications are available to you, go to the library and look at the directories published by Standard Rate and Data Services. These books list thousands of periodicals published in the United States (there are also foreign editions available). They contain information about the editorial content, the names and titles of the chief executives, circulation figures, general advertising rates and discounts, rates for classified ads, whether or not split runs are available (important for testing purposes), and whether or not they publish regional editions.

Before you decide to place your ad in a particular newspaper or magazine, be sure to read several copies. When you're reading the publication, ask yourself these questions:

- Reading over the editorial content, who do you perceive to be the publication's target audience?
- Is the publication's target audience the same as yours?
- Look at the ads. Are there many direct response ads in the publication? If there are, you know that those ads are doing well, and you might choose this publication for your ad.
- Are the ads' target audience similar to yours? If so, this is a publication that is likely to be successful for you as well.
- Does your competition advertise in this publication? Study the magazine for several issues. If your competition's ad shows up repeatedly, that means they're getting good results (you don't keep running an unsuccessful ad). Place an ad that details the reasons your product is the best of its type, and readers will buy from you too.

Call some of the advertisers yourself and find out how successful their ads have been in that publication. Did they get the results they expected? Are they going to advertise in that publication again?

> TIP   A direct response ad carries an implied endorsement of the publication in which it appears. Therefore, you want your choice of publication to reflect the lifestyle and philosophy of your target audience.

Working Within Your Budget

A major influence on your decision about where to place your direct response ad is your budget. Costs of advertising vary with the circulation of the publication. Obviously, the larger the circulation, the more the ad will cost—just like advertising on television, where it costs most for commercial time on the shows with the highest ratings. It's generally much more expensive to buy time on a network show than on a local cable program. So a national publication will charge more for advertising than will a local weekly paper.

There are four basic choices of media for direct response ads. When you're putting together a marketing plan, and deciding which medium is best for your product, you'll need to compare costs for all four choices. They are:

- *Daily newspapers*: The advantages of advertising in a daily paper are that it is a fairly inexpensive way to reach a large number of people, and that, in most cases, you can reach those people quickly (an ad sent to a paper can appear within a few days), and expect a quick response time from readers. However, you're reaching an audience selected primarily by geography rather than by interest or buying habits.
- *Magazines*: Magazine advertising can be very expensive, especially in a popular national publication. However, there are also many special-interest magazines related to a product or service. Some magazines allow you to advertise in a regional edition (the Northeast, for example), which will cost you less than advertising in a full national run. Your advertising also has a longer life span, as people usually keep magazines around longer than they do newspapers. A major disadvantage is that magazines require a long lead time, often three or four months, before your ad will actually appear.

If your ad contains a coupon or order form you want readers to tear out and send to you, there are other factors to consider. You may have a slow response rate because people don't want to tear out the coupon until they've finished reading the magazine, or in the case of upscale shelter magazines (such as *Metropolitan Home* or *Architectural Digest*), they may not want to "ruin" the magazine by tearing out anything at all. In these cases, including an 800 number may be more effective than including a coupon, or you may want to consider an ad with a bind-in-card, which can be torn out without marring the magazine.

- *FSIs:* Free-standing inserts are unattached advertisements which are blown in or inserted into a newspaper or magazine. You'll find many of these in your Sunday paper. Some people find FSIs annoying because they always fall out of the paper. But that may be why they are so effective—when papers are flying everywhere, you can't help but look at them. The disadvantages are that you're once again reaching a nonselective audience, and that there are now so many FSIs that it's difficult to get yours to stand out from the crowd.

- *Weekly newspapers:* Weekly papers often provide an inexpensive way to advertise. These papers usually have limited, community-based coverage—which may be perfect if the paper goes to a community that includes your ideal prospects.

Advertising Discounts

There are also ways to get discounts for your advertising dollars. Most publications offer volume and frequency discounts, which means that if you advertise in more than one publication owned by a newspaper or publishing chain, or if you agree to run your ad a certain number of times in the same publication, you can get a discounted rate. Many publications offer remnant or standby rates, which are special rates on unsold space. This means that you submit your ad to the publication and when the publication has an open spot, they'll publish your ad (within a certain time frame). The advantage is that you can often get a very good discounted rate for your ad. The disadvantage is that you don't know exactly when it's going to run and that you have to do careful follow-up. I once placed an ad for a client on standby, called the paper to find out if the ad had run, and was told that it had. My client was devastated because there had been no response. When we asked for a tearsheet (a copy of the ad as it was printed), we were told there had been an error; the ad had not run after all. It ran the next day.

You can also place your ad through media buying services. These are agencies that buy volume space in various media, and then sell that space to interested vendors. If you have a small advertising budget, you may be able to set up a PI or PO arrangement with a service. PI stands for Per Inquiry and PO stands for Per Order. You then pay nothing for the advertising space, but give the media service a percentage of every order or inquiry you receive (and that is negotiated).

One such service is Stephen L. Geller, Inc. (no relation to me), a Connecticut-based print media buying service with expertise in the direct response market. President Sue R. Geller (also no relation to me) outlined the seven main points her company, and other media buying services, consider when buying advertising space for their clients:

1. *Demographic/psychographic research*: Based on the product, and the agency's experience with similar products, they analyze the demographics—for instance, "this is a product that will probably appeal to women age 18–34 with an income level of $30,000 or more." They also use psychographic data, which refer to a person's attitudes, habits, activities, and behavior patterns. These data might tell them, "this is a product that will probably appeal to women who participate in sports." The agency also has access to research tools such as the Publisher's Information Bureau, which prints reports on thousands of products, and in which publications their advertising has appeared. This gives the agency information about competitive products.

2. *Cost per thousand*: This refers to the ad's cost per thousand readers. This is extremely important in direct response because it's possible that the audience profile of a magazine you've chosen fits your product to a T, but if you're paying too high a cost per thousand, that magazine won't produce enough responses to make the ad worthwhile.

3. *Product history*: Media buying agencies rely on their experience with other products to give them information for future products. SLG, Inc., has a developed a database that includes information on all previous clients, the types of products they sold, the publications in which they advertised, and the results of those placements. They probably won't share specific results with you—they won't tell you the names of the companies, for instance—but they can tell you in which publications similar products to yours were successfully advertised.

If you don't go through a media buying service, you can use your own experience as a guide. What publications have been successful for you in the past? Did specific times of the year produce better results than any other? Were there other seasonality factors, such as holidays? Did you advertise in a Sunday paper? Were there outside factors that influenced buying decisions? I once created a beautiful ad for a collectible item which, based on previous ads, should have been very successful. However, the day the ad appeared turned out to be Super Bowl Sunday—and there was a blinding snowstorm. Half the potential customers couldn't even get the paper, and the other half were busy watching the game.

4. *Rollout potential*: What is the rollout potential of the publication you're considering? If you have a product geared to motorcycle enthusiasts, there are several publications that target that audience, most with small circulations. Even if your ad is successful in those publications, where do you go from there? You need to test your ad in mass-market publications as well, so that if it is successful in a regional test, for instance, you can roll out to a much wider national audience.

5. *Creative approach*: Each newspaper and magazine has its own individual style for both editorial content and advertising. Some publications feature ads that are beautiful four-color illustrations with very little copy. An ad that contains a lot of copy surrounding one small photo might not pull very well in that magazine. The same ad will not work in every magazine, so you either have to change the ad to fit the particular magazine or newspaper, or alter your choice of publication.

6. *Price point of product*: In order to determine whether or not a particular publication works within your budget, you must figure out how many units of your product you must sell to pay for the ad. For instance, if an ad for your software program costs $12,000, how many programs do you have to sell to pay for it? If your product costs $49.95, you'd have to sell more than 240 to make a profit. Is that realistic, given the circulation of the publication you've chosen? For a more detailed explanation of these cost factors, see Chapter 9, "Costs and Mail Order Math."

7. *Objective*: How much you are willing to pay for advertising space also depends on your objective. Do you want to make money "off-the-page"—to get people to respond by sending in their check or money order or calling to order from your 800 number? Or are you interested in a two-step lead generation process, where interested readers call you to get more information, and then must be converted to a sale? Larger companies may be less concerned with the price of an individual ad if they have ancillary businesses that can cover the costs. In that case, the company's objective might be to get names for their mailing list so that they call sell them other products down the line. The objective of a small business with one product to sell is a large number of immediate sales; therefore that company will be more concerned with advertising at a cost that will be covered by the resulting sales.

How to Make Your Ad Stand Out from the Crowd

To be effective, a direct response ad has to leap right out and stop you from turning the page. Your ad has to immediately answer two questions: Who would want to buy this product? Why would they want to buy it? You have to get people immediately excited with an attention-grabbing headline and benefit-laden copy.

The headline doesn't have to be clever or complicated. Some of the most successful headlines are the simplest:

GROW GIANT STRAWBERRIES

HUNDREDS OF TOMATOES FROM A SINGLE PLANT

MIRACLE WINDSHIELD WIPERS

Who wouldn't want hundreds of tomatoes from a single plant, or miracle windshield wipers? One of the most successful direct response ads ever was created more than 50 years ago by advertising pioneer John Caples, a member of the Advertising Hall of Fame. The headline for that full-page ad for an at-home music study course read: "They laughed when I sat down at the piano but when I started to play!—" The extensive copy in the ad went on to tell the story of a young man who became the hit of the party when he surprised his friends and sat down to play Beethoven's *Moonlight* Sonata. The ad painted such a vivid picture that the product was almost irresistible to any would-be musician.

The object of a headline is to create an instant relationship with your targeted reader—something that will make the reader stop, look, and read on. Here are six types of headlines you can use (and you'll probably want to test several of them):

1. *The problem/solution headline.* Readers who experience similar problems to the one posed in your headline will immediately identify with your product.

> **DO YOU SPEND SLEEPLESS NIGHTS WALKING THE FLOOR?**
> **TRY OUR ALL NATURAL HERBAL REMEDY AND**
> **CURE INSOMNIA FOREVER.**

> **MISS AN URGENT MESSAGE FROM YOUR CLIENT**
> **BECAUSE YOU'RE STUCK IN TRAFFIC? NEVER AGAIN!**
> **ACME CELLULAR WILL HAVE YOU BACK ON THE ROAD AND**
> **WORRY-FREE WITHIN JUST ONE HOUR.**

   Pose a problem and provide an answer with benefits for the prospect. The answer can be contained in the headline (as in the examples above) or at the beginning of the ad copy.

2. *The historical event.* In 1986, America issued its first gold coins. Joe England's simple but effective headline, placed above a photo of the coins, read, "American's First Gold Bullion Coins." That ad sold over $10 million worth of coins in four months. If there is something newsworthy about your product, especially if it is a first-time or limited-time offer, it can be an effective draw.

3. *The testimonial.* If someone I know, respect, or identify with tells me they use a product, I might be inclined to give it a try. So if I see an ad for athletic footwear featuring Michael Jordan saying, "THESE ARE THE SHOES THAT HELPED ME SCORE!" or an ad for a hair care product with a photo of Cher and a headline that reads "I NEVER USE ANYTHING ELSE," I think, "If it's good enough for her, it's good enough for me." A testimonial doesn't have to be from a celebrity. For instance, if I came across an ad with this headline:

"I USED THE ACME EXERCYCLE FOR JUST 15 MINUTES A DAY, AND AFTER ONE MONTH, I LOST EIGHT POUNDS AND CAN FIT INTO MY FAVORITE JEANS AGAIN!"
—Betsy Jones, Long Island, New York

I'd be tempted to read on, even though I don't know Betsy Jones. I'm still inclined to think, "If it can work for Betsy Jones, it can work for me."

4. *Product claims.* A product's credibility can be increased by including statistical claims about its effectiveness. The more factual and/or scientific you can make your claim, the better. If nine out of 10 doctors recommend a product, it must be safe and effective. It also helps to reveal the source of the claim you're making. If a report by the American Medical Association confirms that nine out of 10 doctors recommend your product, your credibility is sky-high. Just as with testimonials, the source does not have to be well known. A headline that reads "70% OF THE FORTUNE 500 EXECUTIVES WHO HAVE READ THIS BOOK WERE PROMOTED WITHIN SIX WEEKS" might be followed with an asterisk and a line at the bottom of the ad saying, "According to a 2002 poll by Smith and Associates." You may not know of Smith and Associates, but you'll be comforted by the fact that the author of the book did not simply make up the number.

5. *Outrageous statements.* You can often catch readers' attention by making a statement that provokes their curiosity and almost forces

them to read on. A few years ago, Rodale Press used a headline in a direct mail letter which I always thought would have been perfect for a direct response ad:

**ALL WOMEN WHO DIE BEFORE THE AGE OF 120
ARE DYING PREMATURELY.**

Figure 6.2 shows an ad that I wrote for Olympic coins, which features the story of Robert Garrett, captain of the Princeton Track Team in 1896, who wanted the U.S. to compete so badly he financed the entire team's trip to Greece. This is an unusual story that even most diehard Olympics fans don't know. The photograph of Garrett in his strange-looking Olympic garb helped to increase the curiosity factor.

6. *Questions.* Questions are an excellent involvement device. Leaving a question unanswered is like ending a song just before the last note—extremely frustrating or provoking. A headline that asks a questions makes you want to read on to find out the answer. Some examples of this type of headline are:

**IS YOUR BOSS DRIVING YOU CRAZY? NEED TO GET AWAY
SOMEWHERE PEACEFUL AND QUIET?**

**REMEMBER WHEN THE SMELL OF GRANDMA'S HOME-BAKED
APPLE PIE WAS THE SWEETEST SCENT ON EARTH?**

The copy for these ads would then contain the answers. After the first headline, the copy could read, "Come to our island paradise and get away from it all." The second headline might be followed by "Then let Mrs. McCormick's old-fashioned pies bring those memories home again."

The Copy

Direct response advertisements can be as large as one or more full pages, or as small as a three-line classified ad. Whatever number of words you

Figure 6.2

The headline introducing Robert Garrett (pictured in his nineteenth-century sports garb) intrigued prospective coin buyers to read on.

The story of Robert Garrett who financed the first U.S. Olympic team... and brought home 9 victories for the United States.

Robert Garrett was the captain of the Princeton Track Team in 1896, the year of the first modern Summer Olympics.

At that time there was no U.S. Olympic Committee or coin program to help finance the U.S. Olympic team.

Mr. Garrett wanted to compete, but he couldn't convince his teammates to join him at the Games in Greece... until he volunteered to pay their expenses! After adding a Harvard student and five athletes from the Boston Athletic Association, he had organized the first U.S. Olympic team. They won 9 of the 12 track and field events!

It's with this same dedication to the fine spirit of competition, determination and endurance that the President and Congress have authorized the issuance of extraordinary silver and gold coinage to commemorate the 1984 Games in Los Angeles. It's also the first time in some 50 years the U.S. has minted a gold coin!

All profits from the sale of the coins will go toward our Olympic effort.

Athletic training today is far more sophisticated than it was when the coach's "pep" talks were all an athlete had. Today, the competitive athlete is tested, measured, and even *fed* in a scientific fashion.

All the profits from the sale of these special coins will go toward the U.S. Olympic effort, including paying for today's advanced training of our gifted athletes – their coaches, trainers, equipment, special training aids and travel expenses to the Games.

You too can be a star... for as little as $32.

Your purchase of these magnificent Olympic commemorative coins will ensure that our athletes at the Los Angeles Games and in the future will have the training they require and deserve, while bringing you and your family great pleasure as historic and meaningful heirlooms.

History of Olympic Coins

The tradition of issuing modern Olympic commemorative coinage started with the 1952 Games in Helsinki.

The coins commemorating the 1984 Games are planned to enhance the illustrious traditions of the past.

The 1983 silver one dollar coin was designed by Elizabeth Jones, the chief engraver at the Mint. The obverse (or front) of the coin represents a dramatic depiction of the classic Greek discus thrower.

The 1984 silver one dollar coin was designed by Robert Graham, a Los Angeles sculptor. The obverse of the coin will bear a representation of the Gateway to the Olympic Coliseum. The 1984 gold ten dollar coin was designed by John Mercanti, a member of the U.S. Mint engraving staff. He captured the Olympic Torch bearers in delicate detail developed from a concept created by James Peed.

These "proof" coins are produced by a technique involving specially prepared dies and planchets and a special multiple striking.

How you can own the 1984 Olympic Commemorative Coins.

The U.S. Mint offers three purchase options. The single 1983 silver coin, a two-coin set with the 1983 and the 1984 silver coins, or a three-coin set featuring the 1984 gold coin and the 1983 and 1984 silver coins.

The more coins you purchase, the more you will help our fine athletes.

Support The Home Team.

Option #1 Single-Coin Set
One 1983 Silver Coin $32

Option #2 Two-Coin Set
One 1983 and one 1984 Silver Coin $64

Option #3 Three-Coin Set
One 1983 and one 1984 Silver Coin plus one 1984 Gold Coin $416

need to get your message across is the right length for a direct response ad. Even the smallest ad should tell a story, from the headline to the lead sentence, down to the ordering device.

How do you decide what to write? I always start by making a list of all the product's features and benefits. Then I start writing until I think I've covered everything. Inevitably, when I look back at what I've written I realize that the first two paragraphs are unnecessary, and the third one is the grabber. That becomes the lead (the first sentence or paragraph after the headline).

One of the many decisions you have to make when writing ad copy is who is telling the story. Most ads speak through an omniscient narrator. Figure 6.3 shows another ad I wrote, this one for "The Amazing Super Foods Diet." The headline, spoken by some unseen presence, declares, "Lose 7 Pounds a Week...Or Your Money Back!" The copy goes on to describe all the benefits of this risk-free offer.

More unusual is the ad in Figure 6.4. This ad we created for RCA Victor tells a story from a first-person point of view, as if the young woman pictured in the ad is speaking directly to the reader. This ad was first created speaking in the third person. It was okay, but too much like every other ad we saw for music collections. Then we turned it into a real story, told by Susan Alexander, an actual employee at RCA Victor. This gave the ad the distinctive difference it needed to stand out in a crowded field.

There is one rule of thumb when you're writing ad copy: edit, edit, edit. The writing should be as tight as possible so that everything you need—no more, no less—is included. Keep sentences short, and the language simple but descriptive.

The copy is always followed by the ordering device. In a small space ad, that may be a mailing address or a phone number. In a large ad, an order form or coupon is usually included. Be sure to repeat all the important information about your product, including the offer, in the order form. Remember that some people may tear off only the coupon and not save the entire ad. If there's not enough information on the coupon, they may forget what they wanted to order. As always, the object is to make it as easy as possible for an interested reader to become a loyal customer.

Figure 6.3
An omniscient narrator announces the bold headline of this ad.

This is the last diet you'll ever need...to stay thin

THE AMAZING **SUPER FOODS DIET** NEW!

Lose 7 pounds a week... or your money back!

PROVEN

NO MORE HUNGER ★ NO PILLS ★ MEETS U.S. DIETARY GUIDELINES

- ★ **Counting calories is the only way to lose weight. Right? Wrong! See page 70.**
- ★ **Diet sodas have one calorie per glass — but they are *not* good for your waistline. Read why, page 48.**
- ★ **That one cup of orange sections can be good for you, but (surprise!) it's fattening. See page 46.**
- ★ **Gorging yourself at the salad bar... then don't expect to get into that bikini this summer (page 45).**
- ★ **Cutting down by using margarine instead of butter? Forget it, and see page 45.**

The Super Food Diet...
is a sure-fire way to lose weight without the tedium of counting calories, weighing food or going hungry. There are no pills, no drugs, no gorging on protein, carbohydrates or fruit that promise to "wash away" the fat! If you follow THE SUPER FOOD way — you will be thin and you deserve it!

It is your dream-come-true, a way to quick and permanent weight loss while you dine on gourmet meals you never *ever* believed could actually help you lose weight!

We know it works, but you don't have to take our word for it. THIS IS THE ONLY DIET BOOK THAT COMES WITH A 30-DAY MONEY-BACK GUARANTEE. Try it for one month in your home — and if it doesn't work for you, we'll refund your money.

That is how sure we are that this is the last diet book you will ever ever need.

Mary Ann Crenshaw has been there...

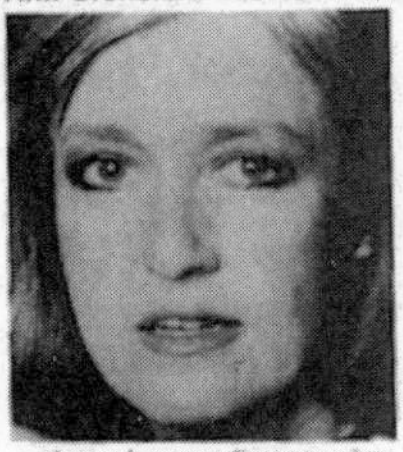

...through every diet maze imaginable. "I've fallen for all the hype. I've tried every diet conceived, and — probably just like you — I've always ended up fat again."

This breakthrough new diet grew out of her need.
As a beauty, diet and fashion writer for The New York Times for ten years, Mary Ann Crenshaw had experimented with hundreds of diets to no avail! She still was carrying an extra 25 ugly pounds — and not feeling very good about herself. That is when she went to work to discover the special Super Foods and sixteen "Star" Super Foods that are the greatest single aid to your losing weight quickly — and comprise the core of the diet. These same foods keep you radiantly healthy. She took off one pound every day... 10 days — 10 pounds gone! It was easy, effective and most important the weight stayed off. And, that was ten years ago.

Now, Mary Ann can show you how to do it too!
You will no longer have to "get by" on cottage cheese and melon, because the Super Foods are the foods you love to eat. These are the dense, chewy foods you can really sink your teeth into; the ones you love when you are "eating" and crave when you are "dieting" — things like bagels, cream cheese, turkey, bananas AND potatoes.

And, since the idea is to enjoy these delicious foods, you can get simple recipes and menus that stand up to even the most finicky appetites. Best of all, it is all there for you — no thinking — just follow the easy diet and lose that pound each and every day!

If you are itching to see those pounds melt away...
...there is a super-fast version of the diet called "No Thrills" that will enable you to lose the weight, safely and fast! There are recipes for the "No Thrills" plan too.

She will show you how to:
- **Have that lovely thin and youthful body, you've always dreamed of having.**
- **Eat and never go hungry. Hunger only leads to binges — and more weight.**
- **Glow with new healthy radiance.**
- **Get away from traditional diet foods — from carrots (fattening if you munch on them a lot) to hard boiled eggs (2 eggs — 200 calories). You will be allowed snacks.**
- **Enjoy the same meals as your family does, and save all that energy of cooking separate ones.**

You'll reap the benefits of this exciting new diet in two hundred and forty pages (hardcover) filled with all the help you'll need to attain your goal — a beautiful slim body! You will have the complete diet, many many delicious recipes, menu plans, and easy ways to maintain it — so the scale will show a daily weight loss of one pound. The mirror will show it even clearer.

Aren't you tired of the diet merry-go-round of hunger, then overeating — weight gain. Get off that unfulfilling cycle and get this amazing new book. Give yourself this special gift, and you'll be glad you did for years to come. Mail the coupon now, while you're thinking about it. There is a money back guarantee, so there is no risk!

Mary Ann Crenshaw is the author of the best-selling THE NATURAL WAY TO SUPER BEAUTY, which included her amazing Cider Vinegar, Lecithin, Kelp, B-6 Diet. Now she is taking you further to the most perfect no-hunger plan with
THE SUPER FOOD DIET

NO-RISK GUARANTEE

To: Success Books, 6 Commercial Street, Hicksville, NY 11801

YES, please rush me my copy of THE SUPER FOODS DIET. I am enclosing my check or money order for $12.95 plus $1.25 for postage and handling charges ($14.20 total). It's a small price to pay for being thin! If I am not delighted with the results, I may return the book (within 30 days) for a full refund.

Name ______________________________

Address ______________________________

City ______________ State ________ Zip ________

11007 Please add applicable sales tax. SFD1

Figure 6.4

This ad was made more effective by changing the narration from the third person to the first person.

We're not going to make this available in stores. And I don't think we're going to run this ad forever, so you should call right now: 1-800-341-6633. Just pick up the phone and call. It's toll-free. You can use this coupon, if you like. And I guarantee you're going to love the music!

Susan Alexander

Here's the deal:
- 2 CDs or 2 Cassettes
- Plus A FREE CD or Cassette (you get 3 for the price of 2!)
- Over 3 hours of the world's greatest music by the most acclaimed performers
- Digitally remastered for the clearest sound
- 10-day audition. Your satisfaction guaranteed
- Not sold in stores

No risk 10-day audition. You must be absolutely delighted or simply return your CDs or Cassettes within 10 days for a full refund.

FREE CD or Cassette!

1-800-341-6633
Call now. It's Toll-Free!

Last week I finally asked Michael over for dinner. And I was...nervous. I planned everything: best table cloth, good silver and china and crystal, candles. I called Mom for recipes, then I thought...music! Music makes the mood, right?

I wanted the best of everything... including the music.

No problem. I work at RCA Victor and who knows more about music? I called my friend Laura. She puts together all our classical compilations. And I wanted *classical*. I mean, I had the best of everything else, so I wanted the best romantic music.

Laura's terrific. She put 22 of the greatest romantic musical selections ever written onto a special one-of-a-kind demo tape. I played it the night Michael and I had dinner

at my place. And it was great. I mean... just great.

Suddenly, everybody wanted my tape. Where else can you get two hours of the most wonderful romantic music ever? I told my boss about it. And now my tape is available on 2 CDs or 2 Cassettes.

They're called *Romance* and *Dinner For Two*. They cost just $19.95 for both CDs or $14.95 for both Cassettes plus $2.95 so we can ship them to you.

You get a FREE CD or Cassette, too! As important as *Romance* is, it's not everything. We need to relax, too. So you'll get our CD or Cassette called *Relaxation*... it helps soothe frazzled nerves...FREE when you order the romantic music Laura put together for me.

RCA VICTOR

Get the Most for Your Advertising Dollars

There is no guarantee that any ad, no matter how creative, will produce the desired results. There are always outside factors.

There are, however, some tips that can help you get the most for your advertising dollar:

★ *Don't forget to use source codes.* You can use any kind of code, any combination of letters and numbers, that will tell you in which publication the ad was printed. That way, if you have ads running simultaneously in more than one publication, you'll know which one(s) produced the best response. If you include an 800 number for response, the code can be "Ask for Barbara" in one publication, and "Ask for Elizabeth" in another, or you can include two different extension numbers. If you're doing an email promotion, you'll want to create a "landing page" that will take people right to your offer. Also, if you are directing people to an offer on your website through a print or direct mail campaign, instead of directing them to your homepage, you would probably create a dedicated landing page by sending them to something like www.yoursitename.com/greatdeal.

★ *If you include a coupon with your return address, use a street address instead of a post office box.* A post office box often seems temporary, and people are more likely to trust your company name if it is followed by a street name and number.

★ *If your budget allows it, use bind-in cards.* These are business reply postcards that the reader fills out and returns to your company, either with an inquiry or an order with a "bill me" option (most people don't like to put their credit card numbers on postcards). Bind-ins catch people's attention and make it easy for them to order, which is your goal in every ad you place.

★ *Request good placement.* Ads that attract the most attention are usually on right-hand pages near the front of the publication. The worst placement is on the left near the gutter (the inner edge of the page). Although the publication will not usually guarantee your placement, you can make your requests known.

★ *Ask about special-interest issues.* Many publications produce special-interest issues over the course of a year. For instance, a hobby magazine may concentrate on needlecrafts one month, and the next month feature model airplanes. If you're selling a quilting kit, you want to be sure to place your ad in the needlecrafts issue. So when you're considering advertising in any publication, call and find out if they are planning any special issues related to your product or service.

★ *Evaluate your direct response ads.* Make a chart that lists the various publications in which your ad has appeared, and what the revenues were from each of them. Measure the results carefully. It's easy to look at the highest revenues and determine that publication to be the "winner." However, you have to take your up-front costs into account. It may have been expensive to advertise in that publication. A smaller publication, which may have produced fewer orders, may actually have produced a higher profit. So it's important that you keep a tally of how much each ad cost to run, how many responses it produced, what the break-even point was on each ad, and which one produced the highest profit.

Broadcast Media

If you're considering space advertising, you might want to consider direct response radio and direct response TV, as well.

For many products, direct response radio can be a very cost-efficient way to sell a product. One of the reason's for radio's effectiveness is that radio programming has become increasingly segmented to target special-interest groups. Some of the current station formats around the country include hard rock, alternative, classic rock, classical, jazz, all-news, all-sports, and all-talk. Some stations are aimed at specific ethnic groups. Radio stations, and sometimes individual shows on those stations, are reaching groups of people with very specific demographics and psychographics.

The idea is to choose the station that caters to your target audience. If you're selling skateboards, you'll probably get a better response from an alternative music station as opposed to an all-sports station.

According to Larry Schatz, VP of Business Development for Corinthian Media, one of the largest privately-held media buying agencies, "In direct response, radio is generally used to support television. Of course this depends upon the product or service. If you're an accountant during tax season, local radio might work fine. However, with most products, we find that radio generally does not perform as well as television. We use it to target and increase frequency."

The most popular (and the most expensive) advertising times on the radio are 6.00 A.M. to 10:00 A.M. and 3:00 P.M., also known as drive time. This is the most expensive because there is the biggest audience. These are the hours when many people are commuting to and from work, and are listening to radio in their cars. Even with cell phones, it seems that people usually won't start dialing to respond to a radio advertisement when they are in their cars. For direct response radio, pre-afternoon drive time, the 1:00 to 4:00 slot is usually the best. But it depends on the target audience as well.

Another advantage to radio is the implied endorsement. According to Schatz, "On one end of the spectrum, radio stations might air a 20 song uninterrupted music block and then run 4 or 5 minutes of commercials. Listeners often tune-out of long blocks of commercials and running direct response there is difficult. On the other end, you have radio personalities that will do live reads. The commercial stands out, it can be perceived as part of the radio program and it's essentially an implied endorsement."

Direct Response television has experienced phenomenal growth in the last few years. DRTV includes any TV promotion from a 30 second to an hour-long infomercial, selling a product or service, or creating a call to action with a URL, a phone number, or both. On average, U.S. viewers watch more than seven hours of TV a day. 79 million households tuned into QVC last year and the station adds more than 25,000 new customers each month. Sales on QVC and the Home Shopping Network are in the billions. And then, of course, there are DRTV ads on nearly every channel offering cosmetics, exercise equipment, music, vitamins, and a variety of hot new products.

Direct response is not new to television. According to Fred Schwatzfarb, Manager of National Direct Advertising for CNBC cable television, when television was in its infancy, programming was not as tightly scheduled as it is now. "A program that started at 7:00 might end at 8:17, and the next program would be scheduled to start at 8:30," he says. "To fill the time, local stations would feature live product demonstrations, which would include a local phone number to call or an address for sending in your check or money order."

In the 1970s, satellite technology spawned the growth of cable television. By the 1980s, the advertising and Direct Marketing industries began to see the potential of the cable market, and the infomercial was born. Americans are watching and responding to infomercials in record numbers. "Today, some of the larger cable stations receive 30 to 40 percent of their revenue from infomercials," says Schwartzfarb. "The proliferation of cable TV stations has made affordable commercial time available to many more businesses." So, while a 30-second program on *Larry King Live* can cost close to $30,000, and a 30-second spot during Superbowl can go for over a million dollars, one minute of overnight time on a cable station can cost as little as a few hundred dollars.

The reason DRTV works is that it's good for the broadcasters and cable networks and it's good for the Direct Marketers. Schatz explains, "To the extent that inventory has not been sold to conventional advertisers, the opportunity exists for Direct Marketers to come in at lower rates. Obviously there are restrictions. You're not buying program specific, you're buying on a preemptable basis, and you're restricted in terms of the kind of ad you can run—it must have a call to action."

The outlook for DRTV remains good. According to Schatz, "With long-standing and well known brands like Ronco and Time-Life, DRTV has lost much of the stigma attached to products sold over the air. It's another way for marketers to reach the consumer with attractive offers and another way for the consumer to respond."

Checklist

SETTING CLEAR OBJECTIVES

☑ The three objectives for direct response advertising are:
   1. To make money
   2. To build your customer list
   3. To learn something

WHERE TO PLACE YOUR AD

☑ Carefully read any publications in which you are considering advertising. Ask yourself:
- ✓ Who is the publication's target audience?
- ✓ Is that target audience the same as mine?
- ✓ Are there many direct response ads in the publication?
- ✓ Are the ads' target audience similar to mine?
- ✓ Does my competition advertise in this publication?

☑ The four basic media for direct response print advertising:
- ✓ Daily newspapers
- ✓ Magazines
- ✓ Free-standing inserts
- ✓ Weekly newspapers

☑ Advertising discounts
- ✓ Volume and frequency
- ✓ Remnant or standby rates

MAKE YOUR AD STAND OUT FROM THE CROWD

☑ Six types of headlines to test:
- ✓ The problem/solution headline
- ✓ The historical event
- ✓ The testimonial
- ✓ Product claims
- ✓ Outrageous statements
- ✓ Questions

CREATIVE COPY

☑ The right length for ad copy: as long as it takes to tell your story

☑ How do you decide what to write?
- ✓ Make a list of the product's feature and benefits, and decide which are most important
- ✓ Ask yourself, "Who is telling this story?"

✓ Edit, edit, edit

✓ Include a simple-to-use ordering device

GET THE MOST FOR YOUR ADVERTISING DOLLARS

☑ Don't forget to use source codes and landing pages

☑ Use a street address instead of a post office box

☑ Use bind-in cards

☑ Request good placement-right hand pages near the front of the publication

☑ Ask about special-interest issues

☑ Track and evaluate your results

BROADCAST MEDIA

☑ Radio
  ✓ Remember that drive time isn't always the best for direct response
  ✓ If it's talk radio, people are already "listening"
  ✓ Radio can be an inexpensive place to test

☑ Television
  ✓ Cable can be an inexpensive place to test
  ✓ Remnant time can be a good choice for Direct Marketers

7

Catalog Connections

A Tool for Serious Marketers

In 1987, Steve and Lori Leveen placed several tiny ads in *The New York Times* and *The Boston Globe* selling halogen lamps for the home. They got five or six responses. Then they placed a one-inch ad for the same lamps in *The New Yorker* with a headline that read, "Serious Lighting for Serious Readers." The phone started ringing and the Levenger catalog was born.

For seven years, the Leveens had been trying to figure out how to start a business of their own. They both worked in the computer field, were tired of high-tech, and wanted out. Then, in 1987, two factors coincided to make their dreams a reality. First, Lori bought Steve a book on design and he became fascinated with the section on new lighting technologies. Second, he was fired from his job.

"I'll always be in debt to my boss for firing me," says Steve. "My philosophy about working for a company versus working for yourself is that it's essential to work for other people to gain experience along the way. But I sometimes jokingly recommend to people that they try either to become president of the company or get fired. The two tracks are amazingly similar."

The Leveens learned the mail order business through trial and error. "A mail order company is one of the few companies you can start on your kitchen table, which is just what we did," he says. "We sold our car to raise $8,000 so that we could take out a few space ads and put together our first catalog. We didn't know what we were doing, but we had a friend, a graphic artist, who gave us some free advice." The first catalog was one sheet of paper, duo-tone, folded twice. The initial run, in 1987, consisted of 5,000 catalogs. In 2001, Levenger mailed over 24 million four-color, 68-page books.

One of the reasons for Levenger's growth is that the Leveens responded to their customers' needs. When people ordered lamps, they often mentioned other products they were having difficulty locating. "When I talk to people who want to start their own company, mail order or not, I guarantee them one thing—that they can't help but learn as they grow. Even if they think they have everything planned, there are always surprises. And it's how you adapt to those surprises that's fundamental."

There were times in the beginning, however, when the Leveens thought they were not going to make it. "When we were still working at home, there would be days when we'd give a couple of refunds and have no orders—we'd have a negative day, which was a frightening thing to behold." Yet the business slowly grew for the first two or three years, based mainly on the direct response ads which sold a product and offered a free catalog. Rapid growth started when Levenger's made enough money to rent other mail order lists and send the catalog to unsolicited customers.

"This was an expensive proposition," Leveen relates. "To do a legitimate test, I would say you need at least a 24-page color catalog to compete in the mailbox with the great catalogs already deluging customers. To test outside lists, you need a minimum of 5,000 names from every list you test. If you have a viable concept, you'll want to test at least seven to 10 different lists. If you test 10 lists, some will fail and some will succeed. If you only test three lists, what happens if they're the bombs? You'd have to fold your tent. So you're talking about mailing a minimum of 50,000 catalogs. At about 50 cents a catalog, that's $25,000. So you're rolling the dice for a $25,000 minimum."

One of the reasons the Levenger catalog is so successful is because 90 percent to 95 percent of the products are exclusive and made to the company's specifications. The Leveens and their design experts are constantly looking for new ways to allow their customers to be more comfortable and productive when they're reading, writing, and researching. They also pay particular attention to the design of the catalog. There is a collaborative effort between the design team and the merchandise

Figure 7.1

This letter to readers welcomes customers and highlights some of the products featured in the catalog.

DEAR READER

In a letter to her daughter in 1752, Britain's Lady Montagu observed that "No entertainment is so cheap as reading, nor any pleasure so lasting." Whether you read for escape or knowledge or both, you'll find in this catalog tools to enhance the pleasure.

Use our *Reader's Nesting Tables* (page 35) to create a cozy reading cocoon that puts reference books, coffee cup and other reading accoutrements within arm's reach. Then have glasses and pen waiting for you at every reading station in your home, tucked neatly in our *Reader's Table Companion* (page 21).

For lighting at a table or desk, the *Equipoise Lamp* (page 27) will bow gracefully to your wishes for a light source that can come closer to the page. It will also go from bright to soft light with a touch of that magic wand called a dimmer switch.

Enjoy your next book even more!

Steve & Lori Leveen
and the Levenger staff

P.S. Another pleasure of reading this catalog: you'll see our new low prices on *Ink Steps* for bottled ink (page 61), the *Gauge Watch* for eminently readable time (page 51) and the *Wellington Briefcase* (page 41), which can handle a puddle of spring rain as if it had on rubber boots (it does).

manager to give the catalog the look they desire—a warm, inviting, but upscale atmosphere. "In fact," says Leveen, "we're always trying to improve on the catalog. Sometimes we rephotograph products to show new functions and other possibilities."

Leveen is a strong believer in communication with his customers. He begins each catalog with a letter (Figure 7.1). His philosophy is that every letter should give the customers an incentive to buy from that catalog. The letter serves to welcome the customers, and to thank them. "We also use the letter to remind our customers of our guarantee, which in our case is unlimited," says Leveen. "The letter often contains 'something special' that's available for a limited time and in this catalog only, so it's a call to action."

"We're in the marketing business, but we're also in the entertainment business. The catalogs that arrive in the customers' kitchens compete not only with all the other catalogs, but with everything else going on in their lives. And most things rank higher than the catalog sitting there. You have to entertain and inform, try not to waste words, get to the point, and offer them something."

The Catalog Boom

According to the Direct Marketing Association and the United States Postal Service, there were over *16 billion* catalogs mailed in 2000. In 2001 there were 10,000 different catalogs mailed in the United States. Four out of five pieces of fourth-class mail are catalogs. More than 60 percent of the U.S. adult population are Direct Marketing customers. Most of those who made catalog purchases were women, married, between the ages of 36 and 50, college educated, earning an income of over $30,000, and owning (or co-owning) a residence valued at $70,000 or more.

The most popular types of merchandise purchased through catalogs were:

clothing
electronics
food
gardening
hardware
home furnishings (bed and bath)
housewares
nonfood gifts
sporting goods
toys and games

The growth in catalog shopping can be attributed to its convenience. People don't have as much time to shop as they used to—especially in today's two-career households. The evolution of the credit card has also enhanced the popularity of catalogs. In our instant-gratification society, even filling out an order form and making out a check seem too time-consuming. The ability to pick up the phone and place an immediate order via a credit card makes catalog shopping both speedy and easy. It also gives us an opportunity to speak directly to a customer representative of the company, and have that person check to be sure that the item is in stock. Another factor that influenced the growth in catalog shopping was the introduction of the 800 number. This allowed customers to order merchandise without incurring long-distance charges.

And finally, the Internet has greatly contributed to the boom in catalog sales. According to H. Robert Weitzen, President and CEO of The DMA, "The days of single-channel retailing are over. With over 90 percent of catalogs doing business online, pure-play Web companies launching catalogs and catalogs opening retail stores, added to the strong continuing growth of Internet and catalog commerce, it is clear that both consumers and businesses are exercising more control over when, and where they make transactions."

There are three basic types of catalogs:

★ *Retail catalogs*: These are put out by retailers who want to bring traffic into their store and to expand their customer base outside of their immediate geographical area. Stores such as Neiman Marcus, Staples, Bombay Company, and Pottery Barn are examples of retailers who also produce mail order catalogs.

★ *Business-to-business specialty catalogs*: These catalogs came about when sellers of big-ticket items (overhead projectors, computer systems, copiers) were looking for cost-efficient ways to sell after-market supplies. If a company bought a copier for several thousand dollars, it didn't pay for the salesperson to make repeated visits to sell them paper and toner supplies. A catalog was a much better solution. Today, or course, there are many business-to-business suppliers, such as Dell Computer and MAC Mall, that sell only through catalogs.

★ *Consumer specialty catalogs*: This is the largest category of catalogs today—catalogs that appeal to a particular lifestyle or special need. You can find catalogs for just about every need and interest imaginable, including catalogs for short people, tall people, large sizes and petites, golfers, cat fanciers, dog lovers, lovers of animation art, and collectors of Samurai armor, and catalogs that feature automotive tools, dragons, equestrian equipment, and even live seafood!

Almost any line of merchandise can be sold through a catalog. I first realized this years ago working at Wunderman Cato Johnson (then Wunderman Ricotta & Kline), the largest Direct Marketing agency in the country. We were given the assignment of designing a catalog for IBM word-processing supplies—an exciting array of printer ribbons, which all looked the same, and photographed like big black blobs. How were we going to sell anything that looked like that?

What we did was invent the first "magalog": a catalog in magazine format (for which we earned a prestigious ECHO Award). The magalog still contained those boring photos of printer ribbons, but it also contained a lot of copy by and about the people who actually used these products, and a variety of colorful charts detailing how to match the ribbons with the correct machines. It also included short articles by industry professionals about such subjects as the future of computers. The phones rang off the hooks in one of IBM's most successful Direct Marketing efforts.

But designing a catalog is not easy. There are many different phases and hundreds of details. This chapter will provide a step-by-step guide for putting together a successful catalog, whether you have 20 products or 2,000.

Make a Statement with Your Catalog

When customers browse through your catalog, it's as though they just stepped into your store. You want to make this a place your customers will remember, and one to which they'll want to return. When catalogs really work, they have a distinctive personality. The personality that comes through is that of the store owner.

There is no better example of this than L.L. Bean. Since 1912, when L.L. Bean started his mail order company selling a rubber-bottomed, leather-topped hunting boot he had designed, he has been selling reliability. As Bean added other items of outdoor clothing and equipment, one of the most distinctive aspects of the catalog, and one that has continued through the years, is the guarantee. In a 1917 catalog, a boxed-in item on the front page read, "Maine Hunting Shoe—guarantee. We guarantee this pair of shoes to give perfect satisfaction in every way. If the rubber breaks or the tops grow hard, return them together with this guarantee tag and we will replace them free of charge. Signed, L.L. Bean." Today, the guarantee applies to the Bean Boots and everything else in the catalog. Products are guaranteed to give "100 percent satisfaction in every way" and will be accepted for return at any time. The philosophy remains the same as it was in 1917: "We do not want you to have anything from L.L. Bean that is not completely satisfactory." Bean found a niche early and stuck with it (although the catalog wisely expanded from products for the true outdoorsman to products for an out-door lifestyle).

There are many ways that a catalog can express a distinctive personality:

★ *Specialty merchandise:* Sometimes the merchandise you offer is enough to create a distinct persona for your company. A catalog from American Girl (Figure 7.2) for instance offers high quality dolls, clothes, accessories and books that often tie in with historical themes. Because of the type of merchandise offered, the catalog automatically has a different personality than a general toy catalog.

★ *Style:* Mark Cross sells upscale, elegant, high-end leather goods and accessories. Their catalog is also upscale and elegant, using clean, crisp design and high-quality paper featuring one or two items on a page. The catalog reaffirms the company's classy image by showing close-up glamour photographs of each wallet and purse so that you can see the grain of the leather and can almost feel the softness and quality of each of their products. Other catalogs, such as Comfortably Yours, choose a more casual, down-home feel, as if you were leisurely browsing through a small-town general store. The items offered in this catalog all have a personal relevance to the "store owner," Elaine Adler. When describing the comfy cat bed she's selling, she'll tell you about her cat, Farina, who constantly shed all over the chintz bedspread and refused to sleep anywhere else until Elaine found her this oh-so-cozy bed. Or how her

Figure 7.2
The specialty items contained in the American Girl catalog give it a distinct personality.

mother-in-law was having difficulty reaching items high in the cabinets until she found this hand-dandy shelf-picker.

★ *Story line*: Some catalogs simply display a collection of items described by their utilitarian features and price. Many of these catalogs are very successful. But the catalogs that have been most successful over the years are the ones that take catalog shopping out of the ordinary, adding fun and pizzazz by telling a story. The best of these no longer exists (at least in its original form). Banana Republic began as a catalog mail order company, and published a catalog that resembled a travel diary. The Spring 1987 catalog, for example, was entitled "Rambles and Scrambles Around the English Lakes with Mel and Patricia Ziegler." Interspersed amongst the beautiful drawings (not photographs) of the clothes for sale is the "Fellwalking Journal," founders Mel and Patricia Ziegler's account of their trip to the English Lake District which begins, "Like the great poet Wordsworth nearly two centuries before us, we're heading to the lakes on 'nature's invitation.'" It goes on to describe a leg of the journey climbing Skiddaw, England's third-highest peak (also known as a "fell," or mountain), where the climbers

find ourselves lost in a yew forest, sludging through mud, brambles tearing our hands and pants legs. We have conflicting maps. Which way to turn explodes well beyond whether the "stone wall" on my map is the "boundary marker" on hers. ("We always go your way!" "We never go my way!")...

Reading this story, you could just image yourself walking alongside the couple, joining in their banter, and, of course, wearing the 100 percent cotton Mayan shirt featured in the catalog. Banana Republic was then sold and the catalog was phased out in favor of the launch of many retail stores throughout the United States.

Stories can also be used to help strangers get to know you, or your product, in a personal way. The J. Peterman Co. catalog, for example, which read like a collection of short stories that happen to feature items of clothing, put readers into a situation and helped them imagine themselves wearing Peterman clothing. For instance, the following copy was on the page with illustrations of a group of sweaters and skirts, known as "hanging out" wear (Figure 7.3):

Figure 7.3

The text in this catalog evokes a strong mood that was the trademark style of the J. Peterman catalog.

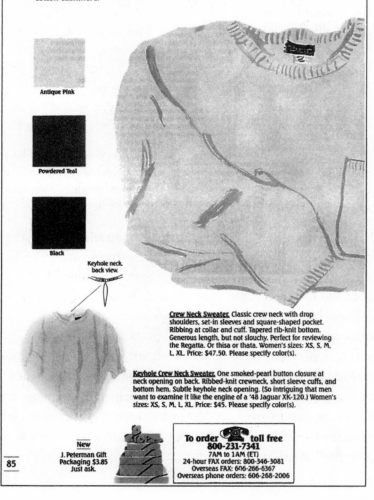

"Hanging out" wear.

The invitation you hoped most to get you just got. You're invited to come and "hang out." For a long weekend. That could mean anything. And usually does.

Walking 6 miles on the beach before breakfast. (As healthy as running, say the latest theories.) Cups and cups of fresh Blue Mountain decaf, fresh Irish soda bread, fresh huckleberries, fresh trout. Biking into town. An hour of Killer Volleyball. Rowing across the sedge pond to talk to the in-residence Hollywood types. Dinner outdoors at twilight. Talking deep and late. Laughing to the point of soreness. Sleeping in. The first time in how long?

And that's just Saturday.

A weekend like this once required a station wagon full of clothes. Now it's a one-bag weekend.

That single bag holds just enough of these inventive, spring-weight tops and bottoms to change your look, your mood, your style, as fast as you can change your mind.

Even more latitude combining colors: Antique Pink, Powdered Teal, or Black. Each executed in that softly luxurious type of cotton loosely called "cotton cashmere."

Antique Pink

Powdered Teal

Black

Keyhole neck, back view.

Crew Neck Sweater. Classic crew neck with drop shoulders, set-in sleeves and square-shaped pocket. Ribbing at collar and cuff. Tapered rib-knit bottom. Generous length, but not slouchy. Perfect for reviewing the Regatta. Or thisa or thata. Women's sizes: XS, S, M, L, XL. Price: $47.50. Please specify color(s).

Keyhole Crew Neck Sweater. One smoked-pearl button closure at neck opening on back. Ribbed-knit crewneck, short sleeve cuffs, and bottom hem. Subtle keyhole neck opening. (So intriguing that men want to examine it like the engine of a '48 Jaguar XK-120.) Women's sizes: XS, S, M, L, XL. Price: $45. Please specify color(s).

New
J. Peterman Gift
Packaging $3.85
Just ask.

85

To order toll free
800-231-7341
7AM to 1AM (ET)
24-hour FAX orders: 800-346-3081
Overseas FAX: 606-266-6367
Overseas phone orders: 606-268-2006

The invitation you hoped most to get you just got. You're invited to come and "hang out." For a long weekend. That could mean anything. And usually does.

Walking 6 miles on the beach before breakfast. (As healthy as running, say the latest theories). Cups and cups of fresh Blue Mountain decaf, fresh Irish soda bread, fresh huckleberries, fresh trout. Biking into town. An hour of Killer Volleyball. Rowing across the sedge pond to talk to the in-residence Hollywood types. Dinner outdoors at twilight. Talking deep and late. Laughing to the point of soreness. Sleeping in. The first time in how long?

And that's just Saturday.

A catalog's story doesn't have to have the beginning, middle, and end of conventional form. It can represent a theme carried throughout the catalog. For example, a recent L.L. Bean catalog featured Bean's most popular products for fall and winter. On the inside front cover, the copy states that the catalog is "full of L.L. Bean products that have stood the test of time" because "if you are like us, you want everything you own to do its job well and keep on doing it until it is honorably worn out." Sidebars throughout the catalog tell the story of the products, such as, "We introduced our original Canvas Field Coat in 1927. Its heavy, tightly woven canvas withstood thorny brush and other hazards of the wild." Now, the only hazards of the wild I'm likely to run into are on the New York City subway system, yet this copy makes me want to buy the jacket and be part of the L.L. Bean experience.

Develop a Catalog Plan

Although some catalogs we receive seem to have been put together hastily and with little rhyme or reason, the most successful are extremely well thought out and carefully planned. Producing a catalog is expensive, especially the first time out, so you want to make as few mistakes as possible. Catalogs that are successful have usually taken all the necessary planning steps. Those steps include:

★ *Define your objectives*: Before you even begin to design your catalog, you must know what it is meant to accomplish. Your objective may be to increase the number of orders you get with each successive catalog. Or your objective may be to build up a database for future mailings. Your objectives may differ depending on which of the three major categories your catalog falls into: retail, business-to-business, or consumer specialty.

Retail: One objective might be to build store traffic and get people into your retail site. You might then mail your catalog to people who live within a reasonable distance of your store. These people are not necessarily mail order buyers; your purpose is to build name recognition and to get them to shop at your store. Sometimes the store and the catalog are separate entities, featuring different merchandise. In most cases, however, the merchandise found in the catalog is also available in the store, and vice versa. Another objective might be to extend your store's reach—that is, to make it possible for people to order your products through the mail in areas where you don't have actual retail sites. A third objective might be to test various items in the catalog before you place them in your general retail inventory.

Business-to-Business has a different set of objectives. One might be to build a solid relationship, so that you become a company's primary supplier of the type of merchandise you offer (e.g., stationery goods, computer hardware and software, uniforms). Another objective might be lead generation. Business-to-business catalogs often have a high pass-along rate—one person in the company passes the catalog along to another person in the company who might also be in the market for your merchandise, so you often get several exposures within one company.

Specialty catalogs: Your objective with a specialty catalog is to reach your most highly targeted audience with a product you know they want or need. The more specific your targeting gets, the higher the likelihood you'll build a strong and loyal customer base.

★ *Merchandise analysis*: Make a list of every product you plan to offer, and its projected price point (how much you plan to charge for each item). If you've sold any of the products before, through a retail outlet or through other types of Direct Marketing, note which are your best-sellers, and if there are any items that customers buy repeatedly or buy more than one of at a time.

Ask yourself these questions about the items you've chosen:

- Do the items on the list go together well? Do they fit the catalog's niche, personality, and style?
- Does each item on the list meet or exceed your standards of quality?
- What is the availability of each item on the list? Are you working with vendors you trust to deliver the items in a timely manner?
- Can any of the items on your list help to sell any of the other items? For example, do you have matching sheets and pillow shams to offer with your down comforter? Or a matching purse to go with your best-selling shoes?
- Will the product be aesthetically appealing in the catalog? Will it be easy to photograph? Will it be difficult to show its true size, color, or design? Will it need a lot of copy to explain its features and benefits, or will a photograph speak for itself?

★ *Competitive analysis*: Study your competition. Find as many catalogs as you can that offer merchandise similar to yours. It's not difficult to locate the catalogs you need. Look through advertisements in your favorite magazines for companies that offer catalogs similar to what you have in mind. Not surprisingly, this industry has evolved to the point where there are now catalogs of catalogs. Two that come to mind are the *Shop At Home Catalogs Directory* (1-800-338-8484) and *The Best Catalogs in the World* (1-800-315-1995). Keep abreast of what's happening in the catalog industry. Read *Catalog Age* magazine, which you can contact at the address listed in the Appendix.

Ask yourself questions about the catalogs you see:

- Regardless of the products they sell, which catalogs have a look and a style similar to what I'd like to achieve?
- Which catalogs don't appeal to me at all, and why?
- Which catalogs are most similar to mine, in product and price point?
- What can I do to make my catalog distinctive from theirs?

★ *Market analysis*: Who is most likely to buy the products offered in your catalog? If you're a retailer, you already have a pretty good description of your typical customer. If you're starting out with a catalog, you must be like a police artist, and draw up a composite sketch of your ideal customer, including age, gender, income, lifestyle, and special interests. Then you can consult with list brokers to get a general idea of the potential size of your market.

What Goes Where

Once you've put your plan together, and decided to go ahead, it's time to start designing the actual catalog. The first thing you need is a pagination chart (Figure 7.4), which is really just a series of small boxes, each representing one page of the catalog (use as many pages as you need). Underneath each box is a list of the merchandise you will feature on that page. You'll probably create many versions of this chart, as you arrange and rearrange the products so that they fit well and look good on the page.

Research has shown that the "hottest" areas, or the spots that produce the most sales in a catalog are:

- front cover
- back cover
- inside front cover
- first right-hand page
- inside back cover
- center spread
- surrounding the order form

Front Cover. The front cover is analogous to your store window. You may actually want to design the cover last, after you've settled on the arrangement for the rest of the catalog, since that may change many times. The cover should make a statement about who you are. It can feature your best-selling item, depict a lifestyle scene (a family on a picnic, a corporate executive at the airport), or display a beautiful graphic. Whatever you choose must be attention-grabbing. You want your cover to catch customers' eyes, because as they go through their mail they're making split-second decisions about whether to save the catalog or toss it in the circular file.

Figure 7.4

A pagination chart helps to determine which products will appear on which page of the catalog.

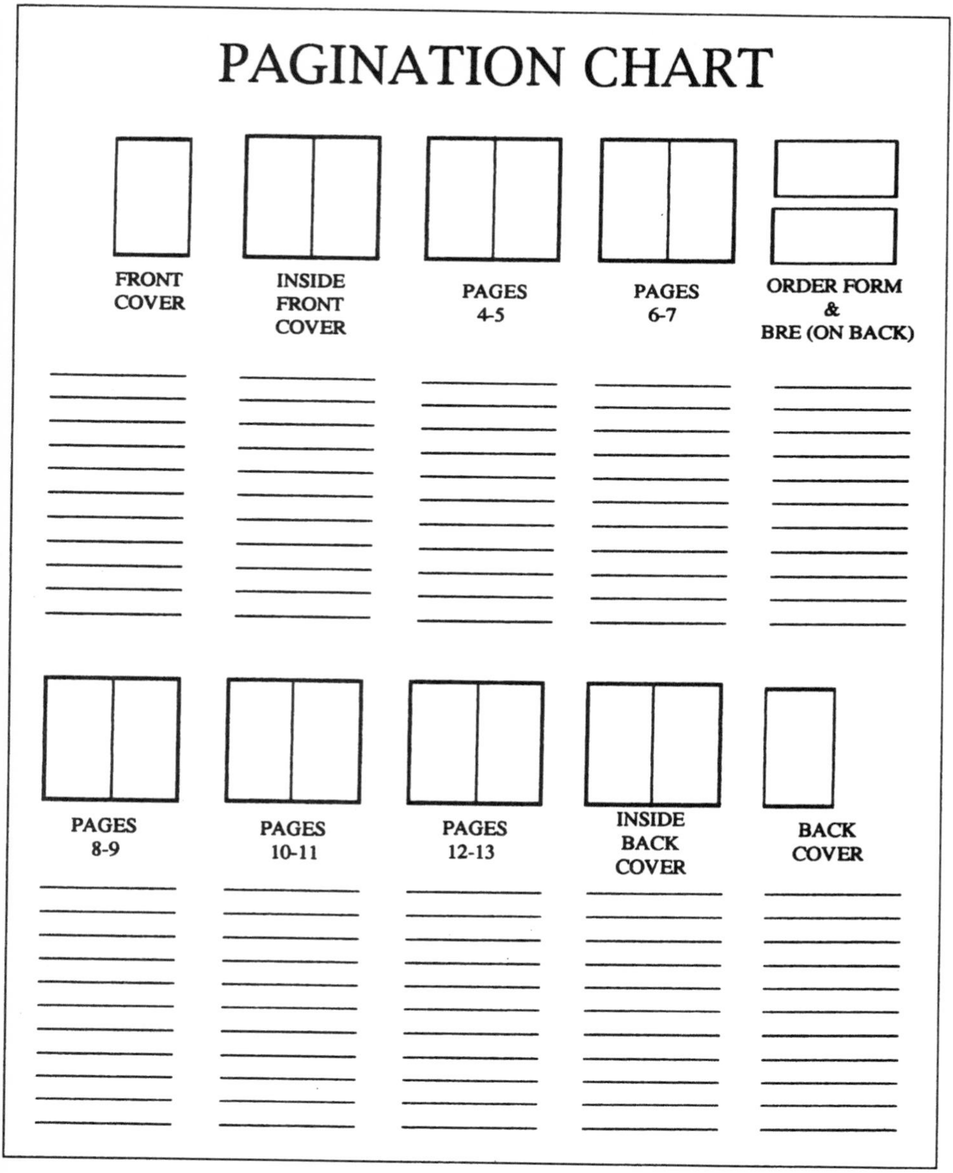

PAGINATION CHART

FRONT COVER	INSIDE FRONT COVER	PAGES 4-5	PAGES 6-7	ORDER FORM & BRE (ON BACK)

PAGES 8-9	PAGES 10-11	PAGES 12-13	INSIDE BACK COVER	BACK COVER

A variation on the front cover is the wrap. The wrap cover is actually attached over the normal front cover of the catalog. This allows you to print special messages to targeted customers without having to reprint entire catalogs. For instance, the Roaman's catalog featured in Figure 7.5 contains the message "Welcome back... we've missed you," targeted toward a customer who recently made a purchase after not responding to several catalogs. The wrap also announces catalog highlights, including the offer of free shipping and handling on the customer's next order from this catalog. Using a wrap makes it possible to personalize customers' catalogs according to their special interests or their frequency of purchase, to thank them for their first purchase, or, as some catalogs do, warn them that "unless you order from this catalog we'll have to drop you from our mailing list mailing list." Since the wrap is often printed on less expensive paper stock than the rest of the catalog, it is often a more cost-efficient way to personalize your message.

Back Cover. This page serves the same purpose as the front cover, although it usually suffers from the second-class-citizen syndrome. Who says customers will see the front cover first? Your store had two big picture windows, and you should take advantage of both.

Inside Front Cover. This actually refers to a spread, or two facing pages. These two pages establish the character and personality of the entire catalog. They should let the customer know immediately what type of merchandise you offer, and in what price range.

The left-hand page can be used for a very special purpose—to address a letter to your customer. The one thing that catalogs lack is the human contact you get when shopping in a retail store. A letter to your customer is a way to restore that human connection. It's your chance to let the customer in on your overall philosophy, on exciting news, or on a specially featured item they'll find inside. Going back to Figure 7.1: Steve and Lori Leveen address their readers (an appropriate salutation, since they sell items relating to books, stationery, pens, and home libraries) in order to bring attention to several items. The first item they talk about is the Nouveau Reader, designed to hold newspapers and magazines so you can read hands-free:

Figure 7.5
This wrap cover allows Roaman's to print a special message to customers who had not ordered in several months.

Welcome back...we've missed you

Free!
Don't miss our special offers:

 **FREE!shorts**
(see pages 2-3)

FREE!big shirts
(see page 71)

FREE!one-pocket tees
(see back cover)

Free!
Shipping and handling on your next order from this catalog!

Look for lots of *new!* **styles through-out!**

Look for **best buy** **symbols** to **save** **even more!**

Special 8-page **clearance** **section!**

One of our designers stumbled on the original in a tiny antique store. With some difficulty, we finally found craftsmen who could still make a reproduction as nice as the original (p. 4). We hope you enjoy it!

This makes their customers feel they're getting a custom-made product. There are two other items featured in this letter to the readers. Not only does the letter alert customers to merchandise they might find useful, but the Leveens have wisely featured three items: one in the beginning of the catalog, one in the middle, and one at the end. What better way to get your customers looking through the whole book!

Another catalog that uses the introductory letter well is Fran Lewis's Bear-in-Mind. Her letter accurately portrays the personality of the catalog: homespun, cute and cuddly, friend of the family. The letter begins:

Two years ago, I posed with a bear called Nickie, who had been given to me by a friend. Well, guess what?... I married him (not the bear, the friend), in January of this year.

This letter doesn't focus on any particular items in the catalog, but it does let customers know that the prices in the catalog "will be good through next July" and that the company welcomes questions and comments from its customers.

Business-to-business catalogs use these letters as well. When IBM Direct came out with their combination catalog and magazine called *Connections*, the inside front cover contained a letter that introduced prospective customers to the concept of the magalog. The letter read, in part:

Connections combines magazine-style articles with a catalog of IBM quality supplies, services and information for your business.

Why the name *Connections*? Simply because this new publication is your connection to the full line of IBM Supplies to keep your IBM equipment working at its best. And, we hope, your connection to the kind of information you can use to make your job a little easier.

First Right-Hand Page. The first right-hand page of the catalog is also a key position. It can serve as an introduction to the type of merchandise readers can expect throughout the rest of the catalog, set the tone, and reflect your personality. Some catalogs use the inside front cover and/or the first right-hand page for a table of contents. Staples, the national-chain office supply company, includes both a table of contents and an index. If your catalog offers many different types of merchandise, you want to make it as easy as possible for people to find what they need. Most catalogs, however, do not need to include these features.

TIP   The first right-hand page should feature some of your most attractive merchandise, something that has a very good price point, and/or something that is unique to your book. You want to put a best-seller (or something you feel will become a best-seller) on this page.

Inside Back Cover. This is another hot spot you can use to feature best-selling items. Again, these should be items with high visual appeal and attractive price points.

Center Spread. Most often, the order form is inserted on matte-finish paper stock into the center of the catalog (it's usually matte-finish because that is easier to write on than the coated stock used for the bulk of the catalog pages). Creating an order form for a catalog is the same as it is for any other type of direct mail. The principles discussed in Chapter 5 apply here as well. When people turn to the order form, they automatically also focus on the two pages that come before and after. Even if your order form is elsewhere in the catalog, the center spread is a natural focus area.

Surrounding the Order Form. Often the back side of the order form provides another space for merchandise. This is a good area for special bargain items and impulse buys—the kind of things you might find near the cash register in a retail store.

Pricing the Catalog

After you figure out how many pieces of merchandise you're going to sell and where they're going to fall on the page, you're ready to start figuring out production costs. There are a number of elements you'll need to include:

Printing Costs

★ *Catalog printing*: One of the first steps is to call at least three printers, give them your specifications, and ask for an estimate. You might say, for instance, "I want to produce a 16-page catalog on 60 lb. coated stock with a separate matte-finish order form. It's going to have 64 four-color photographs, 10 of which will be bleeds, plus a bleed front and back cover, and it will have a label on the back cover." A bleed is a photograph that reaches to the edge of the page, as opposed to having a white-space border around it. Bleeds are more expensive to print. You also have to know how many catalogs you want to print, because the unit cost drops as the quantity increases. Keep in mind that you're not just searching for the least expensive printer. Poor printing quality may cost you later in decreased sales.

★ *Color separations*: Although you see the final printed version of a color photograph, it has most likely gone through a printing process called separation, in which each of the colors included in a photograph is printed on a separate piece of film. This is an expensive, but necessary, part of the process and should be discussed thoroughly with your printer so that all costs can be included in your estimate.

Personnel Costs

★ *Creative director*: A creative director develops the vision of how the entire catalog is going to look. This person is analogous to the director of a movie—he or she interprets the script (in this case the assembled merchandise) according to his or her own personal style. As the company owner, you will work closely with the creative director to come up with a look that pleases you both. The people that translate this vision are the copywriter and the art director. The creative director oversees the entire job and makes sure that everything runs smoothly.

All of the personnel involved in putting together your catalog can be either freelance or in-house, depending on how your company is set up. If you don't have this staff, you can hire a creative director as a freelancer for the project. The creative director is often responsible for hiring the rest of the personnel. Or, you can hire a Direct Marketing agency to do all the work for your company. In any case, you'll still need...

★ *Copywriter*: The person who writes the actual copy for the catalog.

★ *Art director*: The person who puts together the final layout and typesetting of the catalog. The art director oversees the photography, chooses type styles, prepares the final copy and photography on a disk or a mechanical, and oversees the final printing of the catalog. The art director also specs the type to make sure it fits in the spaces around the photographs. If not, the art director sends it back to the copywriter and says, "Cut two lines here, cut three lines here, I need four more lines on these pages."

★ *Photographer*: A few unique catalogs, such as J. Peterman, use only drawings to show their merchandise. Most catalogs, however, rely on photographs. When hiring a photographer, choose someone who has experience in photographing what you're selling. A fashion photographer may not be very skilled at shooting office supplies. You want someone who knows how to make your products look most enticing.

★ *Models*: Some types of merchandise need models to show them to their best advantage. Models can also be expensive, but in some cases are necessary. Obviously, most fashion catalogs have models in almost every shot. But other types of merchandise use models as well. For instance, exercise equipment is often pictured in use by a fit and attractive model. A pillow specially designed for reading in bed may look unappealing by itself, but become a best-seller when demonstrated by a relaxed, comfortable model enjoying a steamy romance novel at the end of the day. Merchandise for children usually sells better when young models are included in the shot— especially babies. Everyone loves to see pictures of babies!

Mailing Costs

★ *Computer service bureau and lettershop*: How much will it cost to send the final printed catalog to consumers? You need to add in the cost of any list work that must be done, and the costs for the letter-shop to do the actual mailing.

★ *Postage*: The lettershop should be able to provide you with an estimate of the postage necessary to mail your catalog.

What's the Good Word?

If the catalog is your store, the written copy is your salesperson. It provides you with the details you need to know before making any purchase: size, material, function, cost. These are the features. But good copy contains more than features. Like any good salesperson, the copy concentrates on a product's benefits. It answers the customers' questions: What will this product do for me? Will it make me happier, more attractive, healthier, save me time?

A good example of this comes from the Levenger catalog of "tools for serious readers." When describing a lamp designed for reading in bed the copy states that what makes this particular lamp the best light for that purpose is "that it gives the reader—and only the reader—superb illumination, leaving the other person in darkness." The copy goes on to talk about the low-watt halogen bulb the lamp requires, and the fact that it's available in styles that can sit on a table, clamp onto a headboard, or be mounted on the wall. The first benefit is obvious: this lamp makes it possible to read in bed without disturbing your mate. But it does more than that. It saves you money by using energy-conserving bulbs. And it's flexible—it can fit in whatever space you have available.

Another unusual catalog is called Rent Mother Nature. Through this catalog you lease a fruit tree, a coffee tree, a lobster trap, an acre of wheat. Then, when the crop is ready, you share in the harvest. The copy reflects the unusual nature of the merchandise, for instance:

Rent-a-Sheep. Adopt a lovable Dorset lamb or sheep for a season: we'll custom weave a wool heirloom for your for generations of satisfaction. Experience the luxurious qualities of nature's own premier fiber milled into a blanket unmatched for warmth, comfort and durability, from the wool of your own sheep.

Writing Effective Copy

Here are some other suggestions for writing effective copy:

★ *Write the copy as if there were no photographs available.* You want your words to motivate the customer to buy. The photograph (or drawing) might catch their attention, but the copy will clinch the sale. Good copy makes the photograph, and the merchandise, come alive.

★ *Suggest a variety of ways of using the item.* An antique-looking wooden bucket, for instance, might be used as a planter, a magazine stand, a popcorn server, or a pot for dry flower arrangements. Your suggestions get readers thinking about ways they might use this item in their own homes and increase the temptation to buy.

★ *Write, edit, rewrite.* A direct mail letter or brochure can be as long as it takes to describe the product, but catalog copy is severely limited in space. Therefore, it's necessary to get your points across quickly and efficiently, no matter what your style of writing.

★ *Use testimonials.* We don't always believe people who say good things about their own products. But when someone else attests to the high quality of the product or service, we're more likely to take her word for it. Figure 7.6 shows a page from a Lands' End Corporate Sales catalog. This page accomplishes several things at once: it tells a story (including a problem which was solved by Lands' End clothing), it shows the clothes being worn by real people in a real-life situation, and it includes a testimonial from the owner of an auto parts company in Wisconsin who tells the reader that his staff likes Lands' End clothes so much, "They wear them on their free time too."

★ *Use powerful language.* The first several words of your body copy are crucial. If you start off by saying "Here is our wonderful new Terrific Tub Cleaner" you're in danger of losing your readers' attention. Try using language that paints a picture, that places the reader in the middle of ongoing action: "Stop scrubbing that tub! Rinse dirt and stains down the drain with our new Terrific Tub Cleaner."

Figure 7.6
The testimonial of this shop owner from Wisconsin gives prospective customers added
confidence in Lands' End clothing.

"Our staff likes your clothes so well, they wear them on their free time too."

So says Dan Argall, owner of Diamond Auto Parts in Fond du Lac, Wisconsin. He'd had problems finding good-quality clothes for his office staff, that they'd wear with comfort and pride as they deal with walk-in customers, field three to four hundred calls a day, and travel the Midwest buying auto salvage.

"We wanted a soft cotton shirt—not hard and harsh. So we started with your Interlochen. Then rugbys, caps, that high-tech Supplex® jacket…

"Everything looks really nice. The embroidery's sharp. And we got real quick turnaround."

Thanks, Dan. And if you need anything else, just ask.

About our Supplex: it's a new 3-ply nylon fabric that's plenty tough, treated for water-resistance, yet soft as cotton. Both Pullover and Zip Front Jacket have vented back that cools you when you're active. Machine wash. Imported. *Colors below.*

Unisex sizes S-XXL
Men's S 34-36, M 38-40 L 42-44,
XL 46-48, XXL 50-52
Women's S 6-8, M 10-12, L 14-16,
XL 18-20, XXL 22-24

Zip Front
- -
2914-5N88   35.00
Pullover
- -
2914-4N82   34.00

Hunter, Red, Sun Yellow, Navy

★ *Suggest specific actions.* For example, "Buy one for every room in the house," "Keep one in your garage and one in the trunk of your car," or "Stock up now for the holidays."

Capture Your Readers' Attention with Snappy Headlines!

In a catalog, you have three chances to get the customers interested in your merchandise: the photograph, the copy, and the headline. The headline must immediately capture the reader's attention. It should entice a customer into reading the rest of the copy.

The most basic headlines are a simple description of what the item is or does: "Microwave Apple Baker" or "Pet Car Seat." Other headlines add one or two descriptive words that build excitement, for instance "New! Exclusive! World-Famous Muffins" or "All-Time Favorite Christmas Ornaments." One of the most effective headline styles, however, is a full sentence which details a particular benefit of the product and draws you into the body copy, such as "Turn any drawer into a customized jewelry box" or "Safeguard your library with classic bookplates."

Headlines should reflect the same style and personality as the rest of the catalog. Lands' End used its human, conversational style in a recent holiday catalog with headlines such as "For someone who's been very, very good, our deluxe leather-trimmed luggage," and "Our Twill Bomber Jacket says Phooey to the old saying, 'If it ain't broke, don't fix it.'"

Catalog Art

When you're designing a catalog, you have four basic choices regarding what type of artwork you're going to use:

- black and white photographs
- color photographs
- black and white illustrations
- color illustrations

Your decisions in this area will be determined largely by your products and your budget.

Some products clearly call for color photographs. "Glamour" products, such as expensive jewelry, artwork, and fine leather, usually look best when reproduced in full color. I recently produced a catalog for Crayola. Since Crayola specializes in color, we had no choice but to use four-color photos. Other products, like books (which don't depend on their appearance to make the sale), may require only black and white or two-color reproductions.

Illustrations work well only in limited circumstances. As mentioned earlier, J. Peterman is one of the few catalogs that use this technique successfully. Illustrations can be expensive as well. If you're thinking of designing a catalog using illustrations, try a sample of one or two pages to see if your products can be rendered well enough to show them realistically and attractively enough to appeal to prospective customers.

Your budget will also determine what kind of artwork you include in your catalog. Get estimates from several photographers. Let them know what types of products they will be shooting, and how may total shots will be included in the catalog. Can the shots be taken in the photographer's studio, or do you have to go on location? Location shots are usually more expensive. You may have to pay someone to rent their facilities, and you will have to pay travel fees for the photographer and any staff that may be necessary for the shoot. If you travel out of town, you will have to pay for overnight accommodations for everyone involved.

The only way to be sure which type of artwork is best for your catalog is to test several versions and track which produces the best results.

TIP   Be aware of size and scale. I recently saw a catalog where an entire room setting was pictured in the same size photograph as a dinner bell featured on the same page. This made it very difficult to judge the real size of any of the items shown.

Make It Easy To Order

Include your telephone number on every page or every spread of your catalog. Order forms sometimes get separated from their catalogs. In my office, for instance, several people may browse through the same catalog. If one person decides to order merchandise using the order form, and tears it out of the book, the next person who looks at the catalog must also be able to order.

Your Online Catalog

In terms of creating multiple opportunities for customers to find out about and buy products, an online catalog can be very important. Print, however, is still very important. Often consumers review catalogs at their leisure, while riding a bus, or reading in bed. They like to flip through the pages, and share in the excitement of the fantasy...whether it's J.Crew or Victoria's Secret, it is always about something more than just the clothes.

Anyone who has ever done a catalog knows that just as soon as it's printed, there's at least one bit of information that you wish you could change. The beauty of online catalogs is that they are "forgiving" and offer the flexibility to let you go back and make changes. For rapidly developing product lines, being able to access the information over the Internet allows companies to offer customers their most up-to-date products and pricing.

The lowered cost of offering a catalog online can translate to a larger profit margin, although some companies pass this savings on to consumers in the form of reduced prices.

Checklist

THREE BASIC TYPES OF CATALOGS

☑ Retail

☑ Business-to-business

☑ Consumer specialty

MAKING A STATEMENT WITH YOUR CATALOG

☑ Three ways to express a distinctive personality

   √ Specialty merchandise

   √ Style

   √ Story line

DEVELOP A CATALOG PLAN

☑ Define your objectives

☑ Analyze your merchandise

☑ Analyze your competition

☑ Analyze your market

WHAT GOES WHERE

☑ Catalog hot spots:

- √ Front cover
- √ Back cover
- √ Inside front cover
- √ First right-hand page
- √ Inside back cover
- √ Center spread
- √ Surrounding the order form

PRICING THE CATALOG

☑ Include the following categories:

- √ Printing costs
  - √ Catalog printing
  - √ Color separations
- √ Personnel costs
  - √ Creative director
  - √ Copywriter
  - √ Art director
  - √ Photographer
  - √ Models
- √ Mailing costs
  - √ Computer service bureau and lettershop
  - √ Postage

WRITING EFFECTIVE COPY

- ☑ Write the copy as if there were no photographs available
- ☑ Suggest a variety of ways of using the item
- ☑ Write, edit, rewrite
- ☑ Use testimonials
- ☑ Use powerful language
- ☑ Suggest specific actions

SNAPPY HEADLINES GRAB ATTENTION

- ☑ A headline should entice the prospect into reading the rest of the copy
- ☑ Three basic types of catalog headlines:
  - √ Simple description
  - √ Excitement builders
  - √ Full sentences that detail benefits
- ☑ Headlines should reflect the same style and personality as the rest of the catalog

CATALOG ART

- ☑ You have four choices:
  - √ Black and white photographs
  - √ Color photographs
  - √ Black and white illustrations
  - √ Color illustrations
- ☑ What kind of art you choose is determined by:
  - √ Your product
  - √ Your budget

MAKE IT EASY TO ORDER

☑ Include your telephone number and URL on every page or spread in the catalog

☑ Remember that more than one person may want to order from the same catalog, so there must be a way for customers to purchase from you even if the order form is missing

YOUR ONLINE CATALOG

☑ Make it interesting

☑ Test new things

  √ Offers

  √ New products

☑ Online customer service

8

Fulfilling Orders and Expectations

When customers order products over the phone, on the Internet, or through the mail, there's a certain amount of faith involved. Customers must have faith in a product they've never seen, held, or tasted. They must have faith that they will actually receive that product after sending in a check or giving a credit card number to someone they've never met. To be successful, marketers must reassure customers that their faith is well placed. How long it takes for a package to get to a customer, what that package looks like when it arrives, how it's boxed or bagged—all these factors can make the difference between a dissatisfied, one-time buyer and a loyal, steady customer.

Fulfillment, in Direct Marketing terms, means delivering your product to the customer the way it was promised (through written copy and photographs) and on time. This sounds fairly easy, but it's one of the most complex parts of the entire Direct Marketing process. Whether you and your family are sending out products from your garage, or you're using a sophisticated fulfillment house, this step has got to be done right.

Who's Fulfilling What?

The fulfillment process—getting the goods from the shipper to the consumer—breaks down into getting the orders in, shipping the orders out, providing customer service, and taking care of returns.

157

Because there are so many steps involved in the fulfillment process, there are also a lot of decisions to make. One of the first decisions you have to make is who's going to fulfill your orders: are you going to do it in-house, or use an outside service to do it for you?

The three options involved are:

1. Handle both the order-taking and shipping in-house;
2. Receive the orders in-house and use an outside service for shipping the products; or
3. Use outside services for both receiving the orders and shipping the products.

How do you know which option is best for you? There are several factors to consider when making this decision, including:

★ *The size of your company*: If you are a very small start-up operation and you want to keep costs down as much as possible, you may want to start out handling everything yourself. As you grow, you can always turn over one or both functions to outside services. There are computer service bureaus or 800 number services that will take your orders and shipping services that will ship your merchandise to your customers. There are some companies that combine these functions—they take orders for you, and ship out the merchandise as well.

★ *Available personnel*: Do you have enough people available to handle each of the necessary functions (that includes inputting data into the computer, packing up the individual items, and shipping them out)? If you have to hire (and train) people, how do those costs compare with hiring outside services already set up to handle these functions?

★ *Physical facilities*: Do you have the space to warehouse your merchandise? Some people run successful businesses out of their garage or basement storage space. If you work out of a small house or apartment, however, you may not have anywhere to store your goods. You'll also need to consider your merchandise. Storing, shipping, and mailing may not be much of a problem if you're selling only one product that comes preboxed, and each box weighs the same amount. But if you have a catalog's worth of various merchandise, where customers may order any number of items (which would vary the packaging and mailing operations), you may not have the space necessary to keep the different items sorted properly.

If you are manufacturing the products yourself, you can warehouse them in your own facility, or use an outside warehouse. Sometimes, if you're buying from outside manufacturers, you can have them hold the product for you and then drop-ship it to your customer directly from their facility. Some large companies who sell large numbers of products year-round use outside warehousing. Others prefer to have an in-house operation. It depends on the company's own facilities, and whether or not they have the staff to manage the facility.

Prefulfillment Essentials

In this chapter, we're going to follow an order from beginning to end— from the moment a customer calls or writes in with an order to the moment the item is delivered to his or her door. Whether you do it yourself or someone else does it for you, the process remains the same. The only difference is in the scale of operation. We'll discuss an in-house operation first, and then look at outside services.

To follow this process, imagine that you've just started your own business called Cookbooks International. Right now you offer five different cookbooks through a direct mailing piece you're sending to 10,000 prospective buyers. Before you begin your fulfillment effort, there are certain factors you must have in place:

★ *Mailing address*: Cookbooks International is a home-based operation. Do you want your home address to go out to these 10,000 people on your list? Or would you rather have everything directed to a post office box? If you like the idea of having a street address rather than a P.O. box number, some of the private shipping facilities (e.g., Mailboxes Etc.) allow you to use their street address.

TIP Be aware that post office boxes have been the home of many rip-off artists and mail order scams, so customers are often wary of businesses that have only a post office box as a return address. If necessary, use both a street address and a box number. For example:

Cookbooks International
400 West 19th Street
Box 225
Spring Valley, NY 10970

Be sure to check with your post office before you do a major mailing, to make certain that the response mail will be delivered to the desired address.

★ *Telephone number*: Do you accept phone orders? If so, are you going to install a toll-free number? According to the Direct Marketing Association's Statistical Fact Book, calling a toll-free number is by far the most preferred method of contacting companies. More than two-thirds of the people surveyed by the DMA chose calling a toll-free number as their first option for ordering merchandise (as opposed to mailing in order forms, even if postage was supplied). In fact, so many businesses offer toll-free 800 numbers, there are very few still available. In many areas, new toll-free numbers will begin with 888 instead.

If you want to offer a toll-free number, but don't want to install your own, there are services you can use. The advantage of having an outside service is that they are available to answer the phone twenty-four hours a day. If you're running a national campaign, you want to be able to take orders from all time zones. The service will answer the phone with your company name, take the order, and then send it on to you for processing. Most services offer you a choice of a dedicated or nondedicated line. A nondedicated line, which is less expensive, means you'll be sharing the line with several other companies. A dedicated line is used for your company only.

You'll need to work closely with the telemarketing firm to develop a script for the telephone service representatives (TSRs) to use. When prospective customers call the toll-free number, the

TSR will call up your information on the computer screen. It's important to choose a telemarketing company with friendly, intelligent TSRs who can give customers information without sounding like they're reading from a TelePrompTer. Remember that customers don't know they're speaking to an outside service—they assume they're speaking to your company directly. The telemarketing company you choose must be able to treat your customers with the same courtesy and respect as if inquirers had called you directly.

You might also want to consider outbound telemarketing (where TSRs make calls to prospective customers). Although outbound telemarketing suffers from a bad reputation, it can be an extremely effective marketing tool if the TSRs are properly trained. However, there are strict laws limiting the times of day or night you may make telemarketing calls, and whether or not you may call again once a customer has refused your offer. Check the laws in your state before starting on any outbound telemarketing program.

You'll need to weigh the costs of hiring an outside telemarketing firm against the costs of installing your own toll-free number line, and having your own staff handle both inbound and outbound telemarketing. There is a great advantage in having people who are most familiar with your product on the phone; however, you may not have the personnel to handle the volume of calls you receive. Whenever I work with outside telemarketers, I make it a practice to send the TSRs samples of the product I want them to sell. I want to make sure they can describe the product accurately to prospects, and answer any questions they may have—which can be difficult if they've never even seen the product they're selling.

How does one figure out when a toll-free number becomes affordable? You do a test. You can hire a telephone service by the month; if you use the number for two months and your orders increase considerably, you subtract the cost of the toll-free number from the increase in income from your orders. Then you compare the results to your other orders per dollar spent, and you find which made you more money. If you're thinking of installing your own toll-free number, you must take all costs into consideration: labor, space, training, management, electricity, telephone lines.

Whether or not you plan to install a toll-free number, you need to know if your existing phone lines can accommodate your incoming orders, or if you need to add a separate line or lines dedicated to that purpose. If you mail 100,000 catalogs, you might expect a 1 or 2 percent response. That means you should get between 1,000 and 2,000 orders, which will start coming in about a week to 10 days after you mail the catalog. Eight hundred to 1,600 of those orders will be telephone orders. Can your one or two phone lines accommodate that many calls within that time frame? Will callers frequently get busy signals? If so, you may have to add more phone lines (which also means more staff) or hire an outside service.

★ *Payment options*: How are people going to pay for the merchandise they order? Cash? Check? Credit cards? Most Direct Marketers today don't even offer the option of paying by cash, and most customers don't want to send cash through the mail. If your item is extremely inexpensive, you may want to accept cash, but it is not recommended. It's too easy for cash to get "lost" along the processing route.

If you would like to offer the option of paying by credit card, you must set up your accounts either with a bank, in the case of Master-Card and Visa, or with the credit company itself, in the case of American Express and the Discover Card. Opening an account with either a bank or credit card company can be a complicated and time-consuming process.

If you can't get your own Visa or MasterCard account, there are credit card processing services available that will handle these transactions for you, for a fee, of course. The fees vary from one processing service to another. You will pay a setup charge, which can run from several hundred dollars to several thousand dollars (depending on the merchandise you're selling), and then you will be charged anywhere from 2 to 6 percent of each transaction they process. As with the toll-free number, accepting credit card orders can substantially increase your sales. Therefore, you must measure the cost of the service against the additional dollars you receive.

★ *Item numbers*: In order to keep track of your inventory, each piece of merchandise you offer must have an item number. The manufacturer will have already assigned a number, called a SKU number, which you can use as your item number, or you can assign each item your own number.

★ *Computer program:* There may still be some small Direct Marketing businesses that don't use a computer, but I don't know of any. If you are receiving only 10-20 orders a month, you can probably keep track of them pretty easily. But once you start getting into the higher numbers, a computer program is essential. Publications such as *Direct Marketing* magazine, or *DM News,* and *Target Marketing* magazine often publish reviews of Direct Marketing software that can be bought off the shelf. Or you can have a computer programmer design a program to fit your special needs.

The Direct Marketing program needs to contain all the information that's on your order blank, plus marketing information you need for tracking purposes. Information you must include:

- Name
- Address
- Phone number
- Date of order
- Method of payment
- Items ordered
- Dollar amount received
- Shipping and handling payment received
- Sales tax received
- Source code
- Email address

Your computer program must also include some method of inventory control. You need to know how many of each item you have in stock, and how many items you have on backorder (backorders occur when you are temporarily out of stock of a particular item).

The First Step: Order Entry

You now have everything in place for receiving orders. The direct mail packages or catalogs have gone out, the orders start pouring in, and the phone is ringing off the hook. The process for sending the merchandise to the customer begins. The first step in this process is order entry, where you take the information off your order blank and enter it into your computer system.

When the mail arrives and is opened, separate it into "check enclosed" and credit card orders. We'll start with the "check enclosed" orders. Each payment must be matched against the items ordered. For instance, suppose Jane Smith has ordered *101 Fabulous French Recipes* for $13.95, *101 Incredible Italian Recipes* for $15.95, and *101 Appetizing American Recipes* for $12.95. Her base cost would be $42.85.

Unless you offer free shipping and handling, Ms. Smith will have to add these charges to her check. Shipping and handling charges are usually determined by dollar amount ordered; for instance a typical S&H chart might read:

If your order totals:

$0–$10.00	Add $4.00
$10.01–$40.00	Add $5.50
$40.01–$60.00	Add $6.00
$60.01–$80.00	Add $6.50
$80.01–$100.00	Add $7.00
OVER $100.00	Add $8.00

So Jane Smith should have added $6.00 to her $42.85. (On your order form, you might also offer her the option of paying extra for overnight or two-day air delivery, or shipping the books to a different address.) It's possible she should also have added sales tax. As mentioned earlier, if you have a business operation in a particular state, customers from that state must pay tax on your merchandise. Assuming she should have added 8.25 percent New York sales tax, Jane Smith's check should be in the amount of $52.39:

101 Fabulous French Recipes	$13.95
101 Incredible Italian Recipes	15.95
101 Appetizing American Recipes	12.95
MERCHANDISE TOTAL	**$42.85**
Sales tax	3.54
Shipping and handling	6.00
TOTAL DUE	**$52.39**

Suppose, however, that Jane overlooked the sales tax and her check is made out for $48.85. You have to decide whether or not you should absorb the cost (you have to pay the sales tax even if she doesn't), or send her a notice that she owes additional money. In this case, you're probably better off absorbing the cost, since any kind of delay or further transaction with a customer only gives her a chance to change her mind about the order.

But what if the check were $10 short? Would you still want to absorb the cost? You have to determine your own cutoff point. If you decide that you need to collect the additional funds to complete her order, you should have a standard postcard you mail out letting the customer know her options. You have four basic options for dealing with miscalculated orders. You can:

1. Absorb the cost and ship the order;
2. Ship the order and request additional payment;
3. Return the check and request payment in full; or
4. Hold the check and the order until you receive the additional payment, then ship the order.

Unless there is a great disparity, it's not usually a good idea to return the check or hold it until you receive additional payment. You may never get another check back from the customer. Be aware that it does not pay to be greedy. One small business owner I know had a customer who ordered products fairly steadily for several years. The orders were not large, but were fairly frequent. Suddenly the customer placed two large orders in a row, but did not increase the amount included for shipping and handling. The business owner sent the customer a letter requesting an additional $10. The customer then decided to cancel the order and hasn't been heard from since. The business owner has now lost a lot more than the missing $10 shipping charge.

Any orders with payment problems (or any other kind of problem, such as addresses that can't be read) should be sorted and dealt with separately. If the order includes a phone number, you can call the customer to clarify the problem. If there is no phone number, you may want to send a letter requesting that the customer call or write you back, or if you have an email address you can contact the customer that way. The rest of the checks can then be endorsed and deposited. Larger companies use check processing services, similar to credit card approval services, which let you know immediately if there are sufficient funds to cash the check. Smaller companies usually wait for the check to clear before they send out the merchandise.

The next step is to deal with your credit card orders. All credit card orders must be authorized by the issuing agency (the bank or the credit card company). When you're given a merchant account through one of these agencies, you're also given a small computerized terminal in which to enter your charges. When you receive an order, you key in your account number, the customer's account number, and the total dollar amount. Then you are either given an approval code number, or a signal that the card has been rejected. Sometime this is done while the customer is still on the line. If you are using an 800 number service, this may not be done until the order is received by you or the computer service bureau you're using.

Once again, you put problem orders aside, and deal with them the same way you would a miscalculated check. Both the check and credit card orders for the day (or the week, however it works best for you) are put into a batch and given a batch number so they will be easier to trace should a problem arise later.

Now you're ready to input all the necessary information into the computer. The order entry process is completed when you create a shipping label, which contains the customer's name and mailing address, and a shipping manifest, which lists the items that have been ordered and need to be readied for shipping.

There is one more function your computer program needs to perform, and that is to generate reports. One report is for accounting purposes, and should contain a summary by product or item number showing how many of each item were sold; total amount collected for products, shipping and tax; and the total dollar amount collected. Another report is produced for marketing purposes. This report includes source code information, so that you can tell which mailings, which lists, which direct mail campaigns, and/or which space ads are producing the best results.

Sending Out the Goods

Think of it. All this work has already been done, and no cookbook has yet been touched! When all of the order entry processes have been completed, it's finally time to move on to fulfillment, and actually ship the product out to Jane Smith. There are seven main functions of the fulfillment process:

★ *Receiving*: Accepting goods from the manufacturer and making sure the correct number of products have been received.
★ *Inspection*: The merchandise that comes from the manufacturer is checked for consistency of quality.
★ *Storing*: Merchandise is stored for easy packing, in cartons, on skids or shelves.
★ *Picking*: Individual items are chosen for shipping according to the shipping manifests received from the order entry department. The manifests state by product what is to be shipped—for instance, five Italian cookbooks, seven American cookbooks, and four French cookbooks.
★ *Packing*: Items are packaged in bags or boxes, labeled, and readied for shipping.
★ *Weighing and metering*: Bags or cartons of packed materials are weighed and readied for shipping by mail, UPS, FedEx, or other shipping companies.
★ *Shipping*: Items are either sent out directly from your premises, or taken to the post office or an alternative delivery service.

One of the major decisions you have to make at Cookbooks International is how your products are going to be packaged for mailing. One book alone can easily fit into a reinforced mailing envelope. But what happens when a customer such as Jane Smith orders more than one book? Are you still going to use envelopes? Or would a carton be better? If you choose a carton, what kind of filler (also known as dunnage) will you use—foam, paper, bubble wrap? You'll probably have to test the form of shipping you use until you come up with the best and most cost-efficient method.

Remember that the first thing your customer sees is not the product, but the packaging. This can work for you or against you. Some companies, such as PaperDirect, a catalog firm that offers specialty paper for home and business use, prides itself on its packaging as well as its product. Company founder Warren Struhl has stated that a large part of his company's success comes from the deluxe packaging they use. In fact, some of his customers save the boxes and recycle them as packaging when they send gifts to friends and relatives.

On the other hand, poor packaging can turn customers off. I recently ordered some pillows I saw advertised in a free-standing insert in a reputable New York newspaper. I waited almost five weeks for them to arrive. When they finally did, I couldn't believe my eyes. There were two pillows stuffed into a torn plastic sack that looked like a used garbage bag. There were no enclosures in the package, just a tattered label. Needless to say, I will never order anything from that company again.

Test out the packaging you're planning to use. Mail items to yourself, and to friends across the country, in various packing materials and then compare which packages arrived in the best shape. As my pillow experience proves, packaging that arrives dirty and damaged can turn a customer away from keeping your merchandise or ordering a second time.

Using Outside Services

Up until now, you've only been receiving a dozen or so orders a week, which you could easily handle yourself. Suddenly, however, Cookbooks International takes off and you don't have the personnel or the storage space to handle all the orders that are coming in. It's time to search for outside services who can take over the functions of order entry and fulfillment.

The first stop would be a computer service bureau. This is the same service discussed in Chapter 4 in connection with mailing lists. There are computer service bureaus that handle fulfillment as well. Instead of having orders mailed directly to you, they can be sent directly to the service bureau. When telephone orders are taken, either by you or by an 800 number service (they're not usually taken directly by the service bureau), they are faxed or sent by modem to the bureau for processing. All the steps outlined above for order entry are done by the computer service bureau. Labels and shipping manifests are then sent to a shipper, and the accounting and marketing reports are sent directly to you.

The service bureau charges you per order entered into their system. They have standard programs already set up which they use for their other clients, as well as programs that have been modified to fit particular clients. If you need any modifications done to the programs the bureau has already set up, you will be charged for programming time, which can be expensive. Therefore, if it's at all possible for you to set up your parameters to match theirs, you can save a lot of money. The computer service bureau will ask you for a marketing plan up front, and they should tell you whether or not your orders can be entered into one of their standard programs or how to modify your marketing plan so that it fits into their systems.

TIP   Fulfillment expert George McGreal advises that when you go with an outside service, it's important to note that you'll be forming a close relationship with them. "Especially if you're just starting out, the service bureau can provide you with invaluable advice and help you make many of the decisions involved in the Direct Marketing process," he says.

When you're looking for a computer service bureau, there are several questions you should ask to determine if it's the right match for you:

★ *Do you handle the type of business I'm doing (for instance, a single product mailing, a catalog mailing, or a negative option plan such as a book club)?* Some service bureaus specialize in one type of program or another. You want to find someone who has experience in your area.

★ *Can you supply me with references—clients who are using your service for similar types of programs to mine?* Again, you want to know how this service is performing with your type of program. Speaking to clients who use this service for a book club when you have a mail order catalog will not give you the information you need.

★ *How long have you been in business?* As in any business, you want to go with someone who's been around awhile, who has an excellent standing and reputation in the industry and in the community.

★ *What's the size of your organization?* Who will be handling my account? There are service bureaus that handle huge multimillion-dollar accounts, and there are smaller operations that handle small and midsize company accounts. If you're a small, low-volume company, you may choose to go with a smaller house that will give you closer attention. But be sure they have the ability to grow with you as your orders increase.

Whatever the size of the company you go with, you want to know who will be handling your account. Ideally, there should be one particular person you speak with whenever you call. That person will then know all details of your company and your marketing plans, and be able to answer any questions you may have. Also ask if there's a backup contact, someone who is available to you if your original contact is out ill or goes on vacation.

★ *What are your fees? What are your minimums?* Once you've explained your program to the service bureau, they should be able to tell you how their fees work, and give you an estimate of what you'll be spending (depending on how many orders you get). You will be charged separately for:

- Receiving, opening, and sorting mail and preparing deposits;
- Obtaining credit card authorizations;
- Inputting names and addresses and creating shipping labels;
- Any necessary programming changes.

★ *Can you refer me to a shipper?* Most computer service bureaus work closely with one or more shippers, and will be glad to give you their names and phone numbers (if you're looking for a list broker, or a lettershop, they may be able to refer you to these businesses as well).

TIP   How do you know if the outside service you hire is doing its job? Become a customer of your own company. Call the toll-free number and place an order (using another name), or get someone you know to do it for you. Were the operators courteous? Knowledgeable? Friendly? Order the same product using a mail-in coupon. Pay by check; add the total incorrectly and see how it is handled. Pay by credit card, then return the item and see if you get refunded in a timely fashion. When you get your merchandise, check it carefully. Were you pleased with the packaging? Was it delivered on time? Was it damaged in any way?

Shipping Delays and the Mail Order Rule

Whether you run your own computer program or use outside services, the system must be set up so that it notifies you when an item is not available. Suppose you are out of stock of your item No. 200, *101 Incredible Italian Recipes*. When you enter Jane Smith's order into the computer and code in item No. 200, you will get a message telling you that item is backordered. You have three options. You can:

1. Cancel the customer's order and issue a refund;
2. Substitute an item of equal value (with the customer's permission); or
3. Send a partial order along with an explanation.

In this case (in fact in most cases), your best option is to send the available merchandise along with a notice that the other item(s) has been backordered.

The Mail Order Rule, enacted by the Federal Trade Commission 25 years ago, states that a company must ship merchandise with the amount of time indicated in a catalog or an advertisement, or within 30 days if no time is indicated. If the item cannot be shipped within 30 days, you are obliged by law to notify the customer. Now it's the customer's turn for three options. By return mail he or she can ask you to:

1. Cancel the order and receive a refund;
2. Have the item shipped as soon as it becomes available; or
3. Choose a substitute item.

If the customer requests a refund, or if you find you will not be able to ship the item at all, there are certain rules you must follow. If the customer paid by cash, check, or money order, you must refund the correct amount by first-class mail within seven working days after the order is canceled. If the customer paid by credit card, you must credit the customer's account or notify the customer that the account will not be charged, within one customer's billing cycle, after the order is canceled.

Figure 8.1 shows a sample letter you can use to inform customers of backordered merchandise. For further information about the Mail Order Rule, contact the Division of Enforcement, Federal Trade Commission, 6th & Pennsylvania Avenue NW, Washington, DC 20580.

Figure 8.1

This is a typical letter informing a customer of backordered merchandise.

```
              COOKBOOKS INTERNATIONAL
                400 West 19th Street
                      Box 225
                Spring Valley, NY  10970
                  (800) 555-0000


                                   Date:

  Ms. Jane Smith
  79 Main Street
  Anytown, Anycity 10010

  Dear Ms. Smith:

     Thank you for your recent order.  We are sorry to
  inform you that because of [fill in the reason for
  the delay], we are unable to ship your order for
  [name the product] at this time.

     We expect to ship this item to you on or before
  [name date of shipping].  If we do not hear from
  you before then, we will ship the item to you.
  If you wish to cancel your order, or replace it
  with a substitute item, please return the enclosed
  postage-paid reply card.

     We appreciate your business, and apologize for
  any inconvenience.

                                   Sincerely,




                                   Signature
                                   Title
```

Regulations on Selling Through the Mail

If you plan to start a mail order business, you must be aware of the applicable laws. In 1938, the Federal Trade Commission was given the power to prohibit "unfair or deceptive practices in commerce." The FTC published many guidelines, including:

- Guides Concerning Use of Endorsements and Testimonials in Advertising

- Guides Concerning the Use of the Word "Free" and Similar Representations
- Guides Against Deceptive Pricing
- Guides Against Bait Advertising

You can find out about these and other publications pertinent to the mail order business, by visiting www.ftc.gov, or by writing to the Federal Trade Commission at the address above.

Some of the FTC's regulations state that you cannot make false claims about your product. You can't say that your product is a miracle cure unless there is clinical evidence to back up your statement. You can't make false claims about prices—you can't say that an item was "formerly sold at $59.85" unless a substantial number were actually sold at that price. And you are responsible for the truth of any testimonials you print. If you print a quote from John Doe, who turns out to have been lying, you can't claim that you thought John Doe was telling the truth. You can still be charged with false advertising.

Although you can sell almost anything through the mail (including guns), there are four categories of items you cannot sell through the mail:

- Pornographic and obscene materials
- New drugs (you need special permission from the Food and Drug Administration)
- Lotteries
- Pyramid or chain schemes

Checklist

SHOULD YOU HANDLE YOUR OWN FULFILLMENT?

☑ These are the factors to consider when making this decision:
- √ The size of your company
- √ Your available personnel
- √ Your physical facilities

PREFULFILLMENT ESSENTIALS

☑ These are the essentials you need to have in place before you can begin fulfilling your orders:

✓ Mailing address: street address and/or box number
✓ Telephone number: toll-free number, enough phone lines
✓ Payment options: cash, check, or credit card
✓ Item numbers to keep track of inventory
✓ Computer program

ORDER ENTRY

☑ Batch mail into credit card orders and those with checks enclosed

☑ Establish cutoff point for absorbing miscalculated payments

☑ Four options for dealing with miscalculated orders:

1. Absorb the cost and ship the order
2. Ship the order and request additional payment
3. Return the check and request payment in full
4. Hold the check and order until you get the payment, then ship

☑ Generate shipping labels and shipping manifests

☑ Generate accounting and marketing reports

SENDING OUT THE GOODS

☑ The seven main functions of the fulfillment process are:

✓ Receiving the goods
✓ Inspecting the merchandise
✓ Storing the merchandise
✓ Picking individual items for shipping
✓ Packing items in cartons or bags
✓ Weighing and metering
✓ Shipping by mail or alternative delivery services

USING OUTSIDE SERVICES

☑ When looking for a computer service bureau, be sure that:

✓ The bureau handles the same type of business you're doing
✓ They can supply you with references of firms who are using their service for programs similar to yours

√ The bureau has excellent standing in the industry and in the community

√ You will have an account representative who will be your personal contact

√ They explain the various functions for which you'll be charged and supply you with an estimate of all costs

√ They can refer you to a shipper (unless they are performing that function as well), a list broker, and a lettershop, if you should so desire

SHIPPING DELAYS AND THE MAIL ORDER RULE

☑ The Mail Order Rule: A company must ship merchandise within the amount of time indicated in a catalog or advertisement; or within 30 days if no time is indicated

☑ If an item is backordered, you have three options:

1. Cancel the customer's order and issue a refund
2. Substitute an item of equal value (with the customer's permission)
3. Send a partial order along with an explanation

☑ The customer has three options in response:

1. Cancel the order and receive a refund
2. Have the item shipped as soon as it becomes available
3. Choose a substitute item

ITEMS YOU MAY NOT SELL THROUGH THE MAIL

☑ Pornographic and obscene materials

☑ New drugs

☑ Lotteries

☑ Pyramid or chain schemes

9
CHAPTER

Costs and Mail Order Math

Unlike other marketing and advertising methods, Direct Marketing can be tracked precisely and analyzed scientifically. You can calculate exactly how much you spent for a particular campaign and exactly how much you earned or lost. Using the numbers you gather from various tests you run, you can make changes in one or more of the following three areas to increase your bottom line.

1. *Increase your selling price.* You might think that increasing your selling price will decrease the number of orders you receive. However, increasing the price a few dollars may not affect the number of orders at all. Sometimes increasing the price brings in more orders by boosting the perceived value of your product.

2. *Increase your response rate.* In other words, try to get more people to buy your product. Test offers, creative strategies, and lists until you come up with the combination that gives you consistently high response rates. If possible, keep your promotion and production costs low so that you can mail to larger numbers of people. Remember to test only one variable at a time so that you know which elements draw the most customers.

3. *Lower your costs.* You don't want to make any cuts that are going to affect the quality of your product or your service. Go over your costs to see if you can lower product or fulfillment costs without jeopardizing quality. Try to shave off $15 per thousand from your printing costs, for instance. That could add up to large savings. You might decide that the four-color brochure you planned can be two-color, and still be an effective selling piece. That decision alone could save you several thousand dollars and make a real difference on your bottom line.

Determine Your Promotion Costs

Although there are no guarantees about how well a campaign will do, it's possible, through careful calculation and cost quotations, to get a pretty good idea of the profit potential of a campaign before you've laid out any money. To do that, you need to know the production, mailing, and fulfillment costs for your product.

Begin by making up your wish list. Put together a model program that contains all the elements you would like to have if you had an unlimited budget. For example, you might want to have both the letter and enve-lope personalized to each customer, with a separate order form, a lift letter, and an 11" x 14" four-color brochure. As you begin getting esti-mates from various vendors, you will discover ways you can cut costs. The printer might tell you that by changing the size of the brochure to 8 ½" x 11", you can fit many more on a press sheet, which would cut your printing costs considerably. Or changing the shape of the order form and the lift letter will allow both of them to fit on the press to-gether, decreasing your costs further.

Once you have determined all the pieces your dream package will include, set up a checklist that contains every cost component in your campaign (be sure that taxes are included in all costs where applicable). We use two kinds of dollar figures—total cost and cost per thousand (CPM). Cost per thousand makes it easy to make comparisons among various mailings, lists, and media.

Start your checklist by filling in the name of the product, and the specifications for the job, which are detailed descriptions of the package (for instance, you may choose to use an 8 ½" x 11" letter (offset and then lasered), a No. 10 window envelope (two-color), a 5 7/8" x 11" four-color brochure, and a No. 9 business reply envelope. Fill in the number of pieces you're planning to mail. This is important, because some costs vary according to the number of pieces you mail. The unit cost for printing, for instance, will drop as the quantity increases, so it might cost $35/M to print 2,000 letters, and $25/M to print 30,000 letters. There are eight costs to consider:

★ *Creative*: This includes all actual out-of-pocket costs for copywriting, finished design, mechanicals, typesetting, and scanning of photographs.

★ *Photos and illustrations*: This includes costs for the photographer, and for any models and retouching that may be involved, or for any drawings or illustrations you may be using. Be sure you tell photographers or illustrators how you will be using their work. Sometimes you can purchase complete rights to use a photo or drawing whenever and however you want; other times you purchase the rights for a one-time-use only. This must be negotiated in advance with the artists/photographers or their agents. Stock photography services, such as EyeWire or Corbis, offer royalty free usage and save on costs of color separating.

★ *Printing*: Costs are included for each piece in the direct mail package—the letter, the outer envelope, the business reply envelope, the lift letter, the brochure, and any other inserts you may have. A printer may give you an estimate based on the total job, as opposed to giving you separate prices for each of these elements. In that case, you simply fill in the total amount and calculate the total cost per thousand. You may also find that you have to use more than one printer—some printers specialize in printing envelopes, for instance. You may have to do some shopping around to get the best price on your total package. The larger the quantity, the more shopping you should do to get the best price. Choose a printer who is equipped for the quantity; ask what their average runs are.

★ *Lists and computer service bureau*: If you're using outside lists, include rental fees, select costs (gender, zip code, or hotline), label, National Change of Address (NCOA), and merge/purge costs. If you're using only your own house file, include any maintenance or updating costs you may incur.

★ *Lettershop*: This is another area where you may only have one total figure, or it may be broken down by the various services lettershops render. Whichever way you do it, make sure you include the total cost and the cost per thousand in your checklist.

★ *Postage*: "Postage out" is what it costs you to mail your package to your prospects. Outgoing postage rates can change according to how many pieces you send to each zip code. Your lettershop will charge you the highest rate for the number of pieces you're mailing. You will get a postage receipt which will give you the exact cost, and you will get a rebate if the actual cost was less than the lettershop's estimate.

"Postage in" covers what you pay the post office for the postage-paid reply envelopes or cards you get back from customers ordering or inquiring about your merchandise. It's likely that some of these orders and inquiries will come through a company's website, as well.

★ *Telemarketing*: Inbound telemarketing is what you pay when customers call you on a toll-free number to place their orders. You have outbound telemarketing costs when someone in your company calls a prospect to make a sale, or when you hire an outside service to do it for you.

★ *Miscellaneous*: This category includes messengers, faxes, telephone, overnight delivery, travel and entertainment, sales tax—any costs that don't fit into the first seven categories.

Copy the chart in Figure 9.1, and add in any other promotion costs you might have that aren't on the list.

Figure 9.2 shows a sample checklist for a direct mail package for Cookbooks International. The mailing includes an offer for *The Giant Book of Recipes from Around the World* at $45.98, with a free pasta fork as a premium. This will be a 50,000 piece mailing, including a 2-page, 8 ½" x 11" letter, a 4" x 6" lift letter, a four-color 70 lb., 8 ½" x 11" coated stock brochure with 6 photographs, a two-color No. 10 outer window envelope, and a one-color card stock business reply card.

Figure 9.1

Promotion costs checklist.

DIRECT MAIL CHECKLIST – PROMOTION COSTS

Name of Product: _____

Job Specifications: _____

_____

pieces mailed: _____

JOB DESCRIPTION	TOTAL COST	CPM
CREATIVE		
Copywriting & revision	_____	_____
Design	_____	_____
Mechanicals	_____	_____
Typography	_____	_____
Scanning (photos)	_____	_____
PHOTOS & ILLUSTRATIONS		
Photography	_____	_____
Models	_____	_____
Retouching	_____	_____
Illustrations	_____	_____
PRINTING		
Color separations	_____	_____
Letter	_____	_____
Lift letter or other inserts	_____	_____
Order form/reply card	_____	_____
Brochure	_____	_____
Catalog	_____	_____
Outer envelope	_____	_____
Reply envelope	_____	_____
Other	_____	_____
LISTS & COMPUTER SERVICE BUREAU		
List rental	_____	_____
Merge/Purge, NCOA, other maintenance	_____	
LETTERSHOP		
Inserting	_____	_____
Addressing (including laser personalization)	_____	_____
Sorting, mailing	_____	_____
POSTAGE		
Postage Out	_____	_____
Postage In	_____	_____
TELEMARKETING		
Inbound	_____	_____
Outbound	_____	_____
MISCELLANEOUS		
Messenger, phone bill, etc.	_____	_____
Administration	_____	_____
TOTALS:	_____	_____

Figure 9.2

Promotion costs checklist—*The Giant Book of Recipes from Around the World.*

DIRECT MAIL CHECKLIST – PROMOTION COSTS

Name of Product: The Giant Book of Recipes from Around the World

Job Specifications: 2-pg. 8 1/2" x 11" letter: 4" x 6" list letter: 4-color 70 lb. 8 1/2" X 11" coated stock brochure with 6 photos: 2-color #10 outer window envelope: 1-color card stock reply card

 # pieces mailed: 50,000

JOB DESCRIPTION	TOTAL COST	CPM
CREATIVE		
Copywriting & revision	$3,000	$60.00
Design	2,000	40.00
Mechanicals	1,000	20.00
Typography	0	
Scanning (photos)	400	8.00
PHOTOS & ILLUSTRATIONS		
Photography	1,000	20.00
Models	0	
Retouching	400	8.00
Illustrations	0	
PRINTING		
Color separations	200	4.00
Letter	2,000	40.00
Lift letter or other inserts	800	16.00
Order form/reply card	800	16.00
Brochure	5,000	100.00
Catalog	0	
Outer envelope	3,000	60.00
Reply envelope	1,000	20.00
Other	0	
LISTS & COMPUTER SERVICE BUREAU		
List rental	6,500	130.00
Merge/Purge, NCOA, other maintenance	500	10.00
LETTERSHOP		
Inserting	350	7.00
Addressing (including laser personalization)	400	8.00
Sorting, mailing	350	7.00
POSTAGE		
Postage Out	17,000	340.00
Postage In	500	10.00
TELEMARKETING		
Inbound	2,000	40.00
Outbound	1,000	20.00
MISCELLANEOUS		
Messenger, phone bill, etc.	400	8.00
Administration	400	8.00
TOTALS:	$50,000	1,000.00

Finding the Break-Even Point

Once you know your promotion costs (which are sometimes called marketing costs), you can determine your break-even point. Breaking even means that your costs and revenue are equal: you're not making any profit—but you're not losing money either. The break-even point is the number of orders you need to receive in order for your revenue to equal your costs.

It's important to note that your first direct mail promotion will be more expensive than the second one. Many costs apply to the first mailing only. For instance, copywriting, typography, film and separations are basically one-time expenses. You won't incur those costs again unless you make changes. The only recurring costs are for things like printing, postage, lists, and telemarketing. So your break-even point on subsequent mailings will be a lot lower.

Knowing the break-even point helps you determine the feasibility of your campaign. Suppose the numbers tell you that you must sell 5,000 widgets with a mailing to 10,000 people in order to break even. That means you need a 50 percent response rate—an unrealistic expectation. Those numbers would let you know there is something way out of line in your planning. Your production costs are too high, or your selling price much too low.

The first step in determining your break-even point is to calculate *all* of your costs. Figure 9.1 helped you determine the cost of one aspect of your campaign—the promotion. To get the total cost of your campaign, you need to add in everything for which you're laying out money, from manufacturing or purchasing the product, to getting the orders in, to sending the product to customers, and perhaps even getting returns from buyers who didn't like your product.

Figure 9.3 shows the break-even point for *The Giant Book of Recipes from Around the World* mailing:

★ *Product cost*: How much does it cost to purchase or manufacture the product? It costs Cookbooks International $6.98 to produce their *Giant Book of Recipes from Around the World* cookbook. The pasta fork being offered as a premium costs $.35, which brings the total product costs to $7.33.

Figure 9.3

Break-even point checklist—*The Giant Book of Recipes from Around the World.*

DIRECT MAIL CHECKLIST – BREAK-EVEN POINT

Name of Product: The Giant Book of Recipes from Around the World

 # pieces mailed: 50,000

PER ORDER COSTS	SUBTOTAL	TOTAL
PRODUCT COST:		
Purchase or manufacturing cost	$6.98	
Cost of Premium	.35	
Total		$7.33
ORDER PROCESSING:		
Computer input	.75	
Packing materials (boxes, dunnage, tape)	.36	
Pick & pack, seal, affix label	.25	
Cost of shipping completed package	1.62	
Total		2.98
BILLING AND COLLECTIONS:		
Credit Card processing charges	1.07	
Returns	.13	
Bad debts	.61	
Total		1.81
MISCELLANEOUS COSTS		
800#	.60	
Other		
Total		.60
COST PER ORDER		$12.72
SELLING PRICE OF PRODUCT	$45.98	
Plus shipping and handling	5.00	
Total selling price		$50.98
Less total cost per order		$12.72
ALLOWABLE: marketing cost per order		$38.26
NUMBER OF ORDERS NEEDED TO BREAK EVEN		
Total marketing cost	$50,000.00	
Allowable	38.26	
Break-Even Point: marketing cost / allowable		
(number of orders)		1307

★ *Order processing*: This category includes all the costs involved in actually receiving the order and shipping the product out to the customer. Cookbook International's order processing costs total $2.98.

★ *Billing and collections*:

- The first subcategory here is credit card charges. If you accept credit cards, you have to pay for processing charges to the bank or the credit card company. Determine the average processing charge. For instance, if you accept four types of credit cards, two of which charge you 3 percent for processing and two charge you 4 percent, your average charge would be 3.5 percent (assuming the cards are used equally). Multiply the selling price of our product, plus shipping and handling, by .035 to find your average processing fee. In this case, since the total selling price is $50.98 ($45.98 plus $5 shipping and handling), the average fee would be $1.78 ($50.98 x .035 = $1.78). Then you need to determine what percentage of your sales will be via credit card. Cookbook International usually receives 60 percent of its orders that way; therefore we multiplied $1.78 times 60 percent to arrive at the average processing charge per order ($1.78 x .60 = $1.07).
- The next subcategory is returns. No matter how good the product, every company gets some returns. The industry standard (for products other than clothes) is 5 percent. The cost of returns includes shipping and handling, and the cost of refurbishing the product to send it out again (using the industry standard of 10 percent of the cost of your product). Add together your shipping and handling costs, plus your refurbishing cost. For Cookbook International, then, the costs would be:

Shipping	$1.62
Handling	0.25
Refurbishing	0.70
Total	$2.57

Multiply that figure by the 5 percent return rate, and you come up with the cost per unit for returns. So Cookbook International's costs were $2.57, multiplied by 5 percent ($2.57 x .05 = $.13).

- The third subcategory here is bad debt, which happens in every business. If you have no previous experience on which to base this figure, you should allow for 5 percent. To determine this cost, multiply the cost of your product, response management, and fulfillment by 5 percent. For Cookbooks, that came to $.61.

★ *Miscellaneous costs:* These include any costs particular to your business, for instance if you use a toll-free phone service, or a telemarketing company.

- If you use a toll-free number, you need to include these charges as well. To determine this figure, multiply the cost per order for using the toll-free number, times the percentage of orders you get through this medium. Cookbooks International gets 60 percent of its orders over their toll-free number, and it costs them approximately $1.00 to handle each one. Therefore, the average telemarketing cost per order is $.60 ($1.00 X .60 = $0.60).

★ *Cost per order:* Adding together the product costs, order processing and fulfillment, billing and collections, and miscellaneous costs, you come up with the total average cost of each order you receive (cost per order, or CPO). It costs Cookbooks International $12.72 for each order of *The Giant Book of Recipes from Around the World.*

★ *Selling price of the product:* This is what you charge for your product, plus shipping and handling. *Recipes from Around the World* costs the customer $45.98 plus $5.00 shipping and handling for a total of $50.98.

★ *Allowables:* To arrive at this figure, you subtract the total cost per order from the total selling price of your product. In this case, Cookbooks subtracts $12.72 from the total selling price of $50.98, giving them an allowable of $38.26 for every order received.

★ *Number of orders needed to break even:* The $38.26 is the amount of money Cookbooks International can spend in marketing per order without losing money. They won't make money either—they'll break even. To calculate the break-even point, you divide the total marketing cost by the allowable. That means Cookbooks International needs to get 1,307 orders to break even, which is equal to a response rate of approximately 2.61 percent. This is a fairly high percentage, but is acceptable to Cookbooks International because they know this mailing includes one-time expenses that won't be incurred again in future mailings.

Figure 9.4 is a blank break-even point checklist you can use to fill in yourself. Add in any additional costs particular to the product you're selling.

How to Calculate the Break-Even Point for a Direct Response Ad

Use the same checklists in Figures 9.2 and 9.3 to calculate the break-even point for a direct response advertisement. Substitute the cost of your ad for the marketing costs, and divide by the allowable number. If Cookbooks International placed an ad costing $5,000 for instance, they would need to bring in 131 orders to break even ($5,000 / $38.26 = 131).

If you want to know what percent response you need from the magazine's readers, multiply the number of orders you need to break even by 100, then divide the result by the magazine's circulation. If the magazine's circulation is 350,000, the formula in this case is:

$$13,100 \div 350,000 = 0.037\%$$

or a response rate of about 1/25th of 1%.

Analyzing Catalog Sales

To analyze a catalog's sales or determine its profit potential, it's best to think of it as a collection of individual ads. Every item on the page should earn back its costs and make a profit. Suppose your 28-page catalog cost $56,000 to produce and mail. Divide the total cost by the number of pages and you find that each page cost you $2,000. Then you divide each page by the number of items on it. If a page has only two items on it, then it costs you $1,000 to advertise each item. A quarter page is worth $500, an eighth of a page $250, and so on.

To analyze an individual item's sales, you need to know the cost for every product featured in your catalog. You can use the checklist in Figure 9.4 to determine the total cost per order for each item.

Figure 9.4

Break-even point checklist.

DIRECT MAIL CHECKLIST – BREAK-EVEN POINT

Name of Product:

 # pieces mailed:

PER ORDER COSTS	SUBTOTAL	TOTAL
PRODUCT COST:		
Purchase or manufacturing cost		
Cost of Premium..		
Total...		
ORDER PROCESSING:		
Computer input...		
Packing materials (boxes, dunnage, tape)....................................		
Pick & pack, seal, affix label...		
Cost of shipping completed package..............		
Total...		
BILLING AND COLLECTIONS:		
Credit Card processing charges..		
Returns...		
Bad debts..		
Total...		
MISCELLANEOUS COSTS		
800#..		
Other..		
Total...		
COST PER ORDER..		
SELLING PRICE OF PRODUCT..		
Plus shipping and handling...		
Total selling price...		
Less total cost per order..		
ALLOWABLE: marketing cost per order....................................		
NUMBER OF ORDERS NEEDED TO BREAK EVEN		
Total marketing cost...		
Allowable..		
Break-Even Point: marketing cost / allowable		
(number of orders)		

Figure 9.5 is a portion of a per-page analysis checklist for Cookbooks International's Spring catalog. *The Giant Book of Recipes from Around the World* was featured on one half of page 12. Here is how the profit/loss was determined:

★ *Dollar amount of sales generated*: Fifty cookbooks were sold, which gives you a total sales volume of $2,549 (50 x $50.98 = $2,549).

★ *Product cost*: As per the break-even point checklist (Figure 9.3), the product cost for this book was $12.72, multiplied by the number of books sold (50) equals $636.00.

★ *Net profit*: Subtracting the product cost from the total sales generated gives you a total of $1,913.00.

★ *Cost of space allocated*: According to our figures above, one-half page of this catalog is worth $1,000:

$$\$56,000 \div 28 = \$2,000 \div 2 = \$1,000$$

Figure 9.5
Catalog sales analysis checklist—*The Giant Book of Recipes from Around the World* (one-half page).

CATALOG CHECKLIST – SALES ANALYSIS

Per Page Analysis: Page # 12

Item #: 300   Description: The Giant Book of Recipes from Around the World

Space allocated: 1/2 page

$ amount of sales generated	$2,549.00
Product cost	$636.00
Net profit	$1,913.00
Cost of space allocated	$1,000.00
Profit to space ratio	1.91
Profit/Loss per item	$18.26

★ *Profit-to-space ratio*: To arrive at this figure, you divide the cost of the space allocated into the net profit. The profit-to-space ratio for this book is 1.91 ($1,913 / $1,000 = 1.913). If the ratio comes out to less than 1.0, you're losing money. If it comes out to 1.0, you're breaking even, and if it comes out to more than 1.0, you're making a profit.

★ *Profit/loss per item*: Subtract the cost of space allocated from the net profit, divided by the number of items sold, and you get your profit/loss per item. In this case there is a profit of $18.26:

$$\$1,913 - \$1,000 = \$913 / 50 = 18.26$$

You would do the same type of figuring for every item in the catalog. Figure 9.6 shows you what the profit/loss would be if *The Giant Book of Recipes from Around the World* had been featured on a full page of the catalog instead of a one-half page. The profit-to-space ratio would then be .96, which translates into a loss of $1.74. This would tell you that you've allocated too much space to this item. Next time you print the catalog, you probably would want to give it less space. You would then have to analyze the results to make sure the number of sales did not drop off because of the reduced space. You may have to run several tests

Figure 9.6
Catalog sales analysis checklist—*The Giant Book of Recipes from Around the World* (full page).

CATALOG CHECKLIST – SALES ANALYSIS

Per Page Analysis: Page # 12
Item #: 300   Description: The Giant Book of Recipes from Around the World
Space allocated: full   page
$ amount of sales generated $2,549.00
Product cost $613.00
Net profit $1,913.00
Cost of space allocated $2,000.00
Profit to space ratio 96
Profit/Loss per item ....   -$1.74

until you get the desired results. An item that doesn't break even in a half page might do very well featured on a full page. If you have great faith in that product, you may want to run it on a full page and analyze those results as well.

By analyzing each item's profit-to-space ratio, you can adjust your space size and positioning so that every item you continue to offer comes out a winner.

Analyzing List Results

Suppose you've rented five different lists of 10,000 names for your mailing. You'd want to know which of those lists produced the best results, so that you could use the winning lists for your next mailing and look for other similar lists.

To determine the response rate for each list, divide the number of orders you received from that list by the number of pieces mailed to that list, multiplied by 100. For instance, if you receive 250 orders from the 10,000 names on list A, the formula would be:

$$(250 \div 10,000) \times 100 = 2.5 \text{ percent}$$

If you want to know the average dollar amount of an order from that list, you would divide the total dollar value by the number of orders. If the total dollar value of orders from list A was $8,000, the formula would be:

$$\$8,000 \div 250 = \$32$$

To find out the amount of sales in dollars per thousand pieces mailed, multiply the response rate times the amount of average order times X (number of thousands mailed). The formula for finding the dollars per thousand catalogs for list A would then be:

$$2.5 \times \$32 \times 10 = \$800 \text{ per thousand}$$

You will use these charts and formulas over and over again in Direct Marketing. They are what make Direct Marketing both an art and a science. You can have the most beautiful direct mail package or the most creative direct response ad—but that won't help you if your pricing is off, leaving you too thin a margin. If you have unrealistic requirements to break even, you'd better rethink your entire campaign.

Checklist

THREE WAYS TO INCREASE YOUR BOTTOM LINE

- ☑ Increase your selling price, or
- ☑ Increase your response rate, or
- ☑ Lower your costs

DETERMINE YOUR PROMOTION COSTS—INCLUDE THE FOLLOWING CATEGORIES

- ☑ Creative
- ☑ Photos and illustrations
- ☑ Printing
- ☑ Lists and computer service bureau
- ☑ Lettershop
- ☑ Postage
- ☑ Telemarketing
- ☑ Miscellaneous

FIND THE BREAK-EVEN POINT

- ☑ Calculate all your costs to get your cost per order
  - ✓ Product cost
  - ✓ Order processing
  - ✓ Billing and collections
  - ✓ Miscellaneous
- ☑ Set your selling price (including shipping and handling)
- ☑ Calculate your allowable (total selling price − cost per order)
- ☑ Calculate the number of orders needed to break even (total marketing costs ÷ allowable)

DETERMINE THE BREAK-EVEN POINT FOR A DIRECT RESPONSE AD

- ☑ Divide the cost of the ad by the total product cost

☑ To determine the response rate:

   ✓ Multiply by 100 the number of orders you need to break even
   ✓ Divide the results by the magazine's circulation

ANALYZING CATALOG SALES

☑ Divide the total cost of the catalog by the number of pages to determine the cost per page

☑ Divide each page by the number of items on it

☑ Determine profit/loss, including the following categories:

   ✓ $ amount of sales generated
   ✓ Product cost
   ✓ Net profit (subtract the product cost from the total sales generated)
   ✓ Cost of space allocated (how much each page, half-page, quarter-page, and eighth-page is worth)
   ✓ Profit-to-space ratio (divide the cost of space allocated into the net profit); if the ratio is more than 1.0, you're making a profit
   ✓ Profit/loss per item (subtract the cost of space allocated from the net profit, divided by the number of items sold)

ANALYZING LIST RESULTS

☑ Determine response rates for each list you rent

   ✓ Multiply the number of orders you receive by 100; divide by the number of pieces mailed

☑ Determine the average dollar amount of an order from each list

   ✓ Divide the total dollar value by the number of orders

☑ Determine the amount of sales in dollars per thousand pieces mailed

   ✓ Multiply the response rate times the amount of the average order times X (number of thousands mailed)

10
CHAPTER

Planning Your Campaign

The fun part of putting together a Direct Marketing campaign is being creative—coming up with ideas, designs, clever headlines and phrases that sell. But Direct Marketing is not just about being creative. It's also about accomplishing very specific goals; goals that will be different for every marketer and every campaign.

In the first nine chapters of this book, you've been learning about the various components that make up Direct Marketing, including offers and mailing lists, direct mail packages, direct response ads, and catalogs; how to get your merchandise out to the customer; and some of the budgetary principles involved in making any campaign a success. Now that you understand these individual components, it's time to put them all together in a cohesive plan.

Just as in any other complex project, it takes organization and planning to achieve consistent success in Direct Marketing. Planning a campaign requires you to define and implement overall, broad objectives, as well as the tiniest details. As you know by now, there are hundreds of details involved in every Direct Marketing campaign—which means hundreds of things that can go wrong at any given moment. It seems as though Murphy must have been a Direct Marketer—something is *bound* to go wrong somewhere along the line.

That's where the Direct Marketing plan comes in. There are so many processes involved, so many people playing so many different roles (everyone who participates in a Direct Marketing program usually ends up wearing many hats), that you really need a guide that spells out your campaign's purpose and specific details.

There are two reasons for writing out a marketing plan: 1) to force you to think through every aspect of the campaign and every decision that must be made—from the overall objectives to the daily tasks that must be set and accomplished—before you start the actual process; and 2) to provide a road map to which you can refer at any point during the campaign to keep your progress on track.

This plan is the key to the success of any Direct Marketing campaign. Plans come in all shapes and sizes. I'll never forget the day when I was working on the IBM account at Wunderman and the client came in with their Direct Marketing plan—which was about as thick as the New York City telephone book. It included every piece of background information on their products, every possible detail, everything that had ever even been discussed about this campaign. Yet I've seen other plans— good plans, concise and to the point—that are no more than three or four pages in outline form. How you put the plan together doesn't really matter, as long as it contains seven areas of pertinent information you need in order to make your campaign work: background, objectives, strategy, tactics, ballpark estimates, contingency plans, and timetable.

Background

The first section of your direct marketing plan, called the background or situation analysis, is an extensive description of your product (or service) and everything that's happened to your product up until the moment you draft the plan. That includes:

★ *Physical description*: Dimensions, weight, color, materials
★ *Function*: What does the product do and how does it do it?
★ *Benefits*: What needs—real or emotional—does the product fulfill for your customers?
★ *Unique properties*: What makes this product different from its competition?

★ *Pricing*: What is the projected selling price of this product?

★ *Line extensions*: Are there now, or might there be in the future, any products that might be sold in conjunction with or as an accessory to this one? Are there any aftermarket supplies you can be selling? For instance, if you're selling hair care products, might you also want to sell hair brushes, combs, barrettes, and styling aids?

If possible, you might even want to attach samples or photographs to this section.

In assembling background information, evaluating the competition is as important as analyzing your own product. What's available in the marketplace that's similar to your product? How is it different? What is the selling price? Where and how are similar products being sold? What advertising campaigns or Direct Marketing are they using to sell the product?

Everyone involved in selling your product should ferret out information. They should be on constant alert for competitors' products. Ask them to tear out any ads they come across in newspapers and magazines (and be sure they're clearly marked with the name and date of publication), and to save any direct mailings they receive.

When you've collected enough samples, analyze them. Who is your competitor's target audience? What features and benefits are stressed in the copy? What is the offer being made? If possible, get back issues of publications in which their ads have appeared. Has their advertising changed over time? What has remained the same, and what's been added or eliminated?

Become familiar with the product itself and determine if your competitors deliver what they promise. Conduct the same kinds of tests you used for your own fulfillment operation: order the product yourself, and get several other people you know to order it as well. Pay by check or credit card, send insufficient payment, return an item for credit or refund. How do you rate their fulfillment services?

Summarize your findings for your marketing plan. This will give you a better picture of the similarities—and, more importantly, the differences—between your product or service and your competitor's. It's difficult to market a "me too" product. Consumers want to know why they should buy your product instead of your competitor's. The more information you can get about the competition, the more effectively you can differentiate yourself in the marketplace.

Once you've completed the situation analysis and the competitive analysis, you should have an objective description of your product's major strengths and weaknesses, and how your product's benefits compare to the competition's. Given this knowledge, you can then go on and determine your objectives.

Objectives

In designing a Direct Marketing campaign, you must first decide what you want the campaign to do for you. What is it that you want your Direct Marketing to accomplish? It is simply to increase your bottom line? Or are you launching a new product, or expanding into new markets? You can't begin to design an effective campaign until you clearly determine your objectives.

Clients always tell me their objective is to make money. Ultimately, that is everyone's objective—but it's not specific enough to do any good. Your objective must be as specific as possible, with numerical targets and limited time frames. Some clear objectives might be: to build response rates by 2 percent within the next six months; to sell 4,000 additional units by October of two years from now; to increase your database by 25 percent over the next three quarters.

TIP   When setting goals, use your past marketing results as guidelines. If this is a first-time marketing effort, do some research and use industry averages as your benchmarks.

Strategy

Once you know your Direct Marketing objective, you can determine your strategy. The strategy is the "big idea" that takes me from my objective to my tactics. When we were working on the Ford campaign to women, the big idea was to develop a database of women and their car-buying intentions: we wanted to know what kind of car Customer A currently owned, and when she would be ready to buy a new car.

Here's another example of a strategy: We had a client recently whose objective was to sell wigs to women undergoing chemotherapy. We spent several months designing the strategy. After studying the background of both his product and the experiences of cancer patients, we decided the most appropriate strategy was to introduce the product via direct mail to oncology nurses and get them to hand out brochures for the wigs and recommend them to their patients.

Your choice of strategy will be based on your objectives and your budget, your product, your time limitations, and your target audience.

Tactics

The tactic used in the Ford campaign was to develop an ongoing relationship with the customer (the *Canadian Driver's News*) that would bridge the gap between the time we got their name and the time they would be buying a car. The tactic for the wig campaign was to give an incentive to the oncology nurses, giving them a thank you gift for having the brochure on display in the office and handing it out to customers.

The same factors that determine your strategy determine your tactics. The budget is probably your first consideration. How much can you afford to spend to implement the strategy? To make your tactical decisions, you must determine what items are essential to sell your product within the limits of your budget.

Another consideration is your target market. Do you have a house file of names you can use as a base to determine your target market? Or if this is a new product, how do you envision your ideal customer? Where would you find that type of person?

Then you must make all the creative decisions. In Direct Marketing, your tactics will be broken down into the small steps necessary to take a campaign from conception to conclusion. You need to ask yourself questions all along the way, such as: Will I use direct mail, or direct response ads in print or TV? What lists will I use? What do I need to say in the letter? What will my offer be? Do I need to include a brochure? Should it be four-color, or black and white? If you're selling several different handmade stained-glass art pieces, you probably need a brochure with four-color photographs. On the other hand, if you're selling a book or magazine, you may not need any photographs, or decide that a black-and-white photo will show off the product perfectly.

The most important thing to remember is that there is not one right decision to be made in any of these areas. Many different strategies might work, as well as hundreds of alternative tactics. When creating your plan, it's a good idea to develop several different strategies and tactics and review them all until you find the ones that make the most sense within the limits of the budget.

TIP   Don't discard unused ideas, however—save them for another campaign.

It's important that you write out the plan and keep careful tract of its results. Because Direct Marketing is an accountable science, you can keep accurate records of your responses. That way, you will know which strategies were successful and helped you accomplish your goal. Then you can repeat that success.

Ballpark Estimates

Once you've developed your background, objectives, strategies and tactics, you want to know how much it will cost to execute the program you've designed. Your plan should include estimates of what the job will cost based on the various tactics you've outlined. When I'm putting together a marketing plan, I usually include an estimate for a program that includes a lot of bells and whistles (such as peel-off stickers, five-color printing, and die-cut order forms), as well as an estimate for a scaled-down approach.

If you have an extensive budget, you can test both approaches and track which one produces the best response. Usually, however, you compromise and settle on a program that has some of the element of the all-inclusive program and some from the scaled-down approach. Or you can cut down on all the bells and whistles, go with the scaled-down approach, and mail out to more lists. You have to make judgement calls based on your experience and knowledge of the market.

Once you have estimates for each proposed campaign, the next step is to figure out what the response rate has to be in order to break even and to start making a profit (using the charts and formulas in Chapter 9). Then for each estimate, you pose a series of "what if" scenarios:

"What if the proposed direct mail campaign pulls a 1 percent response rate? What if it pulls 1½ percent? What if it pulls 2 percent?" Using these scenarios, you can see the upside potential and the downside risk for each proposed campaign.

There is no way you can accurately forecast what the response rate will be. That's what tests are for. If you mail to 50,000 people in an initial test, those names will come from several different lists. Suppose you get an overall response rate of 1 percent. When you analyze the results, you'll find that some lists produced a ½ percent response rate, some produced 1 percent, and some produced 2 percent. Then you would roll out to the lists that produced the best response.

Any additional sources of revenue would also be included in this section. For instance, I might include a bounce-back offer in my product package. Often, costs for a small package stuffer can be covered in the initial printing estimates (if you're printing a brochure, for instance, and there's room left over on the press—paper that would normally be thrown away for scrap—you can sometimes fit in another small job such as a package stuffer). So the printing cost is taken care of, and whatever response you get to the bounce-back offer is added to your profit.

Contingency Plans

Contingency plans include more "what if" scenarios. For instance:

> *What if the first catalog produces only minimal response?* Instead of mailing a second catalog, we'll test a direct mail piece that includes a four-color brochure.
> *What if the catalog produces greater-than-expected response?* We will roll out as quickly as possible to the best-performing lists.

If these decisions are made up front, you will be prepared for any outcome, you will know what to do as you put each step of your campaign into motion, and you will know what your next steps should be.

Timetable

The timetable should be clearly laid out so that everyone involved knows when deadlines are approaching and how long each step will take. If you're proposing two mailings, one in January and one in May, it's important to know when you must begin and complete each stage in the campaign—when do you need to create the copy, send it to the printer, mail the completed package? Who is in charge of the various stages? Does the copy need to be approved by management? If so, what is the deadline for that approval? Who makes the decision to go on to the next step of the campaign? All these questions must be answered so that everyone understands the program.

A Sample Marketing Plan

The following is a marketing plan for a fictional company called Four Star Laptop Computers:

Background. Four Star Laptop Computers was founded five years ago when Joe Barton, age 45, was laid off from his job as a travel coordinator for a large corporation. He then planned to start his own business producing a travel newsletter. As he put together a business plan and cost analysis, he began to realize that his start-up costs—in time and money—were concentrated in setting up a home-based computer system.

Since traveling was important to him, he knew he wanted a laptop computer. Not being fluent in computerese, Barton has a difficult time figuring out what he needed and what components would work together and fill his needs. Computer store employees were not very helpful. Every time he put together a budget, he'd find he hadn't included all the elements, and it turned out that the system he bought cost him 35 percent more than his initial estimate.

By talking to other first-time laptop computer buyers, Barton realized that there were many other people in his situation. So he founded Four Star Laptop Computers, the first self-contained laptop system, that includes hardware, software, and peripherals, designed specifically for non-computer-savvy, home-based business owners.

Product Description. Four Star Laptop Computers are made of exceptionally lightweight, sturdy plastic. The system includes a 14 inch display, 20 GB hard drive, and DVD drive, expanded memory, internal modem, networked optical mouse, ink-jet printer, and all necessary cables. It is designed to function as a basic transportable business computer—loaded with Microsoft Office, a word processing system, a bookkeeping and spreadsheet program, a telephone directory, a contact management system, a basic graphics program, and high-speed Internet compatibility.

Benefits. The Four Star Laptop Computer is positioned as the Saturn of the computer world. You pay one price, no shopping around for the best buy on each component (which may or may not work with all your other components). It is designed with the novice in mind. The manual is written in plain English with step-by-step instructions and illustrations. The computer comes with preloaded tutorials so that as soon as you turn it on, instructions appear on the screen which tell you how to get to the program of your choice. Each program has its own preloaded tutorials. These tutorials can be easily deleted when they are no longer necessary. There is also a 24-hour toll-free number for technical support, staffed by operators specially trained to help novices.

Unique Properties. This is an all-inclusive system, designed for the small home business and the novice computer user.

Pricing. The projected selling price is $2,995.

Line Extensions. The first line extension is a four-color printer. Down the line, Four Star will offer a variety of products for home-based businesses, such as office furniture specially designed to fulfill more than one function and to fit in cramped spaces.

Competitive Analysis. Four Star's pricing is competitive with both retail computer superstores and mail order companies. However, Four Star offers better support than any of these choices. When buying from computer superstores, customers frequently get conflicting advice depending on which salesperson they talk to. And most mail order companies are not geared toward the novice computer user; buyers must know in advance what they need and which components are compatible with each other. Four Star operators, on the other hand, undergo a comprehensive training program in all aspects of the product, so they have extensive product knowledge. The company mission is to establish on-going relationships with customers, to be there to answer questions and help solve problems, and to help customers with growing computer needs.

Objectives. The objective is to sell 500 computers and line extensions in the first year.

Strategy.

- To define the target audience:

  people going into second careers
  people who run home-based or freelance businesses
  retirees or empty-nesters
  part-time business owners

- Test direct response ads in various media

- Test direct mail with a test panel for each target group, talking to prospects one-on-one in non-computer-oriented language

- Provide education for Four Star's customers, not just hardware and software.

Tactics. To develop a list plan and create a target market. Lists might include:

- Newly incorporated small businesses
- Subscribers:

  Entrepreneur
  Modern Maturity
  Inc.

- Associations

  AARP
  Editorial Freelancers Association

The first test will be a space ad and a direct mail piece. The direct mail piece will include a personalized letter from Joe Barton explaining how he was laid off, how he had to go through the maze of computer information and salespeople, and how he came to develop the Four Star concept. The mailing will also include a brochure and a special offer for a one-year free subscription to Joe Barton's newsletter. The newsletter will contain stories from real people about how they use their Four Star computers, and advice about how you can use them better. It will also include other educational information, such as business travel suggestions, tax saving tips for small businesses, how to manage cash flow, how to get loans for small businesses. It will also feature profiles of Four Star employees—their names, their family life, their personal interests and hobbies, how they use their own Four Star computers—so that customers can feel like they have an ongoing relationship with real people, not just a computer company.

Ballpark Estimates. The mailing of 50,000 pieces is estimated to cost $800 per thousand, or $40,000 total. The projection for this mailing is that it will pull between ¾ percent and 2 percent. Direct response space ads will also be tested. The budget for the ads will be between $23,000 and $25,000. The cost of the newsletter will depend on the quantity mailed, but the projected budget for the first year (when Joe Barton will write the newsletter himself) is $3,000.

Contingency Plans.

1. If Four Star doesn't pull at least ¾ percent, the offer will be re-evaluated. Was the newsletter enough? Was the technical support enough?
2. Lists will be analyzed to determine which ones performed the best so that markets can be more closely targeted.
3. Targeted direct response advertising to get leads. Using the information gained from analyzing the lists and from initial direct response testing, two-step direct response ads will be placed in publications that reach Four Star's targeted audience for the smallest cost per order.
4. Research the possibility of an FSI in a newspaper or magazine with a low cost per thousand, or cooperative mailing opportunity with another noncompetitive product for novice computer users.

5. Discounted offers to appropriate associations, such as AARP. Although this may generate less of a profit margin, it would be worth it to generate more sales.

6. If the response rate is higher than 2 percent, a mailing will be rolled out to the best list immediately. At the same time, advertisers for the newsletter will be solicited.

TIMETABLE

Day 1   The decision is made to run a direct mail program, and the writing of the plan begins. This will take approximately two weeks, including the time it takes to get estimates from suppliers and freelancers.

Day 11   Approve the plan.

Day 12   Brief creative people. Brief list people. Start talking in detail to telemarketers, fulfillment people, computer service bureau, lettershop. Share as much of the plan as possible.

Day 18   Get rough creative to finalize estimates and slot them into plan.

Day 20   Go over list cards from list broker(s) and select appropriate lists. Order them from broker(s).

Day 21   Finalize arrangements with telemarketers, fulfillment house, lettershop, etc.

Day 25   Scripts from telemarketers [what they're going to say when your customers call].

Day 26   First draft of creative. Critique it and send it back.

Day 33   Second draft of creative. Fine-tune it over the next two days.

Day 35   Start setting type and fitting it into layouts. Start taking photos. Have letter laser-formatted by the lettershop.

Day 37   Approve letter formatting. Approve type.

Day 39   Start scanning photos.

Day 40   Art, scans, etc., all sent on computer disk, emailed to printer.

Day 41   Lists arrive at computer house. Start merge/purge and source coding [unless you've ordered them already coded]. Names are formatted for lasering at this time.

Day 48   Magnetic tape sent from computer house to lettershop with all the names and addresses in zip sequence, formatted for lasering and ready to use.

Day 50   Get color proofs back from printer with blue prints. Approve them.

Day 52   Start printing.

Day 55   Material is printed, trimmed, folded, and shipped to lettershop.

Day 57   Lettershop starts lasering and inserting.

Day 62   Inserting completed and envelopes are shipped to post office.

Day 76   The letters are delivered. The phones start ringing. Fulfillment house starts sending out orders.

Day 78   The first mail order arrives. They will continue to arrive for the next three months or so.

Day 90   Start analyzing the program and get ready for the next one.

Use Your Marketing Plan as a Reference Guide

The simplest plan is better than no plan at all. It should include as much information as you need to make decisions and take action toward a successful campaign. It can include ideas for the future of your product or service, such as possible promotion partners or aftermarket offers. The purpose of the plan is to work out as many bugs and avoid as many pitfalls as possible before your begin your program.

The marketing plan is not something you create, glance at, and throw away. It's important that you keep it close by and refer to it throughout the length of the campaign. If you're disappointed in the results of your first mailing, for instance, you may go back to your marketing plan and find that you actually did better than you projected in the plan. You may not remember all the contingency plans you developed, so reviewing your plan every few months can serve as a reminder and keep you from having to reinvent the wheel.

Checklist

YOUR MARKETING PLAN SHOULD INCLUDE

☑ Background:

- √ Physical description of the product
- √ Its function and features
- √ Its benefits
- √ Its unique properties
- √ Its projected selling price
- √ Possible line extensions and/or aftermarket supplies
- √ Competitive analysis
    - √ What similar products or services are available in the marketplace?
    - √ How are they similar to yours? How are they different?
    - √ What is the competitor's selling price?
    - √ Where and how are similar products being sold?
    - √ What advertising campaigns or direct marketing are they using to sell the product?
    - √ Who is your competitor's target market?
    - √ What features and benefits are stressed in their marketing?
    - √ What offer is being made?

☑ Objectives:
- √ What do you want to achieve?

☑ Strategy:
- √ What is the "big idea" that will make the program work?

☑ Tactics:
- √ What specific actions will make the strategy work?

☑ Ballpark Estimates:
- √ How much will it cost to achieve your objective?

☑ Contingency Plans:
- √ What are the next steps you will take, depending on how the campaign works (or doesn't work)?

☑ Timetable:
- √ How long will each step take to accomplish?

11

Loyalty Programs

Frequent Flyers, Frequent Buyers

Remember Plaid Stamps? S&H Green Stamps? Anyone who's over 40 does. When you shopped at your local supermarket or gas station, you would get a certain number of stamps, based on the amount of your purchase. You saved up your stamps, pasted them in special books, and—when you had enough—redeemed them for glorious "free" gifts. Most of us would drive out of our way, clear across town if necessary, to shop with those merchants who gave away stamps.

Those stamps were pioneer loyalty programs. They kept customers loyal to a specific retailer by offering an incentive to return (and to spend more money). A more modern example is the frequent flyer program introduced by American Airlines in 1981.

It may not seem that the frequent flyer program has anything to do with Direct Marketing, but it does. According to Gordon Young, Manager of In-Flight Services (and formally manager of Direct Marketing for Air Canada), the most valuable benefit of the frequent flyer program is that it allows the airline to collect data on its individual customers, and then target mailings and special offers to their specific needs.

"I call this relationship management," says Young. "Up until frequent flyer programs, airlines knew who their corporate accounts were. We knew which travel agencies supported us. But we didn't know the names and addresses, the habits, likes, and dislikes of individual flyers. Now we know how much you fly, where you fly, how regularly you fly. We know what hotels you prefer, and what kind of cars you rent." Once they know their customers, airlines are able to develop Direct Marketing campaigns with special offers that will appeal to their loyal flyers.

In many cases, this gives the airline the opportunity to "sell people up" to higher fares. "If we know a person is traveling frequently and paying full coach fare all the time, we know that we can offer them business or first-class travel for a nominal increase in what they're now spending. This is the kind of person to whom we want to target a direct mail promotion."

You don't have to be a giant corporation to offer incentives. Today, in New York City, there is a small manicure shop on a Midtown corner. The first time a customer frequents that business, she gets a card with ten small squares marked on it. Each time the customer returns to the shop and presents her card, one square is punched. When all the squares have been punched, the customer gets a free manicure. The friendly owners also send frequent customers anniversary cards that say: "You've been our customer for six months now. Please come in for a cup of coffee and a free gift." They also send handmade certificates for discounts on nail and hair care products sold in their shop. Both Air Canada and the corner manicurist are cementing their customer base by getting people to return again and again in order to collect a specific reward.

But we're getting ahead of ourselves—because before you start offering free prizes, premiums, and incentives to attract and maintain customers, you have to establish the three most important elements of building customer loyalty: high-quality products or services, extraordinary service, and ongoing communication.

High Quality Products

Direct Marketing is a long-term business. As we pointed out earlier, there is a lot of work that goes into getting new customers, and it costs money to bring each one in. So it makes sense to make sure that each customer stays with you for a good long time.

If you have a terrible product, even the most valiant efforts at customer service won't keep customers coming back. Conversely, even if you have the highest quality product, customers who are treated badly will find their quality products elsewhere.

When customers are judging the quality of your products, everything counts. Every aspect of your business has to support the quality of your product. Your packaging doesn't have to be the most beautiful, but it does have to be sturdy enough so that your product arrives in good shape. It has to arrive in a timely fashion, and look the way you promised it would. If you have shown a photograph of any item you're offering, the item must look the same when it arrives at the customer's home. If a dress that looks purple in the photo is really dark blue, the customer will not only return the item, she'll probably stop buying from you because she's disappointed with what she got.

This is true no matter what the product. When I put together the catalog for IBM printer ribbons years ago, we often had to reshoot several times to get the ribbons to look as black in the picture as they were in reality. If they didn't come out right, people would return the product saying, "This isn't what I ordered!"

This concept works the other way as well. Your presentation has to be as good as your product. A Direct Marketer was recently trying to sell cardboard boxes for storing baby clothes through direct response ads. The boxes featured a cute little teddy bear printed on top, and black spaces to label what was packed in the box. The boxes were advertised for $19.95. They weren't selling, and this marketer wanted to know what was wrong with her ad. It wasn't until she sent me an actual box that I could tell her what the problem was. The real box, large and sturdy, looked small and fragile in the ad's photograph and, since the dimensions of the box were never mentioned, the product did not appear to be worth the asking price. That made it difficult for customers to determine the value of the product being offered.

Customers will keep buying from you if they feel that you deliver value. Value actually refers to *relative* worth. So if you buy something for $5, and it is worth a lot to you (because of its extreme usefulness, or because of sentimental reasons, for example) its value is more than the $5 you paid for it.

TIP   Customers will be loyal to you if they feel the value they get is greater than the price they pay.

Extraordinary Customer Service

A large part of added value for your product is derived from the type of service customers come to expect from your company. I know that, given a choice of two stores or two catalogs, both with identical merchandise, I will choose the one with better service even if the prices are somewhat higher. Treat me right, and I'm yours for life.

Some of the elements of good service include:

★ *Timely delivery*: You never want to disappoint your customers. According to the Mail Order Rule discussed in Chapter 8, you must keep your delivery promises. You have 30 days to ship your merchandise—but if you promise a customer a shorter delivery time, you are bound by that promise. In other words, if a customer orders by phone and you say, "That item will be shipped within 72 hours," you must abide by that delivery time. If you can't the rules of notification apply.

   Abiding by the Rule isn't the only reason for making timely deliveries. Customers expect and deserve it. If it's something they want or need, and it takes too long to arrive, they may go out and buy it elsewhere (and then return the one they get from you). Customers may be buying your merchandise as a gift for a special occasion. A birthday present that arrives one day too late can easily cost you a customer.

★ *Credibility*: Customers want to be able to trust you. They don't want to have to be on the lookout for the fine print, or for hidden charges. They want to know that you have their best interests at heart.

★ *Accurate billing*: Intellectually, customers know that mistakes happen. But emotionally, nothing damages credibility more than being overcharged for something they've ordered. The convenience customers rely on from Direct Marketing is negated when they have to take the time to contact you or the credit card company to adjust inaccurate billing.

★ *Easy returns/refunds*: The one offer that should be included in every Direct Marketing campaign is a money-back guarantee. Customers need to know that if they make a mistake in ordering, or if they are not satisfied with the merchandise they receive, they have the option to change their minds. They also need to know that this will not be a difficult process. Many companies include preaddressed return labels (with instructions on the back) so that customers know exactly how and where to return merchandise.

★ *Flexibility*: One of the most frustrating experiences a shopper can have is being told, "Sorry, that's our policy." Or "there's nothing we can do about it." Customers want to be listened to by someone with a positive attitude who is willing to help them solve their problems.

★ *Caring*: There are some companies that make you feel as if they are doing you a favor by allowing you to shop with them. Customers prefer to buy from a company that can see their point of view, and cares about meeting their needs.

Loyalty programs help you keep customers by treating them well, but they also allow you to discover when they are dissatisfied. Gordon Young cites as an example the story of an executive who lived in New York and had a six-month consulting contract with a company in Chicago. Part of his contract was that he was to fly home to New York every weekend, which he did. When the contract was over, the executive stopped his weekly flying. The airline, able to track his flying habits through the loyalty program, called the executive about a month later and said, "we've been having the pleasure of your company every Friday for the last six months. We haven't seen you for a while. Have we done something wrong?"

Most customers who are dissatisfied with your service will simply stop buying from you. A very small minority actually express their concerns to the company. "By collecting the information we get from the loyalty program, we can track rapid defections like the man from Chicago, but also those whose buying habits deteriorate over time," says Young. "When we have that information, we also have a shot at getting that customer back."

Many mail order businesses have been built on great customer service. One of the best of these is L.L. Bean. If you buy something from them and have any problem with the product, you just have to call up their 800 number and a kind, smart customer service representative will help you find a solution. A few years ago, I bought my son a pair of boots from their catalog. The boots wore out rather quickly, and I called L.L. Bean to ask them where I could get the boots resoled. Instead of giving me that information, they asked me to send the boots back to them— and they sent me a brand-new pair. I will always be a customer of L.L. Bean. They built their company on a reputation of excellent service, and they keep their promise.

I had occasion last summer to visit their store in Freeport, Maine, and was delighted to find that their salespeople were just as accommodating in person as they are on the telephone. For many Direct Marketers, however, the telephone is the only means of contact customers have with your company. So that phone service has to be the best. Whether you have scores of operators answering your phones, or two people at a kitchen table, they must be trained in the art of dealing with customers.

Ongoing Communication

One of the best ways to develop customer loyalty is to establish ongoing communication with the people who are most important to your business, the same way Ford did when they were developing a campaign to bring more women buyers into their dealerships. There is a computer company that uses this tactic very successfully. Soon after you buy a computer from them, you get a letter asking what you think of the product, how you're using it in your home or business, and if the product is living up to your expectations. The company uses the answers to these questions not only to determine customer satisfaction, but also to adapt future computer designs and new products to meet customer needs.

There are many other ways to keep communication lines open with your customers. Carole Ziter, introduced in Chapter 2, is fantastic about keeping touch with her customers in new and unusual ways—so much so that when she and her family vacationed in Europe, she, her husband, and her children wrote postcards to her entire customer mailing list!

One of my favorite methods of ongoing communication is to offer customers education. This is something that I do with my own agency. I like to invite clients to my offices for lunch and have a guest speaker give a brief talk. The speaker is someone who is an authority in a field related to their business, or someone who has had great success in a similar type of business. I invite some of my best clients, as well as some prospects (so they can see how happy my current clients are). For one such seminar, I invited Pat Cameron, a market researcher, to speak on consumer trends. This turned out to be a win-win-win situation: Pat got some new business from contacts she made at the luncheon, the clients got some valuable information from her, and one of the prospects I'd invited hired us to do some work for him because he was so impressed with what he'd seen and heard.

You may not be able to invite customers to your offices for a seminar, but you can offer them educational materials. Remember Dr. Teitelbaum in Chapter 2? He sends out a simple one-page flyer that contains chiro-practic information. If you're selling makeup, you might send out a free newsletter on beauty tips once or twice a year—not connected with any purchase, but as a service to your customers and a way to keep your company name fresh in their minds.

Another method of continuing communication with your customers is to send them something they can use throughout the year to keep your name in front of them. It can be as simple as a refrigerator magnet or a pen with your name inscribed on it. At Christmas time each year, a direct mail production services company I worked with often, Word-tronics, sends me a plastic holder for a calendar page. Then, each month, they sent me the appropriate calendar page. This is a smart tactic; if they sent out the entire calendar at once, I'd get used to seeing it in front of me and wouldn't even notice their name anymore. But each time I got a new page in the mail, they also sent a short promotional letter (Figure 11.1). This letter, though not perfect in grammar or punc-tuation, expresses the personality of both the company and the indi-vidual who wrote the letter. It's an informal, friendly letter that also reminds me of some of the company's services.

What makes their gift really special, though, is that each calendar month features a personalized cartoon in which the name "Lois Geller" appears prominently (Figure 11.2). Their mailing is so clever that it is well worth whatever it costs them to send it: Because I am constantly reminded of their name, I use them often and recommend them to other clients as well.

Figure 11.1

Wordtronics kept their name in front of customers by sending out a promotional letter and calendar each month.

316 North 6th Street
Prospect Park, New Jersey 07508

Ms. Lois Geller
President
The Lois K. Geller Company, Inc.
333 East 46th Street - Suite 1G
New York, NY 10017

Dear Lois,

Hi!

Summer

A time for relaxing

But also for planning

For that important Fall mailing

Call me now to discuss your plans

And I'll be happy to give you an estimate

With prices that will save you lots of money

Looking forward to hearing from you,

Sincerely,

Jeffrey Schwarz
Senior Account Executive

Figure 11.2

The calendar page Wordtronics sent cleverly personalized each month's cartoon by including the customer's name in the caption.

Calculating Long-Term Value

Suppose it costs Wordtronics $1.00 to print out each calendar page, and $.55 to mail it. It costs $.50 more to produce the accompanying letter. Is it worth $2.05 per month ($24.60), plus $5.00 for the plastic holder, to keep me as a customer? My company may spend thousands of dollars each year with Wordtronics; spending $29.60 to keep me loyal seems a small price to pay.

In order for you to find out how much you can spend on a loyalty program, you need to determine the long-term value of your customers. You do that by calculating the average expenditure of your most loyal customers. Suppose your average repeat customer spends $100 a year. Creating a loyalty program that costs you $29.60 per year per customer is probably not a good idea—it's too high a cost for the return. There is no magic formula to determine how much you should spend on keeping customers. Your best bet is to develop several programs and test your options. You may find that spending $5 per year per customer does not bring the desired results, but that spending $8 does. That $8 a year—or even $10—to keep your customers buying your product or service is well worth the expenditure, but $12 may be too much to spend.

Suppose you decide that a $10 expenditure gives you the best response. You can spend that $10 all at once or divide it up in a variety of ways: you could send out a few personalized notes during the year and a $5 gift at Christmas; you could send out a quarterly newsletter; you could offer a $10 gift certificate on your customer's birthday. Whatever money you spend to keep your best customers is a better investment than spending a lot more money to obtain new customers.

Staying in for the Long Haul

There is one important point to remember about loyalty programs: it does take work and money to sustain most programs. Some can be very simple and inexpensive, such as the hole-punch card the manicurist uses. But others can be extremely complicated, such as the frequent flyer programs instituted by the airlines. Because of the high administrative costs of running the program, many airlines have had to increase the amount of miles you must fly in order to get a free trip. So don't be surprised if your program needs some adjustments once in a while.

But if you do institute a loyalty program, be prepared to stay with it for the long haul. Don't make promises you can't keep. If you say you're going to send a calendar page for every month, you can't just suddenly skip October. When there are games or gimmicks involved, you must make expiration dates perfectly clear. There's nothing more disappointing than for a customer to save up points all year in order to be eligible for your fabulous prize, just to be told that the prize program no longer exists. Your customers will feel they've been left holding the bag, and that you've broken your promise to them.

If you want to institute a loyalty program, you could try a step-up program. By testing a simple, limited-time program, you can determine whether or not it will pay to continue. For instance, you could offer a program that has an expiration date: "Get $10 off every $100 purchase you make until July 1." That way you can get all the kinks out of the program. If your customer service line is busy all day with people asking for explanations of the offer, or wanting to know whether they're eligible for various prizes, perhaps you've made your program too complicated. By holding it within a limited time frame, you can contain costs that might otherwise get out of hand.

If, however, you find that the program works for you, you could then roll it out, or start it up again on a slightly expanded basis. You might send out a letter which says, "Our previous program was so successful we decided to lengthen the offer to help you beat those Christmas shopping blues. So you can accumulate points from now until December 1, and redeem them anytime until Christmas Eve." Then you can incorporate all the changes you made from what you learned during your first offer.

Keep It Fresh and Fun

In order for a loyalty program to be most effective, you have to perk it up every once in a while. The airlines are always adding new ways to increase your mileage accumulation. Recently, one frequent flyer program I belong to added a dining club, which awards mileage points for money spent at participating restaurants.

To keep your own program fresh, periodically change the award or add a new one (be sure to give people plenty of notice if you're going to eliminate something). If you're sending out information, such as a newsletter

or flyer, change the format every once in a while (even if it's just temporary—like a special holiday issue), or alter the content. Send your best
customers a surprise gift, out of the blue. People love surprises; they love
gifts; and they love thank yous. How could you get a better combination?
Make your loyalty program fun, and make it intriguing. Your customers
will stay with you, wondering what you could possibly think up next!

Carole Ziter's $2 million company, Sweet Energy, is not one of the
Fortune 500. But Sweet Energy has grown steadily since it started in
1979 with an expenditure of about $200. One of the main reasons for its
growth is that Carole Ziter has mastered the art of customer loyalty.
Here are some of her secrets for what she calls loyalty marketing:

★ *The power of the personal relationship*: Carole learned about Direct
  Marketing when her husband worked for a company called Garden
  Way, one of the pioneers in the Direct Marketing field. They sell
  garden and farm supplies and equipment. One of the products they
  sell is the Rototiller—not the most exciting of products. However,
  the personalized letters their customers received from Dean Leak,
  Garden Way's Sales Manager, were so persuasive and friendly, people
  trusted his opinion. If he said the product was good, they believed it.

  "Dean's letters were so effective," Ziter says, "because when you
  got one it was like he was sitting on the porch with you talking
  about your garden and telling you how he'd just tilled his."

  Ziter remembers one experience she had while helping her husband out at a trade show. A man came over to look at a Rototiller
  they had on display. "He came over and he put his hands on the
  tiller and his eyes glazed over like this was the one thing he wanted
  most in the world," says Ziter. "When I asked him if he needed
  assistance, he told me, 'I just heard from Dean last week. He told
  me you were having a special sale.' That's when I realized the power
  of the personal relationship with your customers, that one-on-one
  you can't get unless you're selling vacuum cleaners door-to-door.
  The fact is, you can deliver your focused message personally to a
  million people. And it won't be diluted by a sales representative
  who may not deliver it the way you meant it to be expressed. You
  can get directly to the people you want to get to, and you can tell
  them exactly what you want to say."

Carole sends a personalized letter with every order from Sweet Energy. When her company was small, she sent handwritten notes to each and every customer. The note was only two or three lines, such as

Dear Sharyn, thank you so much for your order, and Happy Mother's Day.

That short personal letter produced an unexpected response. "I would get letters back from people telling me all about their families, their gardens, and their lives," says Ziter. "A relationship developed that I didn't want to give up. So when we went to a computerized system, we built in a program that could generate a letter for every single order."

This letter is still an important part of Sweet Energy. Some, like Figure 11.3, are basically a thank you and a bounce-back offer. It is personalized to the extent that it addresses the customer by her first name, and makes reference to the items she has just ordered.

Other letters, as in Figure 11.4, contain news about Sweet Energy and about the Ziter family. You'll also note that this letter includes an apology for a mistake in the catalog. In the letter, the customer is informed she is being given a credit for the difference in price. You can believe this customer not only forgave the error, but continued to be a loyal Sweet Energy buyer.

★ *Keeping in touch between orders*: During the holiday season (Sweet Energy does half its business in the ten weeks before Christmas), Ziter sends her customers a four-color, 25–50 page catalog. The rest of the year, her customers receive an eight-page, two-color newsletter Ziter calls the *Gazette*, which she puts together herself. "I've become computer savvy so I can continue to produce the *Gazette* myself," says Ziter. "I now have a Mac at home and use programs like QuarkXPress. My catalog is done totally on the computer, and I can bring it up in four colors. The technology has advanced so fast and become so affordable that it's easy for someone like me to do much of this myself." Ziter admits to being a control freak, but she likes to be able to communicate personally with her customers (although she does work with a copywriter who helps her polish things up).

Figure 11.3

A thank you letter and bounce-back offer from Sweet Energy accompanies each order.

Colchester Vermont, 05446

Dear Barbara,

   Thank you so much for ordering from our FIVE POUND SALE. We are delighted to help you with your Christmas shopping this year. Your gifts will be shipped as requested.

   We also want to help you with your holiday baking needs. By the first of November, you'll be receiving our HOLIDAY BAKING SALE which features all the specialty items you'll be looking for to make your family's traditional family favorites. Things like -
                  Olde English Candied Fruit
                  New Crop California Walnuts
                  Red and Green Glacee Cherries
                  ALL ON SALE!

   But, you don't have to wait until our Holiday Sale hits your mailbox. You can order right now!

   Olde English Candied Fruit - plump citron, orange, lemon, pineapple, and red cherries all soft and moist - perfect for fruit cakes. #FCM   reg. $4.50/lb   ONLY $3.99/lb

   New Crop California Walnuts - crisp and crunchy halves and pieces as fresh as they can be.
   #01NWL   1 lb. reg. $4.95   ONLY $4.20/lb
   #05NWL   5 lbs. reg. $23.75   ONLY $19.95 ($3.99/lb)

To figure the shipping charges when you order, just use the chart on the order form in the enclosed catalog.

   Have a wonderful holiday season.

                                   Carole

P.S. Remember -you can save an additional 10% or 20% on every purchase if you are a Sweet Energy Health Club member. Details are on the catalog order form.

There are several factors that make the *Gazette* so effective. As you can see in Figure 11.5, the cover page features a picture of Carole herself. This strengthens the personal relationship she's established with her customers. Each edition also announces a special sale. Taking another cue from Garden Way, Ziter believes the words of Lyman Wood, the founder of Garden Way, who said, "When you go out in the mail, always have a reason to talk to people." So every *Gazette* contains a special offer or promotional item.

Figure 11.4

This letter, which apologized for a mistake in the catalog, also contained news of the Ziter family, which creates a personal relationship between Sweet Energy and its customers.

Colchester
Vermont, 05446

Dear Mary,

WE GOOFED! As you've probably already noticed, the prices for the apricots,prunes and raisins on our BIG THREE SALE don't reflect the 5%, 10%, and 15% discounts we promised. We went to press without checking them carefully enough. However, you don't have to worry. We've enclosed a credit for the difference. Thanks for ordering anyway and trusting we would catch our error. These are the items found on pages 2 & 3 of our Gazette.

Hope you're having a great summer. It's been unusually warm here in Vermont, but I'm not complaining. In mid-August, Tom and I are off to Turkey to visit the packing plants where our marvelous apricots and figs come from. We're looking forward to seeing the harvesting, drying, and packing process first-hand. We'll take lots of pictures and tell you all about it later.

You'll find a separate tally sheet enclosed with your 1994 Sweet Energy Christmas Dollars attached. Put them in a safe place until our new catalog arrives around the first of October. Remember, the Christmas Dollars are only good for purchases in the 1994 Holiday Gift Catalog. They may not be used for orders from our Gazettes.

Stay healthy and happy,

Carole

P.S. If you're a Health Club Member, don't forget to take your discount on every order. If you're not a member, just fill out the enclosed application form and start saving TODAY!

★ *The "exclusive club" offer*: Sweet Energy offers its customers a chance to become members of the Health Club (Figure 11.6). As a reward for joining the club, members are given special offers "not available to the general public," an automatic 10 percent discount on all products (note the *deluxe* membership offer), and a subscription to the club newsletter packed with "information to help you enjoy good health."

Figure 11.5

The personal relationship between Sweet Energy and its customers continues in the newsletter customers receive several times a year.

Figure 11.6

Sweet Energy keeps customers loyal by offering memberships in Health Club, which provides special discounts, exclusive product offers, and information on health-related topics.

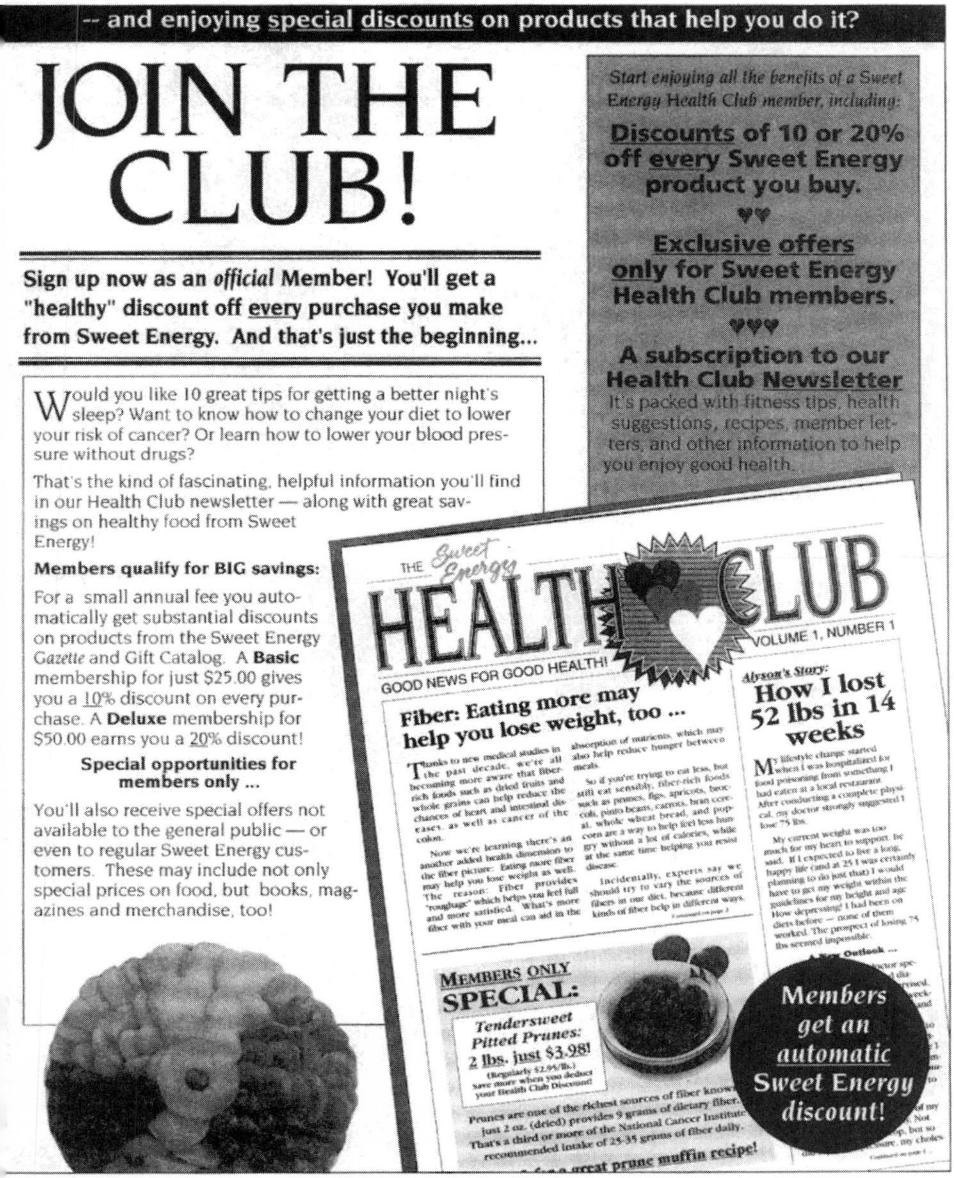

★ *The year-end dividend check*: Every purchase a customer makes from Sweet Energy is entered into their computer system. Every January, customers receive a dividend check, or rebate, based on the dollar amount they spent with Sweet Energy over the previous year. The rebate is applicable toward purchasing more Sweet Energy products. "Not only that," says Ziter, "we keep track of the purchases of any customers you refer to us during the year, and we add their total to your dividend check. We think it's a great incentive for our customers to give us the names of people they think might be apricot lovers."

★ *Happy Birthday, Customers*: Each Sweet Energy order form contains a blank that asks for the customer's birthday (month and day, not year). The birthdays are added to the computer database, and every month a list of birthdays is printed out. Then, just before the customer's birthday, they receive a hand-written card from Sweet Energy, along with a $2 gift certificate. "Customers forget they filled their information on the form," says Ziter, "and we get thank you letters every day from people saying they're amazed and pleased to have received a card from us, and don't know how we knew it was their birthday."

Not too long ago, Ziter got an unexpected payback for her birthday greetings. When she was about to turn 50, her husband wrote a note—which Carole didn't know about—that he had the Sweet Energy employees enclose in all their orders. The note said, "I'd like to have you do me a favor, Carole's 50th birthday is coming up in May. She thinks you're part of her family, and it would mean a lot to get a birthday card from you." Starting in March, about 10,000 of these letters went out.

The weekend before her birthday, Carole and her husband went to New York to celebrate. Before they left, he called Carole's office and asked if any cards had been received. "Oh, yes, we got a few," he was told. When the Ziters returned on Monday, more than 2,000 birthday cards were waiting for them. "I couldn't get over it," says Ziter. "Not only did these people send me cards, but most of these letters were sent out in March. So the people had to mark my birthday on their calendars as a date to remember. That is the power of Direct Marketing, the power of this personal relationship you develop with people. It's so important, and so touching."

Other Loyalty Program Success Stories

★ *Carvel's Birthday Club*. Any child can register his or her birthday at a Carvel store. Shortly before the birthday, Carvel will send a birthday card, with a certificate for a free Carvel cone. This is more than good public relations. It also serves as a reminder to Mom that Carvel makes delicious ice-cream birthday cakes.

★ *Ringling Bros. and Barnum & Bailey Circus pass*: When your child is born, Barnum & Bailey wants to know about it. Send them notification, and they'll send you back a pass good for "ANY PERFORMANCE ANYWHERE ANYTIME," issued personally to your son or daughter by Kenneth Feld, President and Producer of the Greatest Show on Earth (Figure 11.7). The pass is good for a lifetime. As this is an ongoing program, it may seem like the circus would lose money giving away so many free passes. But children don't come alone. With the free pass in hand, mothers, fathers, sisters, brothers, and maybe even doting aunts and uncles will become paying customers. Taking that child to the circus for the very first time becomes a special event for the family who received the pass—and, Barnum & Bailey hopes—a customer who will return for future visits "as long as the joys of childhood shall live within your heart."

★ *American Express customized coupons*: A friend of mine recently purchased a golf club using her American Express card. Her next billing statement included a coupon for a 10 percent discount on golf-related products. It also included a coupon for a local restaurant offering 10 percent off if you pay with American Express. This is part of a program American Express calls The Card for Your Corner of the World. It allows merchants who accept American Express to create customized advertising and marketing campaigns in specific markets. These customized coupons are building cardholders' loyalty to both American Express and to the local merchant.

★ *The Saturn Car Club*: Years ago, Saturn held what some people called a loyalty event. The automaker invited Saturn owners to company headquarters in Spring Hill, Tennessee, for a three-day weekend called the Homecoming. Now Saturn has introduced the

Figure 11.7
This free pass to Ringling Bros. and Barnum & Bailey Circus creates whole families of loyal customers.

Dear Lois Geller,

Congratulations on the birth of your child! As a father, I would like to wish your family a world of special joys, and I wish your baby a happy and healthy childhood. My pledge to you is to keep the magic and wonderment of childhood alive forever in The Greatest Show On Earth!®

May all your days be Circus days,

Lois Geller
1 Maple St.
Anytown, USA

IN HONOR OF ROMEO & JULIETTE,

THE NEWEST MEMBERS OF OUR CIRCUS FAMILY,

LET IT BE KNOWN FAR AND WIDE FOR ALL TIME THAT YOU,

Cody B. Geller

Born on May 10, 1994

shall be the honored guest of The Greatest Show On Earth® for your phenomenal first visit to Ringling Bros. and Barnum & Bailey Circus, at any performance on any day of any year in any city of the United States of America, for as long as the joys of childhood shall live within your heart. Let it be known that as an official Ringling Brother or Ringling Sister, you are entitled to experience all of the magic, mystery and marvel of America's Living National Treasure by virtue of your birth in this Celebration Year!

May All Your Days Be Circus Days!

Kenneth Feld
President and Producer

America's Living National Treasure

Car Club. For a $30 annual fee, members can utilize a trip-routing service and receive travel-oriented discounts, a catalog of special merchandise, and a quarterly newsletter. The company is also encouraging local dealers to run their own loyalty events.

In business, it's the small personalized touches that count. That's why Carole Ziter is so successful. The combination of all the small touches she extends to her customers adds up to a core group of loyal customers who buy from her over and over again—and get their friends to buy from her as well. She started adding these human touches when she was running a very small business straight from her kitchen table, which proves you can create loyal customers no matter what the size of your business.

Here are various suggestions for loyalty programs you can adapt for your own product or service:

★ *Gift certificate programs*: Customers who spend a certain minimum amount of money get a gift certificate at the end of a limited time period. For instance, anyone who buys $500 worth of merchandise during a one-year period will get a $50 gift certificate, good for one year from the date it's issued.

★ *Point programs*: For every so many dollars they spend, you award your customers one point. When customers accumulate a certain number of points, they can then choose their reward from selected merchandise. For instance, you may offer one point for every $5 spent on your products. Then you could offer several choices from which customers can pick—one redeemable for 20 points, another one slightly higher in value redeemable for 30 points, another one even higher in value redeemable for 40 points. It's best to make the reward merchandise different from the merchandise that is normally available form your company. This not only makes the offer more exclusive; it gives the reward a higher perceived value because customers don't know the exact price of the prizes, they only know how may points it takes to get them.

★ *Sticker or punch card programs*: Customers are given special program cards. Every time people buy a product from you, they get a sticker which they then affix to the card (or they get a hole punched in the card). When the card is filled, customers are eligible for their free reward. My local manicurist who offers a free manicure for every ten-hole-punched card uses this type of loyalty program.

★ *Communication programs*: This is where Carole Ziter really excels. Her customers hear from her often, and in a very personal way. Not all communication has to be offer-driven. You can write to give people information, to thank them for buying, to let them know you haven't heard from them for a while, or just to say hello. Of course, if you want to add an offer, that's fine too. I recently received a catalog which included a personalized card that read:

Dear Lois: We notice you have not purchased anything from us since last July. We hate to lose your business, so we're making you a special offer. Buy one pair of earrings from this catalog, and get a second pair for 50 percent off.

I was more than happy to accept their offer. Other forms of communication programs include:

Flyers   Holiday greetings
Newsletters   Thank you notes
Educational materials   Personalized letters
Birthday cards

Partnership Programs

Partnership programs are a way for two or more companies to share in the investment and rewards of Direct Marketing. They're also a way of building loyalty for all the businesses involved.

Almost all airlines that have frequent flyer programs now have partnership programs as well. That means that when you make a purchase from one of their partners, you earn extra miles. Gordon Young of Air Canada says that when customers get involved with partnership programs, it strengthens their ties to your company. For instance, Air Canada is now in partnership with a telephone company. When customers of that phone company make calls, they earn frequent flyer miles. Therefore, when they make their travel plans, they're "married" to Air Canada.

"The benefit to the phone company is that they get a competitive edge in attracting and keeping their customers. The customer benefits by getting whatever discount the phone company offers, plus free miles. Air Canada benefits twice: we get paid by the phone company for the privilege of being our partner, and we get another venue for tying the customer to our airline."

Any type of businesses can form successful partnerships. Stores in a minimall, for instance, might want to get together to entice customers. Each store could send a direct mail letter or flyer to their own mailing list announcing an exciting new offer exclusive to customers of the minimall: "Every time you spend over $25 in any store in the mall, from now until January 1, we'll stamp the enclosed contest card. When you've spent $500, you can enter the card in a drawing for a grand prize of a $5,000 shopping spree in the mall." This is a good way of increasing business for all the stores in the mall.

Loyalty and partnership programs like these do more than build sales. They bring you closer to your customers. They feel like they're getting something extra, that you're doing something special just for them. Then when they're making out their shopping lists, your company's name will be at the top.

Checklist

ARE YOU BUILDING VALUE FOR YOUR COMPANY? DO YOU OFFER

☑ High-quality products

☑ Extraordinary customer service based on:

   √ Timely delivery
   √ Credibility
   √ Accurate billing
   √ Easy returns/refunds
   √ Flexibility
   √ Caring
   √ Ongoing communication

DO YOU KNOW THE LONG-TERM VALUE OF YOUR CUSTOMERS? WILL YOU ENCOURAGE LONG-TERM LOYALTY?

☑ Stay with your loyalty program for the long haul

☑ Keep it fresh and fun

HAVE YOU TRIED THESE LOYALTY PROGRAM OPTIONS

☑ Gift certificate programs

☑ Point programs

☑ Sticker or punch-card programs

☑ Communication programs

  ✓ Flyers
  ✓ Newsletters
  ✓ Educational materials
  ✓ Birthday cards
  ✓ Holiday greetings
  ✓ Thank-you notes
  ✓ Personalized letters

☑ Partnership programs

12
CHAPTER

Direct Marketing for Big Business

The number of Fortune 500 companies that are members of the Direct Marketing Association is increasing dramatically every year. Automobile and oil companies are spending hundred of millions of dollars every year on Direct Marketing, and tens of millions are being spent by computer companies, publishers, appliance manufacturers, and cosmetics conglomerates. If there's any doubt that Direct Marketing works for big business, all you have to do is look at the list of Fortune 500 Companies from Coca-Cola to Seagram's, Hasbro to Harley-Davidson, and Levi Strauss to Sara Lee are all increasing their Direct Marketing budgets—by hundreds of thousands of dollars—every year.

Big-Business Advantages

Although the principles of Direct Marketing remain the same whatever the size of your company, big businesses have several obvious advantages, some of which include:

★ *Existing databases.* Many large companies have an existing database, or customer file, even if it has never been used for Direct Marketing. For instance, when we developed the campaign for Ford of Canada described in Chapter 2, it was the first time they had

231

ever used Direct Marketing. However, they had an existing data-base called the NAVIS (North American Vehicle Identification System) file, which contained the records of everyone who had bought Ford cars in North America for the past several years. So we were able to launch a campaign with a fairly large universe of names already established.

★ *Enhanced databases.* Larger companies have the ability to append or enhance their in-house databases so that they can both seg-ment their own lists and target prospective customers who are highly likely to buy their product or service. Some companies with huge generic databases are finding it is more profitable to segment their customers and target them with specific offers. For instance, Lillian Vernon had a huge database of people who had bought low-priced items from her relatively inexpensive catalog. That doesn't mean her customers were all low-income—high-income people also buy items from an inexpensive catalog. So Lillian Vernon segmented her list into people who had purchased the highest priced items she offered, and created a catalog that would appeal to this more upscale part of her audience. She also segmented her list by pulling out names of customers who had purchased items for children over the years, and created a catalog called "Lillian's Kids" which offers only products for young children.

The days of the big, general catalogs that offered everything to everyone are over. It's simply not efficient to pay for the printing. It's much more profitable to segment the market and send a cata-log that appeals to a particular market niche. Sears and Montgom-ery Ward, both formerly known for their "telephone book" approach—they sent their giant wishbooks to just about every-one—have phased out the big books for smaller, tightly targeted niche market catalogs.

The business-to-business division of the Dell Computer Corpo-ration recently overhauled its entire database because it didn't con-tain enough information to allow for segmentation (and because it contained a lot of unusable names). So the corporation conducted a comprehensive telemarketing campaign to clean up the names and address and add more than 150 fields of information to the database. In the process, Dell got rid of more than 50 percent of its existing list. It cost well over $1 million to accomplish this cleanup; however, the response rate of its remaining customers doubled and the company realized approximately $4 million in annual savings on printing and postage by reducing wasted mailings.

Once a large company knows more about its customers, it can begin predictive modeling or regression analysis: using the information provided by enhancing the database to predict the buying habits of particular segments of its lists, and their likelihood of responding to a particular promotion. The company can then not only offer these segments specific products from its existing inventory, it can design new products especially for these segments.

★ *Testing*. A small company is usually hindered by its inability to test in large enough numbers to provide statistical accuracy. For many years, the minimum test sample has been 5,000 names. However, test sizes are steadily increasing. Several companies, including the Body Shop and Lillian Vernon, do not think a 5,000 name minimum provides statistically sound results, and have increased their test lists to between 10,000 and 20,000 names. When a Fortune 500 company is spending $50 million on Direct Marketing, it's well within their budget to spend $50,000 on a particular test. Therefore, they can test more variables and are more likely to get a higher response rate when they roll out their campaign.

Big businesses can afford to test many different types of things. They can test the offer structure, test the creative, and test price points. They can run A-B splits in a variety of publications. They have the ability to test many factors of a Direct Marketing program quickly, determine what works best, and roll out with their most effective campaign. A smaller business with a limited budget may only be able to run one test per season.

The ability to test a variety of factors and roll out to the winners in a short period of time does more than create new business for a large company, it also gives them a head start over the competition. When I was working at Meredith, we published a Quick and Easy cookbook series. Unfortunately, our timing was not very good— Time-Life had published a similar series six months earlier. They had the ability to test their offers and get their product out much faster than we did. We were both going after the same market. Time-Life was able to get there first, and we were not able to catch up to their success.

★ *Partnership.* One of the fastest growing areas of Direct Marketing is promotion partners, as we discussed in Chapter 11. Car manufacturers, banks, airlines, and telephone companies are joining up in all kinds of combinations to get customers in the habit of using their products and services. Many nonprofit organizations have partnered with long-distance services and credit cards, for instance, so that when a customer uses that phone service or credit card, the nonprofit organization receives a portion of the dollars spent. One example is a company called Working Assets, which offers both a credit card and a long-distance service. When Working Assets' customers use either the phone service or credit card, the company contributes a percentage of the money spent to several worthy causes.

Partnerships between large companies are proliferating because they are obvious win-win situations. When a department store such as Marshalls forms a partnership with American Express, customers are dealing with two easily recognizable entities. Both companies benefit from sharing customers. It may be more difficult for Mom and Pop's corner store to form a partnership with such a large corporation because the benefits are not equal (although programs such as American Express Card for Your Corner of the World may be changing that philosophy).

★ *The Power of Two.* Some large retailers have been reluctant to move into Direct Marketing because they view the two selling methods as competition for each other. Instead, they are finding that retailing and Direct Marketing enhance each other. For example: Not long ago, I received a catalog from Pottery Barn. I glanced through the catalog, saw a few items I liked, but didn't order anything. A few weeks later, I happened to walk by a Pottery Barn retail store. I remembered the items I had seen in the catalog. I now had a second chance to make that purchase—which I did. On my way out of the store, an employee asked, "Would you like a catalog?" and handed me one to take home. I now had a third chance to look over Pottery Barn's merchandise and perhaps buy something else.

The power of two also works for manufacturers who sell via both retail and Direct Marketing. Some manufacturers are reluctant to use Direct Marketing because they're afraid to alienate retailers who sell their products. They forget that a successful Direct Marketing effort may produce a 2 percent response rate. But the other 98 percent of the people who received the mailing have gotten a targeted message, and have that impression in their minds when they go out shopping in the mall. The Direct Marketing effort doubly enhances the likelihood of a customer buying that product.

Those companies that use catalog and retail sales to complement each other are having great success in both areas. Saks Fifth Avenue, which mails more than 35 million catalogs a year, reports that database comparison tracking credit card numbers shows that three-quarters of its catalog customers are also active in-store buyers.

The U.S. division of The Body Shop developed a database of retail customers and plans to use it to grow its mail order business. That's because the company's 450,000 mail order buyers spend an average of $32 per order, as opposed to the $15 average order of the in-store buyer. However, the company always includes a local store listing in each catalog because in-store sales increase every time a catalog is mailed. And Talbots, the Massachusetts-based apparel retailer and cataloger, uses its catalog customer database to locate clusters of Talbots shoppers and then opens retail operations in those areas.

★ *Inventory control.* We developed a jazz program for Polygram Classics, and since this was a new offer, we weren't sure how many CDs we would sell. Because a large company like Polygram controls its own manufacturing, we were able to manufacture these CDs on an as-needed basis. A smaller company, using an outside manufacturer, must purchase a minimum number and then hope they sell. Another advantage large companies have is the ability to create special promotions and offer deep discounts to get rid of excess inventory. When I ran book clubs, I used to have a once-a-year special sale of my "leftovers" which were offered at very low prices.

The large inventory of other books we offered allowed us to take a much smaller margin on these leftovers. A small company doesn't always have the ability to do this.

The Challenges Big Businesses Face

Big business doesn't have all the advantages, however. No matter how much data it gathers, a multibillion-dollar corporation can't establish the kind of intimate rapport a small business can maintain with its customers. They try, often by introducing warm, friendly, amusing spokespeople like Frank Purdue or Dave Thomas of Wendy's. But Purdue chickens or Wendy's fast food can never make one-on-one connections like the ones made by newsletters from Dr. Teitelbaum's chiropractic office, or from Carole Ziter of Sweet Energy.

Although customers want the products and services of large companies, they still want that small-business connection. You can only establish that connection with a real person. Not every customer of Sweet Energy knows Carole Ziter personally—but they feel like they do.

A spokesperson can sometimes help a large company establish rapport with its customers. People who identify with Jamie Lee Curtis are more likely to sign up for Verizon Wireless telephone service. Fans of Michael Jordan might consider buying Hanes underwear because he is featured in the commercials. Large companies that have no individual with whom consumers can identify can never generate that immediate connection.

But the main challenge big business faces is that Direct Marketing is a long-term process and needs a long-term commitment by upper management personnel. Direct Marketing doesn't always produce results overnight. It usually has a cumulative effect. Without a long-term commitment, campaigns can be stopped before they've had time to take hold.

In large companies, top management often suffers from frequent turnover. Whenever new people come in they want to make their mark and often start by dismantling all current programs and starting over from scratch. One administration may make a commitment to Direct Marketing, pay for the development of a database, and gather vital information. When they leave for greener pastures, the new administration comes in, doesn't understand the Direct Marketing process, and stops the program before it can get off the ground.

I experienced this firsthand several years ago when I was working on a corporate level with a major retail store chain to develop a Direct Marketing campaign. We established a large database, which we had just started to segment. We were building a loyalty program and even considering issuing a store credit card. Then came a change in management. The chairman of the board and several other key players left the company. A new advertising director, who didn't understand the purpose and impact of Direct Marketing, was brought in. She decided to eliminate the Direct Marketing campaign altogether, and devote more time and money to television and print advertising. What she didn't realize was that the Direct Marketing effort would have cemented the store's relationship with its customers, and hurt the competition (which had not yet begun Direct Marketing).

A few years later, that advertising director left for another position elsewhere. The company, seeing the success of other retailers who had been steadily increasing their Direct Marketing efforts, wanted to try again—and they're now playing catch-up to get back to where they were before.

Another challenge for big business is that many large companies are divided into several divisions. Each division allocates its own advertising dollars. In many cases, department heads or product managers in charge of allocating these dollars handle one product for three or four years, then move on to another position or even another company. They don't stay with one product long enough to make major commitments to its growth, and they don't have the overall vision of the company in mind.

Often, these product managers are given a yearly budget. It's very difficult to carve a Direct Marketing program out of this yearly budget, because of the expense of setting up the database. They are then forced to act like a small company—setting up the database in year one, testing one factor in year two, rolling out on the results in year three. By that time, this product manager is on the ladder to success and is already on his or her way to another job. It's up to the corporation to make the long-term commitment and allocate funds to set up a corporate-wide database, and then advise each department on the best way for them to develop their own long-term Direct Marketing programs.

Companies often find themselves further divided because there are only a certain number of budget dollars to be spent—and they are spread unevenly over advertising, Direct Marketing, promotion, and public relations. One department's budget goes up only if someone else's goes down. Each department, of course, thinks that their job is the most important and they often fight with each other to the detriment of the product and the company.

Finding Solutions

The challenges big businesses face in Direct Marketing can be met and won. Here are some suggested solutions:

★ *Hire visionaries.* Implementing change and new directions for a company takes people with vision and a strong sense of security. Embarking on a Direct Marketing campaign can be risky, as can any new business venture. The results of Direct Marketing, unlike other forms of advertising, are clearly accountable, and clearly visible to anyone watching. If an ordinary image ad (one that is not direct response) is placed in a magazine, no one knows exactly how many people buy your product as a result. However, if a direct response ad is placed in a magazine, the number of people responding can be immediately counted and recorded. This makes the campaign, and the executive who implemented it, vulnerable as well as visible. So it takes someone who believes strongly in the power of Direct Marketing and has the foresight to carry it through.

★ *Take advantage of your database.* The benefits of a large business owning its own database outweigh the risks of developing a Direct Marketing campaign. If all the retail stores in a particular area close down, or if a recession hits the retail industry, a company with a strong database provides itself with an alternate distribution method it can use to scientifically determine who will continue to buy from them. It allows the company to be more dependent on its own resources, and less driven by the ups and downs of the general marketplace.

TIP   Another advantage a large company has is its ability to make list exchanges. If you find a company whose list is appropriate for your product, they might be willing to exchange a number of their names for an equal number of yours.

★ *Start small.* Big businesses often feel everything they do must be done on a large scale. When Time Warner launched its Sound Exchange catalog, they hired a large staff, brought in outside products, and started out with a huge mass mailing. When, after the first year, the catalog didn't do as well as Time Warner executives had hoped (which often happens in Direct Marketing), their disappointing results were highly visible. Not only was all of Time Warner's organization eyeing them; the rest of the entertainment industry was too. Several companies who had been considering similar campaigns then said, "If they can't do it, how can we?"

There's no reason you must start a campaign with a catalog offering every item in your inventory. You don't have to start with a mailing going to vast numbers of people. Your first program should be a learning experience in which you make all your mistakes. Once you test a small quantity, you can then roll out on a much larger scale.

★ *Develop long-term planning.* Even in companies where there is a commitment to Direct Marketing, there is often a "play-it-by-ear" philosophy. A committee will devise a test and then wait to see what the results are before setting up another meeting to ask, "Where do we go from here?" A marketing plan needs to be set up outlining various contingencies over a number of years, with a commitment for a length of time.

★ *Publicize your results.* When a successful Direct Marketing campaign has been implemented, be sure that the entire organization knows about it. Write up the results in the corporate newsletter or magazine. There may be a product manager in another division who wasn't aware of the campaign and may want to contribute to it. When the results are good, more people in the company become your allies and you may get the support you need to expand your Direct Marketing budget. Alert the news media as well. You don't need to worry about tipping off the competition—you never give away your trade secrets. You're disclosing the results more than the actual tactics. You do want people to know that you're out there, however. The more support you get behind your efforts, the more consumers will be looking for, and responding to, your direct mail packages and ads.

★ *Use professionals.* Many times, a large corporation will bring in an agency like mine for consulting purposes. Then they announce they're going to handle the Direct Marketing program in-house. Too many times that means it's going to become Jane Doe's secondary responsibility, after she oversees the four other programs she's already working on. "She's never done Direct Marketing before, but we're sure she can handle setting up the database," they say. "No need to spend the extra money for outside services."

That's just the story I heard recently while helping a major corporation put together a campaign. They told me, "We offered a product through the mail a few months ago. Go see Bobbie in the back room. She handled inputting the database from that mailing." When I went to see Bobbie in the back room, I discovered that she had hired three temporary employees to input the names from the database. Not only that, the company spent almost $18,000 on the temporary help due to the amount of overtime they put in on the project. The company would have spent a lot less than $18,000 for a computer service bureau to handle the data entry, after which the database would have been formatted correctly and available for future campaigns.

Large companies are often tempted to use their in-house designers, MISs (Managers of Information Systems), and mailrooms to do their own Direct Marketing. These people usually have no experience with it. They may be very good at what they do, but that doesn't mean they're going to know the ins and outs of Direct Marketing. There are too many details, too many things that can go wrong. In the long run, it's much cheaper to go to an outside lettershop, which is fully automated for every step of the mailing process (folding, inserting, labeling, personalization, stamping, sealing).

Companies must take the long-term value of their customers into consideration when deciding how much they will spend on a campaign. It's foolhardy to save a nickel or a dime up front, when your customers are worth thousands to you over the long haul.

Direct Marketing presents major opportunities for large companies. Companies that made the decision early on to test and refine their Direct Marketing programs are reaping the rewards. Corporations such as

Columbia House and BMG, for instance, really benefitted from being among the first to establish themselves in the music-entertainment mail order niche. Companies that are not currently using Direct Marketing are missing out on the opportunity to build strong, long-lasting relationships with their customers.

Big-Business Success Stories

★ A "virtual" bookseller, Amazon takes on "bricks and mortar" icon, Barnes & Noble with its direct Internet sales business. With collaborative filtering, personalization, extreme focus on ease of use, this dotcom is going from Earth's biggest bookstore to Earth's biggest everything store. Amazon.com's main site offers millions of books, CDs, DVDS, and videos (which still account for most of its sales), not to mention toys, tools, electronics, health and beauty products, prescription drugs, and services such as film processing . . . who can imagine what will come next!

★ *IBM goes direct. Again and again.* In 1979, IBM first launched IBM Direct to distribute computer supply equipment via catalogs. By 1984, it was a $1 billion business. However, its success was undermined by a war between the Direct Marketing organization and IBM dealers and the division was closed. In 1992, IBM began a revised $500 million business-to-business Direct Marketing operation to create a cost-efficient international distribution channel for its software, main-frames, and midrange computer equipment. In 1994, sales were 200 percent over the company's original goals, and IBM Direct has now become one of the most successful divisions of Big Blue. By 1995 the company faced a major sales challenge in that they were primarily using reps, but their competitors weren't. The market was changing and customers were demanding more commodity-type pricing and a lower level of service. In response, IBM developed "Gold Service" which began with a handful of customers and eventually was expanded to more than 300 corporate accounts. Each Gold Service corporate customer gets access to a special IBM website developed just for their organization. The result? Average revenues for accounts enrolled in Gold Service increased more than 30 percent per year.

★ *GEICO drives into direct response television.* GEICO Corp., the automobile insurance company, which relies almost totally on Direct Marketing to sell policies, began a direct response television campaign in 1994 that continues to this day with great success. The results were so immediate—10,000 new customers a week, according to the commercial's producer—that Geico had to cut back on its initial media buying schedule so that its operators could handle the calls.

★ Rodale grows into a publishing giant. In 1942, J.I. Rodale started *Organic Farming and Gardening* magazine, which taught people how to grow better food by cultivating a healthier soil using natural techniques. J.I. put his theories into practice on a 60-acre farm near Emmaus, Pennsylvania and truly set down roots which grew. Today, Rodale helps readers keep their gardens vibrant and their bodies vital. In addition to *OG* (formerly *Organic Gardening*) which is the most widely read gardening publication in the world, Rodale's portfolio of magazines includes *Men's Health*, *Prevention*, and *Runner's World*. The company's book unit publishes some 100 new titles a year and has a catalog of more than 500 books on subjects such as cooking, health, and nature. This family-owned company, known for decades of stability and commitment, has built a strong publishing business through Direct Marketing.

Checklist

BIG-BUSINESS ADVANTAGES

☑ Existing databases

☑ Enhanced databases

☑ Testing large numbers and more variables

☑ Forming partnerships

☑ The Power of Two

☑ Inventory control

THE CHALLENGES FOR BIG BUSINESS

- ☑ Establishing rapport with customers
- ☑ Getting long-term commitments from high-level management
- ☑ Dealing with separate divisions, department heads, and product managers
- ☑ Divided allocations of advertising budgets

SOLUTIONS FOR BIG BUSINESS

- ☑ Hire visionaries
- ☑ Take advantage of your database
- ☑ Start small
- ☑ Develop long-term planning
- ☑ Publicize your results
- ☑ Use professionals

13
CHAPTER

Direct Marketing for Small to Midsize Businesses

One Case Study: Smart Research = Small-Business Success

When Geoff and Lynn Wolf's first child was born in 1985, Geoff wanted to buy his newborn daughter a special gift. He rode into town (Durango, Colorado) and quickly realized there was no children's store there. He went home without a gift, but with an idea. He wanted to open a store and managed to do it in 1986. It was called, A Unicorn's Garden, located in downtown Durango, it sold children's clothing, gifts, and toys.

Six years later, the store was going strong and Geoff left his position in the restaurant industry to concentrate on ways to expand the business. One of the options he came up with was to create a mail order catalog.

"When we looked into children's catalogs, we quickly realized that there were already a lot of players out there," Geoff says. "Even though our store's concept was unique, we didn't feel another children's catalog would make it."

Two factors then combined to point the Wolfs in another direction. In studying their existing business, they realized that many of the products that sold well in their store had to do with horses and riding. At the same time, Lynn, who had ridden horses as a young girl, took up riding again, and the Wolfs came up with the idea of producing an equestrian catalog, with an emphasis on horse-related products for children.

Before they began planning the catalog, however, Geoff embarked on an in-depth study of the market. "I looked at all the equestrian catalogs that were out there, and the various markets they were addressing," he says. "Then I did a demographic study on horse owners—who they were, how many there were. I spent quite a few months researching both the equestrian market and the catalog industry. I spent time in the library and called all the horse associations to get their information. I contacted the Direct Marketing Association and studied the Direct Marketing industry. Using that information, we painted a picture of a customer and market niche that didn't have a lot of other players in it."

When it came time to design the actual catalog, the Wolfs began to research again. They read extensively and talked to people in the industry about what makes a catalog work. They pored over hundreds of catalogs, then took elements of design and copy they thought most effective, and put them together to create their new catalog called, Back in the Saddle. They then hired a local graphic artist and photographer to turn their ideas into reality.

The original plan was to test 5,000 to 10,000 catalogs for their initial mailing. "Just as we were about to mail it, another equestrian catalog went Chapter 11 and their list became available," says Geoff. "So we purchased their entire list, even though that meant a significant increase in our costs. But we decided that we had to take advantage of the opportunity." The first mailing grew to 50,000 catalogs.

The first catalog, which was 24 pages long, was a resounding success. The second catalog was not. "We made lots of mistakes in the beginning," says Wolf. "One of them was that we should have brought in an industry consultant earlier than we did. That spring we scheduled our second catalog to be dropped in homes on April 15—tax day. We should have known better, but we never made the connection. People don't want to spend any more money on the day they've just paid their taxes. That catalog was a bomb."

The company was acquired in 1998 by Potpuorri Holding Inc., and it became part of a twelve-title group mailing 50 million books a year. By 2001, Back in the Saddle was mailing 5 million catalogs annually. Much of the merchandise, like the Angel Horse Necklace in Figure 13.1, was created exclusively for Back in the Saddle.

Figure 13.1

Merchandise in the Back in the Saddle catalog includes items made exclusively for them, such as the Angel Horse Necklace.

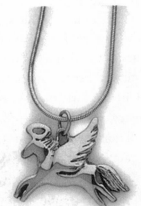

Angel Horse

Honor the spirit of a once-loved, always-cherished horse with this sentimental pin and pendant, carved in wax, then cast in sterling silver, with the halo and wings of an angel. By Silver Pony Designs.

#715256 Angel Horse Pin $22
1" long

#757836 Angel Horse Pendant $30
1" long on a 17" snake chain

The Wolfs' advice for anyone going into Direct Marketing is simple. "Spend extra time up front learning who your customers are going to be and how you want to reach them. Once you start, track your customers carefully. Don't try to save money on your database software, because need to have that information. Ask your local Direct Marketing association where you can get information on the databases available for various levels of business. Many software companies will send you a sample disk of their database programs. I got five samples, played with them all, called their references, and chose one that worked for me. One thing I learned when I was studying Direct Marketing is that you live and die by the information you gather. Even if you're only doing 10 to 20 orders a day, it's really important to get that information."

Wolf attributes the success and growth of Back in the Saddle to the fact that "we were very clear from the start as to what we wanted to do. We identified a market before we started, and we had a very clear vision of who we thought would buy from us. So we were able to put the right piece in the right people's hands at the right time."

The Top Ten List: Ten Secrets to Small-Business Success

One of the reasons that I am so passionate about Direct Marketing is that it is an equal-opportunity marketing tool. Any size business, from a one-person at-home operation to a multibillion-dollar corporation, can benefit from some form of Direct Marketing. The previous chapter showed that big business has both advantages and challenges, and the same goes for small businesses.

There are some insider secrets that can point small business toward Direct Marketing success. Here are ten of them:

★ *Capitalize on the fact that you're small.* Throughout this book, we've talked about humanizing Direct Marketing. This is difficult for big business to achieve, but relatively easy for small businesses. Make your customers feel as if they're dealing with a local merchant, even if you're thousands of miles away. Tell your customers you're a small business. Paint a clear, vivid, memorable portrait of the characteristics that make you and your company unique. Tell them why yours is the perfect company for them to patronize, and how you've earned the right to sell your particular product or provide your special service.

Take a hint from the jewelers' concept of romancing the stone. They take a rough, mundane-looking stone and cut, shape, and polish it until it becomes a thing of beauty—and of great appeal to potential buyers. No matter how mundane your product or service may seem, find a way to romance it so that it becomes a commodity your customers cannot do without. Make it easy for your customers to share your passion for what you're doing.

★ *Test small and think big.* By testing small and spending the minimum budget, you can start building the business step by step. That way you're not as vulnerable as if you blow your entire budget on one campaign. Thinking big means thinking long term. Put together a Direct Marketing plan that starts with a mailing of 5,000, for instance, and a small space ad. If that works, plan to roll out to a mailing of 10,000 to 15,000, and a few more space ads. Have contingency plans if the first mailing doesn't pan out.

Your marketing plan should set you on a path you can follow as your business grows. Plan on adding a certain number of new lists every time you roll out. Be flexible in your goals and plans. When Geoff Wolf had the opportunity to buy a 50,000-name list, he had to adjust his original plan to do a much bigger mailing. But since he had developed a marketing plan up front, with an eye toward company growth, he was able to raise the additional money he needed and take advantage of an unexpected windfall.

★ *Develop ongoing relationships with your customers.* Picture this: It's your first date with someone you like. You've had a good time, but when the evening is over, you simply say "Good night" and drive away. Would you think to yourself, "Since we just went out, I'd better wait six months before I try for another date?" Of course not. You'd want to cement the relationship by saying, "I had a wonderful time. Would you like to go out again?" A small business must do the same. However, small-business owners sometimes think, "Ms. Smith just bought a book last week. I'll contact her again in six months and see if she's ready for another purchase." You have to ask your customer for a second date as soon as the first one is over. That's when he or she is most disposed to continue the relationship and order something else. Always have something new to offer. Make plans for expanding the services you provide, or the number of products in your line.

★ *Emphasize your guarantee.* Customers sometimes prefer to buy from larger companies because they recognize and trust a familiar brand name. They may be reluctant to buy from a small company, especially if they've never heard of it before. Your guarantee gives customers some assurance that they will receive the merchandise in good condition, and that they have some recourse if they're dissatisfied with their purchase.

★ *Keep your database in good order from the start.* Large companies pay thousands of dollars to update and enhance their databases, often because their original customer lists did not contain enough information. You should be able to pull out information on your customers' purchases and transactions (what they bought from you, when they bought from you, and the number of times they bought from you), as well as whatever psychographic and demographic information you can gather.

This is a lesson Geoff Wolf learned when he started his catalog business. It made him reevaluate the marketing techniques he had been using for his retail store. He realized he could also use Direct Marketing techniques to increase sales there. "The first thing we did is develop a better customer base," he says. "Once we got into direct mail, we trained our salespeople to get that information directly from our customers." The Wolfs then started using direct mail in several different ways: direct mail letters, loyalty programs, and specialized newsletters. One area of their store that was doing well, besides equestrian items, was trains. They started an Engineer's Club for children who collect toy trains, and began mailing train newsletters which included special offers. The results were immediately visible—every time they sent a train mailing, sales would rise.

Their advertising budget changed from 15 percent direct mail to 70 percent. One suggestion Wolf has for small businesses is to use a postcard mailing as a way to clean up your mailing list. Figure 13.2 shows a postcard he used to announce a summer sale at A Unicorn's Garden. "For less than a quarter you can mail a first-class piece and get undeliverable mail return to you. It costs less than mailing a first-class letter, and you get to eliminate names that no longer belong on your list. I think every retail business should do this at least once a year."

★ *Give your marketing efforts a chance to work.* Not every campaign or newsletter is going to produce immediate results. Small businesses sometimes don't realize that in Direct Marketing you may not make money for a while. This is a hard pill for small companies to swallow, but a necessary one. Everyone's heard the million-dollar overnight-success stories, but these are the exception to the rule.

TIP   In Direct Marketing, it's often the case that you lose money in the beginning. Don't look at it as losing money, however; look at it as gaining an education. You're a detective, searching for your marketplace. You have to follow every lead, even if it doesn't pan out in the end. If you stick to it, you'll get your reward.

Figure 13.2
The owners of a Unicorn's Garden retail store use postcard mailings to announce special sales and as a way to clean up their mailing list.

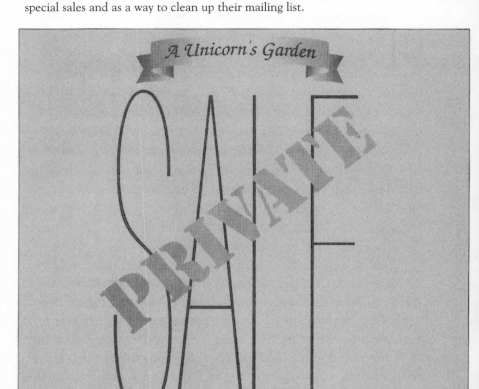

Even big business doesn't always strike it rich right away. When I worked at the Meredith Corporation, we wanted to market a *Better Homes and Gardens* cookbook. For three seasons we tried various marketing approaches, and none of them worked. The fourth time out, we finally found the right audience and the right offer. But the formula took many permutations before we got it right. And when we did, it became a very successful and profitable system.

Figure 13.2 (continued)

Dear friends of A Unicorn's Garden,

I know it sounds incredible, but the new fall clothing will be arriving in a few weeks! I am offering our valued customers **35% OFF** select summer items from Gramicci, Jeannie Mac, Guess and Mousefeathers!

Now is the time to pick up extra shorts and T-shirts at a great savings. We also have climbing pants, sun dresses, and swimsuits. Stop by soon because you know how things fly out the door!

A Unicorn's Garden
120 W. 8th St.
Durango, CO 81301
(970) 247-3947

WHAT'S NEW
at the **Garden?**

Check out the incredible "Air Pogo!" For travel we now have "Magnetic Triazzle." If you haven't stopped by in a while, there are lots of new play-things for summer fun, travel and birthdays. Join our Birthday Club for a free gift and ice cream!!!

P.S. *Bring this card in for 20% off all shoes and sandals.* Offer expires July 30, 1995. Open 7 days a week.

★ *Use a small budget wisely.* The most obvious disadvantage a small business has when it comes to Direct Marketing is a small budget. Careful evaluation of your resources is necessary when beginning a Direct Marketing campaign. Sometimes it may be better to hold off on marketing plans until there is more money available. If you only have enough to do one test and it is not successful, where will you go from there? It might be better to wait, or to look for investors who may be able to give you some marketing capital.

Explore all your options. If you're a manufacturer, it may be possible to test your product in someone else's catalog, or as a package stuffer. For instance, if you manufacture a crafts item, you might approach a publisher of crafts books to include your piece in their fulfillment package. You would pay them a certain amount of money per thousand to get into the package, and it can give you an opportunity to test your product inexpensively in someone else's mailing.

Usually the least expensive way to start is by testing a direct response ad, perhaps in the classified section of an appropriate publication. This may be a good way to introduce your product. If you are offering a service, you'll probably use the two-step approach where the first step is an offer of information related to your product or industry (e.g., "The Decorator's Guide to Winning Window Treatments"), and the second step is converting that inquiry into a sale.

If you have the budget, however, direct mail is usually the best way to spend your marketing dollars, since it's the most targeted media, and produces the best response rates.

★ *Make your offer as interesting as possible.* Let's face it. It takes a great effort to get people to change their buying habits. Many small-business owners say, "I can't afford to discount or give my products away." If you don't want to give your product away, offer an outside product as a premium when customers purchase your product at full price. But be sure you include some kind of offer, something that will make it hard for prospects to resist. (See Chapter 3 about offers.)

★ *Build relationships with your suppliers.* One of the most important things you can do when you're starting out in Direct Marketing is to build relationships with your suppliers, just as you build relationships with your customers. Do your homework. Locate several printers in your area, designers, copywriters, list brokers, lettershops—whomever you may need for your particular marketing efforts. Take advantage of your small business status. If you shop around, you may be able to find a supplier who is willing to give a beginner a break. Sometimes a list broker can arrange a discounted price the first time you test a list. You'd be surprised at how many suppliers are willing to help you get off the ground. They may ask for a large deposit, or even all the payment up front if your credit has not been established; however, they're also usually willing to share their expertise and experience with someone just starting out.

★ *Ask for professional advice.* If you're going to place an ad in several publications, ask the advertising managers if they think it will be effective, and if there's anything you can do to make it stand out in their newspaper or magazine. If you're putting together a catalog, find people who are already successful in noncompetitive areas and ask them for advice. Most people are flattered to be asked, and enjoy sharing what they know. When you're designing an order form, take it to the people who will be doing the order entry, whether it's in-house or an outside vendor. Ask them if you've included all the necessary information, and if the design makes it easy for them to input the data. And always check with the post office before you do any mailings to make sure you have the necessary permit (for bulk mail), and that everything you've designed conforms with their regulations.

Keep Your Vision in Mind

Now here's some advice that's seemingly contradictory to what's just been said. That is: ask for professional advice, but keep your own vision in mind. Don't let anyone sell you a bill of goods because they know "everything there is to know about the Direct Marketing business." There are no hard and fast rules in this business. Something that has not worked for ninety-nine people may be a super-success for the hundredth.

One way to avoid problems is to pay to have a full artist's comprehensive layout (also called a comp) made up for your ad, catalog, or brochure. This is a close mock-up of what your finished catalog, ad, or brochure will actually look like. Sometimes an artist or an agency will tell you, "This rough drawing is basically what it's going to look like. It will give the general idea." But if you're not very experienced, a general idea may not be good enough. The artist may have a very different vision of what you want, and once all the photography and typesetting has been done it's very difficult to change. But comps can always be revised. If you want changes made, discuss them with your designers and confirm the changes in writing so there is no misunderstanding.

Direct Marketing reflects your vision and your personality. No one knows better than you how to sell your product. You know it better than any Direct Marketing agency or any creative person. Take advice that enhances your vision. More often than not, if you follow your gut instinct about your own product, it will turn out to be a winner.

Checklist

TEN SECRETS TO SMALL-BUSINESS SUCCESS

- ☑ Capitalize on the fact that you're small
- ☑ Test small and think big
- ☑ Develop ongoing relationships with your customers
- ☑ Emphasize your guarantee
- ☑ Keep your database in good order from the start
- ☑ Give your marketing efforts a chance to work
- ☑ Use a small budget wisely
- ☑ Make your offer as interesting as possible
- ☑ Build relationships with your suppliers
- ☑ Ask for professional advice

14
CHAPTER

Relationship Building in the 21st Century

The Internet and Beyond

I intended this chapter to be about Internet and email marketing but once I got into writing it, I remembered that Direct Marketing isn't about using just one medium. It's about getting and keeping customers. Electronic, interactive communications can help you do that but only if you use them as tactical tools and not as strategic building blocks. So let's start with the notion of what we can do to keep customers and then move on to how we can do that online.

Building Relationships One at a Time

When I worked at Meredith Corporation years ago, the strategy for selling cookbooks and gardening and craft books for *Better Homes and Gardens* was to mass mail the "women of middle America." We had no idea who these women really were, so we wasted a lot of company time, money, and energy with this shotgun approach.

As technology evolved we fine-tuned our database and began to target customers by their interests. We identified segments of women who bought cookbooks, or gardening books or craft books, or all kinds of books. We stopped the shotgun selling to middle America, and began "rifle" selling to individuals. It's a lot easier to cater to your customers when you see them as individuals, when you can almost imagine their faces. It's a lot easier to care about them too. And, almost by accident, we began developing relationships with each of these wonderful individual customers.

Customer relationships … individual customer relationships … are the real future of Direct Marketing. If you ask 100 industry insiders about the future, probably 95 of them will tell you about the incredibly advanced technology just over the horizon. Although the technology is indeed dazzling, fundamental "low-tech" (even no-tech) programs need to be in place before high-tech can do you any good: service, loyalty and aftermarket sales.

These aren't new concepts—we've discussed them in earlier chapters—but they are taking on new meaning as technology pushes Direct Marketing along at a rapid clip.

Back to the Future: Servicing and Caring For Customers

In my neighborhood in New York, there is a Chinese restaurant I have never visited, but I'm one of their best customers. When they mailed menus to everyone in the area, I placed an order on the phone. The food wasn't great but it was good enough that I called them again a week later. When I gave my address, the lady on the phone recognized it immediately, called me by name and asked if I wanted General Tso's Chicken again. There are many other Chinese restaurants in my neighborhood, some probably better than this one, but none of them treat me as an individual. Because of the excellent customer service, I nearly always call the restaurant that knows me.

As consumers, the number of choices we have is staggering. Lots of vendors offer the same products and as product quality improves, there tends to be fewer differences among them. Just about everything from coffee to computers to German cars is becoming a commodity. So, it's probably not going to be product superiority that determines which companies survive and thrive, but rather how well they meet individual customers' needs. Good marketers try to meet customers' needs; great marketers do that, too, but they also try to anticipate prospects' needs.

Simple example. A few years ago, one of the home shopping channels introduced a terrific idea. The host invited the audience to fax him questions and he answered them on-air as they were received. This is the ultimate in customer service—answering individual customer concerns *before* they purchase your product.

One of the biggest concerns is convenience. More than ever we buy from one vendor instead of another because of convenience. A product doesn't have to be the best or least expensive if we can order it easily and get it quickly. People are very busy, these days, men and women, but especially women and women still make most of the purchasing decisions. Not too long ago, social scientists thought we would be less busy than we are now. In fact, they theorized that new technologies would create more leisure time. But that hasn't happened yet. Life is easier in a lot of ways, but certainly not simpler. It seems the more time-saving devices we have, the more time we need. So we go for the quick and easy whenever we can. And the Internet helps us do that. Sometimes.

We access vendors, compare prices, and research products online. This so-called "time-saving" approach . . . isn't always. In my case, getting on the Internet is like opening an encyclopedia. After I find what I want, I keep looking at all the other interesting things that pop up. I have spent hundreds of hours wandering the Internet. There are a lot of people like me.

We thought email would save us a lot of time and effort. It turns out we still get the same number of phone calls each day . . . fax use is actually up about 15 percent . . . and now we get hundreds of emails to sort through! Email has actually added more work and you see people checking their "in boxes" on their laptops in restaurants, at special computers at the airport and in their "tech-ready" hotel rooms. Sometimes technology adds stress, but it isn't going to go away.

For a while, it looked like technology might trump common sense. Our agency met a lot of potential clients who thought that more and better technology is the answer to their customer service challenges, or that it will help them cut their acquisition costs. Some companies still think this way. Maybe they're right but it hasn't happened yet. In the meantime, essential concepts of direct marketing still drive businesses no matter which tools you use to implement them. Customer service is customer service if you do it in person, on the phone, in the mail, or online.

Good service means everything to consumers. Companies that help our lives run smoothly will be the ones we'll depend on for the long term. Good service is a mindset more than a handset and when technology catches up to that simple concept, then we'll really have something great.

Loyalty Programs: The "Mom and Pop" of the 21st Century

As Direct Marketing grows, we are going to have to develop more and better loyalty programs. Why? Because if we don't make it worth their while, there's almost no reason for customers to remain loyal. They don't know us. They don't care whether we're located nearby (in fact, with toll-free numbers and URLs, most people have no idea where we are). And customers know that if we don't have exactly what they want, chances are they'll find it somewhere else, easily.

Effective loyalty programs create bonds between company and customers. One of the best and simplest definitions I've ever read came from the chief protagonist in Nelson DeMille's 1985 novel *Word of Honor*. He said "The essence of loyalty is reciprocity." He meant give and take. You scratch my back, I'll scratch yours. As the sense of loyalty grows with more and more give and take, customers realize that you will scratch their backs and the bonds become difficult to break. Loyalty programs create a customer base with a vested interest in your success. They want to continue doing business with you, so they can reap the reward they've been promised, whether it is free miles, discounts on merchandise, free shipping, surprise and delight features or an information-packed newsletter.

Businesses can take advantage of high-technology to maintain personal relationships. For starters, technology helps us learn (and remember) more about customers. They will respond to recognition from a large company but most of them would rather have a relationship with a person at a company rather than with the company itself. (We all know the company's soul-less.)

Businesses will need to use creativity and high-tech resources to develop "personality"—kind of like the Mom and Pop stores did years ago. Examples from general advertising include spokespeople like Frank Perdue, Tom Carvel, Aunt Jemima, Orville Redenbacher, Ronald McDonald. Home shopping channels depend on recognizable hosts with strong personalities to form relationships with their viewers. Direct marketers are going to have to find similar ways for people to equate their product or brand with a real person or character. It's more difficult to abandon a relationship with a real person than with a large corporation; just think about the anxiety when you consider changing dentists, or going to a new hairdresser.

Aftermarket Selling

The concept of aftermarket selling has been around for many years, yet many marketers still don't take advantage of its potential. Aftermarket selling means offering customers continuing service and new products after their initial purchase. A bounce-back offer is a simple example. (That's the little buck slip that comes with the product you order.) Think of a good restaurant. When you finish your meal, the waiter will ask, "Can I get you anything else? Coffee? Dessert? Cognac?" That "can I get you anything else?" is the heart of aftermarket selling, and it's a question too many companies fail to ask.

Aftermarket selling is continuous selling. It doesn't pay to put together a database unless you're going to continually sell to the same customer. It means constantly planning, "What's the next thing I can sell to these customers?" Usually your customers want to hear from you and are disappointed when they don't. A few years ago, I responded to an offer on a box of teabags. For three proofs-of-purchase and $3.95, I could get a brightly decorated tea tin. I bought two more boxes, sent in my money, and the tin arrived. Then I never heard from them again. They already had my name and address, knew I'd tried their product and had taken the trouble to respond to an offer. Wouldn't it have made sense to send me more offers, coupons, announcements of new products? But they didn't do that. They didn't take advantage of a perfect opportunity to create an ongoing relationship. So I ended up switching to another brand. Remember, the essence of loyalty is reciprocity and that's our future.

Most experts agree. In their ground-breaking article "The End of Mass Marketing," authors Don Peppers and Martha Rogers (*Marketing Tools*, March/April 1995) wrote that one-to-one marketing is the wave of the future. And they explained that, ". . . the primary marketing task in the one-to-one future is not finding customers for your products, but finding products for your customers."

Computerized databases make it possible to know a great deal about customers. We can use that knowledge to tailor products and services to individual customer needs.

For those of you who are bottom-line driven (as we all have to be), this isn't a cost; it's an investment. It is much more cost-efficient to keep a customer than to acquire a new one. When we continue to sell

> TIP   Individualized service is the key to the future of direct marketing. It's what keeps customers coming back for more. Companies can no longer afford to sell us a product and then abandon us. There are too many opportunities to go elsewhere to get what we want.

to customers (defined as people who have demonstrated they will buy something directly from us), we increase their lifetime value.

The Internet

At the beginning of the twentieth century, the most common form of Direct Marketing was the catalog, which was a boon to people who lived out on the farm or the edge of the frontier. It took months for them to get a catalog in the mail, and months to get their merchandise, but they did it gladly because catalogs gave them access to things they couldn't make. Gradually, direct marketers added print ads, solo mailers, co-ops, TV commercials, take-ones, mini-catalogs, etc., etc., then, along came the Internet.

New computer and wireless technologies, innovations in cable and broadband, smarter websites will all continue to propel change faster than a speeding bullet. These technologies are already bringing us closer to the real goal of Direct Marketing: relationships with each individual consumer and immediate cost-effective responses.

It is estimated that the interconnected network (that is the Internet) which started in 1969 with four computers, will connect more than 200 million people by 2003.

The Internet was developed as a research and communications tool. Over time, as we realized the potential for commercial applications, Direct Marketers started testing the Internet as a medium to communicate with customers and prospects. Adapting basic Direct Marketing techniques to the new communication channel made sense. Then, in an incredible (and totally insane) frenzy, direct marketers got pushed out of the way as literally everybody jumped on the so-called "Information Highway." The phrase "dot com" got burned into our brains, and then we watched in astonishment as it imploded and almost all of the dot coms went broke and disappeared.

That first seismic wave of dot coms (defined as Internet companies) failed because most of them ignored the basic tenet of Direct Marketing: plan a profitable business model. Direct Marketers *always* plan how they are going to make a profit. Another reason they failed is that they focused their businesses on a medium rather than products, services and customers. It's as crazy as if you started a business solely to exploit the power of radio. (What you do, of course, is identify your target audience and then find the right media mix to communicate with them. The early dotcom-ers did it backwards.)

Some companies survived. Traditional brick and mortar companies (retail stores), and established catalogers (like Lillian Vernon and Lands' End) did pretty well. But they were just moving established businesses to another channel. Genuinely innovative dot com companies like Amazon and Ebay survived and thrived by developing truly revolutionary ways of servicing and selling to customers.

By the late 1990s, enthusiasm for all things Internet waned, although people still use it, still rely on it for shopping, information, communication and entertainment. According to the DMA, U.S. Direct Marketing Web-driven sales will increase dramatically over the next few years. The Internet isn't going away.

The Internet makes the world smaller. We are all closer because of our access to each other and to mountains of information. For example, medical research and information used to seem almost top secret. Now, you can practically diagnose and treat yourself with a little online research. When my cat got sick, I researched his ailment online and found out about treatment options before I got to the veterinarian's office.

As a result of information accessibility and the ability to communicate with other Internet users, there are huge markets for really esoteric things! I collect figurines that were "made in Occupied Japan." I used to have to rely on chance to find any of them and if I ever wanted to sell, I knew the dealers were charging twice what they had paid me for them. Now on the Internet, it's easy to buy and sell, and there are no longer "secrets" about their worth.

As anyone who has ever typed www.google.com can tell you, the Web is a phenomenal tool for finding whatever it is you happen to need. It empowers consumers to do research and compare products and prices, often side-by-side. And because consumers have so many choices right off the bat, competition is at a ferocious new level.

In addition, consumers communicate their opinions about companies, brands, products in a variety of forums. There are websites, such as **eComplaints.com**—which offer consumers a "chance to fight back" and "be heard" by the company at fault and, more important, by your fellow consumer. There are sites that offer users the opportunity to review products, like **Epinions.com** or **Amazon.com**. There are online forums, where users can rant and rave about anything. There's an astonishing variety of tightly focused rant (or rave) sites, for example, **BeautyBuzz.com** is all about cosmetics.

Marketers are adjusting their perspectives and strategies to serve the newly empowered online consumers. The buyer's in charge of the process now. Where once they waited for offers to come to them, now they go out and find them themselves. And, if we're smart, they'll find us.

The Internet is a terrific channel to reach consumers (actually to lead them to us), give them tons of information and options, test offers constantly, and provide absolutely excellent and up-to-date customer service. It lets us talk to them regularly and it's a two-way conversation. They can tell us how we're doing, (some companies don't listen, believe it or not) and, once they get to know us online, they'll tell us more about themselves. All this information is entered into a database automatically with the customer doing the keystrokes. Best of all, perhaps, the Internet is a great opportunity to create and reinforce brands.

Website Basics: The Virtual Storefront

B2B or B2C, it's usually a real live person doing the looking around and making the decision to buy. So, when it comes to developing a website, the key issue doesn't change: create an intuitive, "user-friendly" interface.

PhotographyTips.com is an example of a well-organized, useful site that's doing a great job. According to the home page (Figure 14.1):

PhotographyTips.com is for everyone with an interest in photography. It is intended to help beginners get started in photography, and become so good at it in that they turn into advanced amateurs. But, accomplished photographers will also find useful tips and hints here. Our primary objective is to help people like you to take better photographs.

Figure 14.1

PhotographyTips.com

The Photographer's Online Information Place

PhotographyTips.com is for everyone with an interest in photography. It is intended to help beginners get started in photography, and become so good at it that they turn into advanced amateurs. But, accomplished photographers will also find useful tips and hints here. Our primary objective is to help people like you to take better photographs.[About this site]

EXPLORING OUR SITE:

- *A good starting point* where you can discover many tips about good composition, learn the basics of light and pick up several useful techniques to improve your photography is our Technique section.
- *Or, you might want* to take the bull by the horns, and go straight to our Subjects category, where you can find tips on just about everything you might wish to photograph, from babies to wild animals.
- *Here you'll come across* our handy Posing guides and practical tips on Choosing a wedding photographer.
- *If your interests* lean more towards the tools photographers use and how they work, then check out our Equipment section. Find out how to buy a used camera or the basics of digital photography.
- *Looking for fun?* Try our Humor in photography pages or our What in

The site is exceptionally easy-to-navigate. According to Dan McCormick, the Founder of PhotographyTips.com, "People love a tremendous amount of well explained detail. I get letters from all kinds of people telling me it sounds like their father talking to them about photography! I really wanted it to be very friendly and thorough. It seems people really like the organization, because they can find whatever they are looking for quickly and in many ways."

McCormick opted for no outside advertising. He generates revenue by promoting his own products and selling listings in the Products & Services Business Directory. "At the outset I thought that advertising would provide more of the revenue for the site, but people seemed to find it annoying. I looked at the emails I was receiving and many people were requesting the posing guides I was offering free online, in another format. They wanted something that was easier to work with . . . and though the online version was free, they had to download it. So I created the CD version and it's doing extremely well."

McCormick is developing other products now. He wants to grow his business "organically"—meaning that he wants to create something of value that people tell him they want.

When customers, or prospects, go online they want information and they want easy access to it. And when they're ready to buy, they want the process to be as simple and seamless as possible. When they have questions, they want answers, fairly quickly. Sometimes customers want to be part of a community of people with shared interests. And, to top it all off, sometimes they want to be entertained.

Keep it Simple

Being user-friendly is key. Users will leave if a site isn't easy to navigate; if it takes "forever" to download; if they can't find what they want; if the type is too small or all reverse (dark background with white type), or if there is a distracting background graphic. People will leave a site if they find any element troublesome or confusing. They just hit the back button and they're gone, often leaving a full "shopping cart" sitting at the virtual checkout counter. And they'll probably never come back. This can trickle over to the non-virtual world, too. If the site is part of a retail or catalog operation, a single bad experience can tarnish the relationship between the customer and the company or brand. And while some companies are "not getting it" others are definitely doing all the right things.

eBags.com does a great job. They're a truly customer-focused online-only merchant and they've begun reaping the rewards. Since launching in March 1999, they've sold 1.4 million bags and have become the world's leading online provider of bags and accessories for all lifestyles. Here are some reasons people love the site (Figure 14.2):

- Even with 150 brands and more than 4,000 items, it's easy to find whatever you need. You can shop by product category, subcategory or brand or enter a key word in the search engine.

Figure 14.2
eBags.com

Internet Pioneer, Regina Brady, Offers These Tips for Creating a Great Home Page

According to Brady, a world-class expert in interactive media, when someone lands on your URL, you've got about 22 seconds to keep that person's attention. So, here are some tips you should consider for your home page to get people to stay...and respond to what you are offering:

- A three-column format seems to be most effective.
- When people arrive at your home page, their eyes generally go to the upper right hand corner. This turns out to be the best place to collect email addresses. In fact, a recent client moved their email collection area here and almost doubled the number of sign-ups!
- Including a guarantee, your return policy, 800 number and some testimonials on the home page establishes credibility.
- Your home page will include navigation tools which serve as a clear path into and around the site. Navigation should be intuitive and consistent. Most people expect to see subject categories on the left-hand side of the screen.
- Use self-banners, Web-only specials, and exclusive offers.
- Include a viral component "Refer this site to a friend!"
- Change your home page regularly, through new offers, "newsy" features— (but don't change your look, your colors, or your navigation).
- Help people relate to your site by highlighting "bestseller lists," "customer favorites," "Frequently Asked Questions," and pictures of people using your product or benefiting from your service.

- On the home page, they show you how many units the company has shipped and how many people are actually online shopping while you are. This really adds an element of credibility.

- The ability to comparison shop is a great benefit because users can select several items and have all the information about them displayed in one easy-to-read chart.

- With each item, under a "May we suggest" heading, the user is also presented with an array of other items which compliment the one chosen (an interesting approach to aftermarket selling).

- They even have an interactive "Design Your Own Bag" feature.

Online Branding

Branding is about having a unique personality. It is who you are as a company, what you're like, your very reason for being from the customer's point of view! Most important, a brand is a promise of exactly what your company will do that provides "distinctive" customer satisfaction.

If you already have a clearly articulated offline brand, it's critical that you continue it online. Your site should have the same "look," "tone," and "feel" as your other marketing materials. That doesn't mean the brand people (or general advertising people) determine what you do. It just means that if you're Coca Cola you don't suddenly start acting like Budweiser. Branding isn't just a visual representation of your company, like a logo or a "look" you pull from a style manual. You need to have a clearly defined idea of "who you are" before you begin to communicate.

Your personality should act as a magnet to your target audience. As a direct marketer, it is to your benefit to determine your identity as a company, then figure out how you can translate that identity into qualities that ingratiate you with your customers—just as you would in a one-to-one selling process. (If you're selling surfboards, it's okay to wear cut-offs and sandals; if you're selling Rolls Royces, I recommend a Savile Row suit.)

It all goes back to the fact that customers buy from people they like and trust. Even when they're buying from a catalog or a direct mail piece, they like to feel as if they're dealing with a person, not a company. You have to give your company human qualities.

Stonyfield Yogurt does a great job of bringing their brand online. **Stoneyfield.com** (Figure 14.3) has a strong personality that's consistent with their offline image and they've found a way to combine humor with their core mission.

The site is easy to navigate and has the kind of information that interests people who eat organic yogurt. This includes chats with a pediatrician, women's health specialist, online forum, information about the environment, games for kids, newsletters called "moos-letters," recipes and a gift shop!

By creating a compelling website experience that communicates "who they really are" and offering relevant content, Stonyfield Yogurt has been able to solidify its relationships with their customers.

Figure 14.3

Stonyfield.com is a unique site because it creates an interactive environment for its customers.

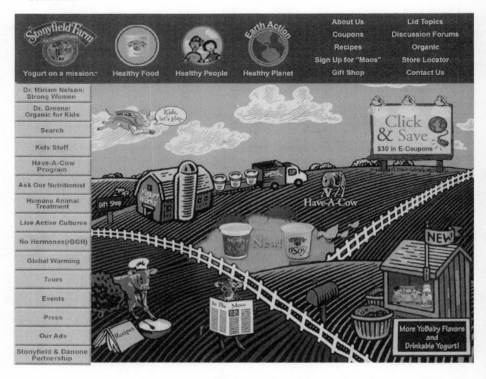

> TIP   Realistically, not every company has the resources to be like Amazon.com and develop a site that learns user preferences with collaborative filtering and rule-based software. But developing a unique and dynamic brand doesn't cost any more money than developing a mediocre one!

Interactivity

Interactivity is about letting customers choose their own online experiences and decide for themselves what they will look at (content). Opt-in newsletters are an example of users choosing content. Chats with experts and forums, like Stonyfield Farm offers, are examples of allowing users to choose how they'll get more involved with your site and your company. Additionally, Stonyfield Farm uses their website as a research vehicle, polling their strong opt-in email lists and posting live interactive polls and surveys. The site also offers consumers ways to find and request products through the use of an online Product Locator and Product Request Form. Using an innovative E-couponing program, Stonyfield Farm is able to get coupons into the hands of unlikely consumers and, with high redemption rates, drive product trial.

We're just discovering interactivity's potential. Faster connections and developing technologies like multimedia will make it possible. Many sites offer "home tours" complete with music. There's a site called, **sumerset.com**, that lets you watch your houseboat being built step-by-step. Websites that offer games and "e-cards" add another interactive dimension. **Evite.com** lets users invite people to parties!

On **LandsEnd.com**, you can create a virtual model that looks like you so you can try on different outfits and combinations. The site also will suggest certain outfits to flatter and fit a particular body type.

Even B2B (business-to-business) companies use interactive tools to show what they can do for current and potential customers.

ThomasRegister.com, the largest industrial database on the Web, through its e-business offering, Order Online, lets buyers and designers find the exact product they need and either buy it online immediately or send a "Request For Quote" directly to the supplier. Through Thomas Register's **CADRegister.com**, users can download detailed technical drawings of industrial parts directly into their plans, so they don't need to redraw them, which is a laborious process.

Developing a Great Site…Over Time

For most companies, the process of getting a website in order is, well, a learning process. My agency has had a website presence for a long time, and, in hindsight, I'm pretty embarrassed by some of our early attempts. Here are a few of our website incarnations:

Back in 1995 our site was a single page (Figure 14.4). I was pretty excited about it, though. We learned to add information that would benefit our visitors. We compiled a "Resource Center"—printers, list brokers, fulfillment houses, compilers, etc. We added text from my monthly Target Marketing columns, and slides from my speeches. Of course we included samples of our work so that people who were look-

Figure 14.4

www.interport.net/~gellerco. This was my own "first attempt" at a website.

Welcome To The Lois K. Geller Co. Page.

We've been expecting you.

As you may know, we are a full service direct marketing advertising agency in New York. We do everything. And anything. If it's direct marketing, we do it and do it well.

Over the years our people have created winning programs for corporations like IBM, 3M, Ford, Crayola, the Canadian Government, Marshalls, PolyGram, RCA Victor, American Express, Bell South, Bell Atlantic and dozens of smaller companies like Grace Labs. in Connecticut, and Heritage Resources in Ireland.

We're not normal. Most agencies charge you a lot of money up front just to talk to you. We do it a little differently.

First we listen to you and ask questions and we don't charge you anything for that. Then we come back with an outline of what we think will work best for you. We tell you what it will cost and why it will work. And we don't charge you anything for that, either.

Then, if we agree, well, that's when you pay us to write an exhaustively detailed direct marketing plan for you. That will take three weeks or so. Then we present the plan to you and you decide if we're going ahead.

We can do a lot for you. We can:

- find you new customers, revive lapsed accounts, charm your existing good customers into becoming better customers
- build relationships between your company and your customers that will pay off handsomely for you over the years...
- create loyalty programs that will bond your customers to your company so firmly that your competition won't have a chance to steal them away.

You have nothing to lose by calling us. Oh, we'll take up a few hours of your time and we might pester you with questions. But then you don't have to do another thing until you see the outline of your new program. And there's no commitment beyond that.

Why not call us now? You can reach us on the Internet at gellerco@interport.net or write to us at 333 East 46th Street,

ing for an agency could see what we've done. We added information about new services, like Direct Marketing Boot Camp, where we go right to companies and teach their people about Direct Marketing. We offer visitors the opportunity to register and then we include them in our on and off line mailings. We have interactive contests and visitors can send Direct Marketing questions to our resident curmudgeon "Dr. Direct" and he'll answer them. **Masongeller.com** (Figure 14.5) is still a "work in progress" and will continue to be as we try to find a balance between promoting our services and providing visitors the information they find useful. By adding features, we have increased the time spent on our site to an average of fifteen minutes, which is pretty good.

Figure 14.5
Masongeller.com

mason&geller
DIRECT MARKETING

A full service direct marketing agency, offering services from planning through implementation.

About us   Articles   Jobs   Contact Us

Articles
About Us
Jobs
Affiliations
Boot Camp
Subscribe to our newsletter

Tip of the Day! In a direct mail package, the most important component is the letter. To make it interesting, start out with a story or an attention-getter. Maybe even begin with some bold face type to grab the reader's interest.

We are a full service, strategic direct marketing agency.

Our strength is developing strategic marketing plans and executing them with creativity and innovation. Most importantly, we focus on response rates, profitability and results. Regardless of media used.

We want to be your partner in developing breakthrough DM programs, engaging creative and response that exceeds your plan.

What makes us unique…

We are one of the few agencies completely devoted to direct marketing. Also, unlike many agencies, we offer our clients the ongoing hands-on leadership of our principals. We take ownership throughout all phases of a program to provide enhanced value and solid solutions for our clients.

Click here for more information about Mason & Geller M&G's President, Lois Geller's latest book- Now available.

Customers for Keeps

8 Powerful Strategies to Turn Customers into Friends and Keep Them Forever

"This is an important book for every company struggling with an increasingly cynical and indifferent consumer."
Dom Rossi, Vice President and Executive Publisher, Reader's Digest

As consumers become more discerning and value-conscious than ever, the success of every business depends on its ability to find and keep customers. To survive and thrive, companies need to make themselves absolutely exceptional in the eyes of their customers.

In Customers for Keeps Lois shows through hundreds of stories and examples

If You Would Like to Lift Response, Read Lois Geller's Book

Response

Lois K. Geller

Response!

The Complete Guide to Profitable Direct Marketing

Inside Stuff

Inside information from some of direct marketing's most renowned experts - Case studies of successful direct marketing campaigns -And Dr. Direct!

Subscribe Now!

DIRECT MARKETING

Lois Geller, our President is featured on Fortune's website, as the Direct Marketing Diva. Click here to see the latest article.

Dr. Direct
is our favorite in-house curmudgeon and direct marketing expert. He answers questions we get from Lois' students at NYU, from newsletter subscribers and from anyone else who asks.

Ask a Question

Resource Center
A rich information center for anyone involved in direct marketing.

If you are searching for a supplier to the DM industry such as Printers, List Brokers, etc., check out our Resource Center. We have hundreds of companies listed, across the US and Canada.

If you would like to have your company listed, email us your company info or use the registration sign up in the Resource Center.

Enter the Center

The Survey Says...
We are finalizing a white paper on retail loyalty online and

Caring for Customers Online

Unlike a regular store, if you are doing business online, you can't charm people with your smile, your warm "thank you!," your dazzling ambience.

The basic truth in any business—including e-commerce—is that it's repeat business from loyal customers that builds your bottom line. And it is much more profitable to keep customers than it is to replace them.

About 20 percent of your regular customers will generate 80 percent of your e-business. So, it really pays to keep current customers happy. If the best use of the Internet is to develop relationships with our customers and prospects, the first step is to take care of their needs and address their issues. There can be no dialogue or communication or relationship if they are experiencing problems and we don't help them!

Online customer service, known as "live help," seems to be the best solution. For example, on Lands' End's site, they offer Lands' End Live™ which lets visitors "chat" in real-time with Customer Service Representatives who can send them pages of products they might like. It's expensive and not all business models can support it. Whether or not you decide to offer online customer service, there are several options you should consider:

- FAQ: Frequently Asked Questions
- A search feature: A natural language searchable information base
- Email response: Accept customer service and sales questions by email and respond in a timely manner
- Acknowledging customer orders via email
- "My account" function with order tracking and options for changing settings
- Providing an 800 number on your site, and handling sales and customer service inquiries by phone
- Letting customers give you their phone numbers, then calling them back in real-time
- Community building: provide a forum for your customers to communicate with each other (and answer each other's questions)

Customer expectations drive customer service innovations. Too many people are frustrated with the online buying process. They want someone to answer their questions *when they ask them.* They want reassurance.

As evidenced by the huge number of abandoned shopping carts, consumers are experiencing obstacles to what should be a seamless process. Recently I spent 20 minutes trying to input a gift certificate number…and no matter what I did, it just wouldn't work! There was no "live help" and I was put on hold forever when I dialed the so-called customer service number.

The catalogers who pioneered customer service offline are leading the way online. Lands' End and LL Bean were among the first to offer live customer help and are among the best at satisfying customer service expectations. **eBags** is one of the few Internet only companies at the forefront of meeting customer needs with:

- Low price promise and guarantee on home page.
- Toll-free number, prominently displayed on each page.
- Carry-on regulations for each airline and links to eBags products that meet those requirements.
- An estimated arrival date button on every product page so you don't have to wait until you order to find out that a bag can be mailed to you now, or is backordered, and will be mailed at a later date.

Creating Traffic

There are a lot of steps involved in building a profitable e-business. You need a strategically designed website, a quality product or service, irresistible benefit copy, and a flawless buying process. But you can have all that and still have no customers. So, you also need to build traffic to your site. Here are some of the ways to do that:

★ Search engines

Most Internet shoppers find what they're interested by entering keywords in the major search engines and directories. If you're not high on the list of search results, they won't find you. It costs money to get placed in the first few entries of YAHOO! or Google, and it's usually worth it.

★ Direct Mail

Direct mail pieces can drive people to your website, if you give them a compelling reason to go there. This OfficeMax mailing (Fig-

Figure 14.6
OfficeMax mailing

ure 14.6) offers $25 off your first purchase when you go to their website, which is pretty compelling. Your mailing piece doesn't have to be expensive. A simple postcard can drive people to your site for a contest, free information, a special offer or even a free sample.

★ Promote

Promote your website on your business cards, your stationery, even your invoices and envelopes. Put it in your ads, your flyers, your sales letters. Get your URL into press releases, holiday cards, everything, you can think of, including your packaging.

★ **Spread the word through links**

You can exchange banner ads or links with other websites that have a similar target audience. So, if your company sells charm bracelets for teenage girls, reciprocal links with a site that sells clothes to this population could increase sales for both sites. If you pay for links, or banners, try to negotiate a pay-for-performance deal so you won't waste money. That means you give a percentage of each sale that comes in through a link.

★ **Content**

You can drive traffic to your website once, but if you want them to stay there for a while, and if you want them to come back, you must show them something they want to see. That takes fresh, interesting content. If it's interesting, new, involving, charming, compelling, they'll come back again and again. But it's tough to come up with great content day after day. So you need help. Two great sources are partners and your customers. Encourage these two groups to provide you with relevant information; things like tips, personal stories and testimonials.

★ **Partnership Opportunities**

At the end of this Chapter, I highlight some examples from eBags about how they partner with a wide variety of companies and don't pay anything until someone makes a purchase. Just remember that whatever you offer in terms of a discount can be a value-add to another company. Your content linked to their site and vice versa keeps both sites fresh and interesting.

★ **Viral promotions**

A "viral promotion" is when you get your customers to "spread the word" about your site, your product or your offer. Their involvement in your site is fresh content and it helps drive traffic. If you can provide something that people want to "pass on" to their friends, they will. Jupiter Research shows that nearly 70 percent of all respondents are willing to pass along information. The average forwarding rate of an interesting email is 4–7 percent. They'll be more likely to forward your email or a page from your site if you put a graphic next to the words, "Please forward to a colleague/friend." Just a picture of an arrow or an envelope that looks like it's moving will do the trick.

Stonyfield Farm harnessed the power of word of mouth (viral marketing) through its "Adopt-a-Cow" program in the early 1990s, which created a bond between yogurt buyers and the cows on its farm and gave consumers something worth telling friends and relatives about. The program was so successful that some people had to share adoptee cows!

Privacy and Security

Trust is a huge issue in online marketing. According to a Harris Interactive Online Poll, consumers' top three "major concerns" are:

1. That companies will sell, trade or provide their personal information to other companies without permission (75 percent);
2. That transactions may not be secure (70 percent); and
3. That hackers could steal their personal data (69 percent) which sounds like #2, doesn't it?

Consumers don't trust companies to handle their personal information properly, but most say independent verification of company policies would make them feel better. Sixty-two percent of consumers say that independent verification of company policies is the single action that would satisfy them and make them feel more comfortable. In fact, 84% say verification should be a requirement. A privacy policy is great, but independent proof that you're sticking to the policy is even better.

Companies who ignore privacy issues will suffer. 83 percent of consumers who responded say they would stop doing business with a company entirely if they heard or read that the company misused customer information.*

---

*"Privacy On and Off the Internet: What Consumers Want" conducted from November 5 to 11, 2001 by Harris Interactive for Privacy & American Business, a nonprofit public policy think-tank. Ernst & Young LLP and the American Institute of Certified Public Accountants (AICPA) sponsored the research, which was conducted online. 1,529 adults aged 18 or over participated. The margin of error was ± 3 percentage points.

Email Marketing

Email can be a very cost-effective, high-response-rate vehicle. You can use it to acquire and retain consumers, sell and promote products, drive loyalty, offer exceptional customer service, and reinforce branding efforts. And email campaign costs $30 to $90 per thousand. Compare that to direct mail costs of $500 to $700 per thousand or even more. Responses to a direct mail campaign start trickling in after a week and you won't get them all in for about 6 weeks. Email responses start almost instantly and you get them all in a few days.

According to a 2002 Study by GartnerG2, commercial email is on the rise and direct mail is on the decline. Email advertising revenue is projected to reach $1.26 billion in 2002. That's up from $948 million in 2001. By 2005, revenue is forecast to total $1.5 billion. Gartner projects that direct mail, will account for less than 50 percent of mail received by households by 2005, down from 65 percent in 2001. According to Denise Garcia, Research Director for GartnerG2, "As email use and trust increases, consumers will become more comfortable accepting advertisements through their computer."

There are many companies that disagree. They believe that email responses will level off, and then decline and then traditional direct mail will be back in favor. With the volume of opt-in commercial email accelerating, marketers are going to have to come up with clever campaigns to get great results.

- email click-through rates show a wide variance of effectiveness based on best practices.
- email is becoming a strategic issue in upper management. Issues of permission and privacy are making it imperative that senior level personnel become more involved.
- email marketing is a double-edged sword: it can be a tremendous boost to branding efforts, or it can be disastrous. For example, large companies with a lot of departments are discovering that they have to coordinate email management so that the divisions don't interact with customers independently . . . and drive them crazy with over-stuffed inboxes.
- Companies are working to leverage all available channels to capture email addresses and they're becoming more conscious about maintaining message and tone consistency across all media.

Email deployment is much more cost-efficient than snail mail. However, that's true only when email is targeted to the right audience, at the right time, with a solid offer. Otherwise it's a waste of time and money and you risk annoying your customers. Here are some of the guidelines for developing email campaigns.

★ Customize and give 'em what they really want

Some companies really understand their database, really know their customers, and carefully target offers. Other companies just throw it out there and hope some of it sticks. If I register at a music site and all I ever buy is jazz music, please don't email me about The Dixie Chicks' latest music!

Ask recipients whether they prefer HTML or text. HTML messages deliver higher click-through rates (on average, rates twice as high as plain text messages) but not all email services support HTML (AOL in particular). Formatting will probably get more complex with growth in handheld computers and email-enabled cell phones. Technology lets us recognize these preferences, and deliver content in the right format.

★ Be a prig about permission and privacy

Successful email is based essentially on trust. Permission and privacy are the keys to that trust and without them you don't have a viable email program. There are no shortcuts to permission, and no gray areas in issues of privacy.

"Opt in" is better than "opt out." That means getting customers to say "Yes, I'm in" rather than just "No, I don't want in." It's active vs. passive consent. Also, remember to remind your opt-in recipients of your relationship and always give them the opportunity to opt out. Perception of privacy disappears when you include all the names and email addresses of everyone who gets the email. I've received email messages where I had to scroll past hundreds of other addresses to get the message. I'm sure the sender meant to blind carbon copy these addresses, but instead they put them in the "To:" field. And, though it's tempting to increase revenue by letting other emailers use your list, just say "NO" to the new revenue stream. Don't sell your customers' data. Email isn't like direct mail. For some reason the privacy issue is much more sensitive online.

★ Writing for electronic media

Email's a tricky medium. It's much easier to get rid of than printed mail. You just hit delete and it's gone. The computer screen isn't paper. It's more like TV and the delete button is like the remote control. If they don't like what they see, they zap it. Ideally, your email copy should fit on the screen so people can read it without scrolling. If you have more to say, provide a link to a website with all the info. You can't oversell in email. It just doesn't work. What does work is friendly, honest copy that connects on an emotional level. That means "all business" copy is out; casual, personal, and down-to-earth is in.

But there is one similarity between direct mail and email that's very important. Highlight benefits! People want an immediate answer to their first question "What's in it for me?" So, instead of going on and on about your product, tell them in a straight-forward way, exactly what it's going to do for them. For example:

Dear John,

XYZ corporation is pleased to announce the formation of a new and easy-to-use service to facilitate bill paying.

This email is clearly about "me." The prospect doesn't care about XYZ Corporation.

OR

Dear John,

Wouldn't it be great if there was a way to effortlessly keep track of all your bills...and then pay them with a few clicks?

This copy talks about the immediate benefit for the prospect.

The most important parts of an email are the "Subject" and "From" lines. You want people to open your email, but it isn't worth it to trick them. They'll get mad and they won't respond. The best subject lines are interesting and with almost no hype. The effect of words like Save, FREE!, etc., in an email subject line is exactly the opposite of their effect in regular direct mail.

I don't know why but something bizarre happened when the world went online: We forgot what we learned in third and fourth grade about punctuation, spelling and grammar. Your business writing style reflects your company and there is nothing endearing about typos and poor grammar. If you're not a good proofreader, hire one. There are plenty of freelancers out there. Email your copy to them and you'll have the corrections within a few hours. It is well worth the cost. If you're really on a tight budget, ask a few friends to check your copy.

Be sure to make your offer easy to understand, easy for the reader to access information, easy to contact you. Make it easy to use your order form and purchase your product. The best test? Do all these things yourself and ask other people to test the process for you.

★ Track and Test

Tracking results in email is just as important as it is in snail mail. You can track click-throughs (which don't mean all that much but they can be marginally useful), conversion rates, cost per order, etc. Mostly you want to know how much money you spent and how much you got back. There's all kinds of other useful information you can track, but when you start, focus on the important stuff.

★ Personalize

Personalizing the body of your email message can lift response rates, and it's pretty straightforward:
- Consider using a customer's name in communications.
- Use the sender's real name in the email and in the "From" line, and put the sender's contact information at the end of the message
- Make sure to include all contact information (including phone numbers) at the end of the email message.

★ Leverage your Email Opportunities

There are lots of good reasons to be communicating by email. In addition to promoting products it's also important to develop non-commerce communications with customers to solidify your relationship. When a customer registers at your site or buys a product, that should always be acknowledged with a "thank you." Other

types of customer communications include new product announce-
ments, upgrades, sales, news that impacts customers, follow-ups
on inquiries and orders.

An online newsletter is a great tool for relationship-building. If
you can deliver interesting information, information of value, your
newsletter can drive traffic to your site and make it much more
likely that your other emails will get read.

Surveys are an excellent way to gain understanding of your customers so that you can better meet their needs. Surveys allow companies to access the power of email as a two-way channel of
communication—using the "dialogue" to drive improvements to
both business and services.

Ten Tips for Writing Email

Here is a list of 10 tips to get the most from your email efforts:

1. Define your objectives.
   The very first step is deciding what, exactly, you want to accomplish. Your objective will determine who you send to and what
   you offer. Remember that trust is key in this medium and your
   primary objective is always to build a relationship.

2. Develop an offer that supports your objectives.
   An offer is a "call to action." You need to give people a compelling reason to click and buy now … before they go off to the
   next email in their in-box.

3. Write a "subject" line and a "from" line.
   The first step in getting response to your email is getting it
   opened. The subject line and from line are what recipients see
   first—and they want to know, "what are you writing to me about"
   and "who are you?"

4. Write concisely.
   Get to the point. Online, people have little tolerance for long-
   windedness, so "write tight." Use links so that recipients can
   access additional information.

(continues next page)

5. Be well-organized.
   Break the copy into blocks. Use headings so that readers can skim and understand your message.

6. Make sure your communication is error-free.
   No grammar or spelling mistakes. Also, check that your links work!

7. Use a conversational tone.
   Just pretend that one of your customers was sitting next to you and write, as you would speak, using natural language. People respond to real people, not faceless organizations.

8. Focus on benefits, not attributes.
   When we read any solicitation or announcement, there is only really one question that we want answered, "What do I get out of this?"

9. Personalize and customize content.
   Develop online promotions with relevant and targeted content.

10. Make it very easy for the recipient to opt out or unsubscribe.
    Take the high road with issues of privacy.

Keep 'Em Coming Back

Getting visitors to your website is a challenge and should be a primary objective. But it's just the beginning. Ideally, once they visit, they should: a) get so much of value from your website that they can't wait to come back and b) come back because you'll invite them back with an email offer.

Inviting is one of simplest ways to get visitors to come back. To do this, you need to get your visitors' email addresses onto your prospect list. And, if they love your site, they'll give them to you. If you ask nicely, they'll give you all sorts of other valuable information, too. They'll tell you how they heard about our site. They'll tell you who they are and what they want and what they will look for in the future. What's the best way to ask? Ask them to register with your site the first time they visit. That will give you the information you need and the opportunity to invite them back again and again.

Making the Most of Opportunities and Customer Relationships: Conversations with a Profit-Driven Internet Entrepreneur

The Life Time Value of a Customer (LTV) is the net value of what the customer will buy from you, minus the cost of acquiring them as a customer.

Ideally, you want to spend as little as possible to acquire a new customer and then do whatever it takes to make sure the customer purchases again and again. **eBags.com** has found a formula that works. Peter Cobb, one of the founders, shared it with me.

★ Acquisition

"Our customer acquisition cost last month was $6.50 and an investment banker told me that's the lowest CPA of any retailer he's seen. We keep it low, because we only pay when we have a purchase. One way is through our affiliate programs. We have over 30,000 affiliates, and we pay our affiliates only when people end up buying."

"The other way is through partnership promotions with leading consumer companies. For instance, right now the eBags logo is on 55 million 12-packs of Pepsi soda. That's a lot of exposure for us. Last summer, the eBags logo was on 40 million bags of Frito Lay products. These kinds of promotions benefit us in several ways: First, they give us a lot of credibility—people think these companies wouldn't align themselves with eBags if it wasn't a good company. In this era of e-retail and who's going to make it, this is very important. Also, it's just a lot of great exposure, as you're eating your chips, there is our logo. And, inside the bag, we've also included a game card, and it says, "get $5 off your purchase at eBags." So it's a value-added for a company like Frito-Lay; a customer is incentivized to buy the chips, because he'll get the $5 back at eBags. It's good for the manufacturer . . . it's good for the customer . . . and it's great for us. We have eight of these programs. We're on aisles 2, 4, 6, 9 of every grocery store in the country. We track these programs by sending consumers to landing pages like fritolay.com/eBags or pepsi.com/eBags."

"Of course, the best part is we don't spend any money on any of these programs. We've gravitated to this as an option. One of our objectives has been to find ways to get the message out to the masses of people who may not be online."

★ **Driving Repeat Purchases**

When you think about a company that sells bags, you can't help but wonder…how many bags does one person actually need? Cobb, explains, "When we started raising money, venture capitalists said, 'Why would we give you money if people buy a piece of luggage and then don't need another for 5 years?' But our point was that if you do buy a piece of luggage from us, we'll learn a little bit about you. First, you probably travel and you will need accessories, like toilet kits and packing aids, and you are probably a business person and you might need a laptop and a PDA case. And you're probably active so you'll need a golf bag, travel duffel, gym bag. And you have kids who need backpacks for school, and you might be married, and your wife needs a handbag. It turns out there are plenty of opportunities for repeat buying. It's just about having the products and promotions."

"We drive most of our repeat purchases through our email marketing program. It's called "My eBags." We have over 2 million members now in this program. We found that asking too many questions initially greatly reduced the number of people who would sign up. Now we ask people to be a member and then update their profiles. "Tell us more about yourself and we'll give you an extra 10% off."

"The other way we drive repeat purchase is to try to deliver a great shopping experience on the site, and great service and products, so people want to come back."

eBags has come up with a very interesting and effective pop-up /sweepstake strategy. Visitors to the site on the front-end, get a pop-up for a contest for a trip to Italy, and then at the back-end they get a pop-up to enter to win a PDA. These don't cost eBags anything because they team with the airlines, hotels and PDA manufacturer. At first Cobb wasn't sure these pop-ups were such a good idea, "Pop-ups are somewhat controversial, but our feeling is that we always test things. So, half the people for a certain period of time would get eBags without pop-ups and the other half would get the site with pop-ups. Then we monitor, is there any difference in how long people stay on the site? How fast they click off the site? How much they purchase? What's the average purchase price? The average gross margin dollars per purchaser? We found that people who get the pop-ups actually have a higher conversion rate. They engage with the site more than those who don't. It's counterintuitive, but we structured this promotion so that if you enter one of these contests, you'll immediately get an email that says, "Thanks for entering to win . . . here's an extra 10% off." It turns out that a lot of people take that email and go in and buy."

Cobb says that as a company, the philosophy is to "Use your brains instead of throwing money away. We call this way of thinking 'Mind Over Money.'"

To budding Internet entrepreneurs, Cobb recommends an ironclad business model to start with. Figure out how to get to sustained profitability quickly. He also stresses a willingness to sacrifice. He explains that at eBags everyone makes substantially less than they would make on the open market. But they all believe in what they are doing and they all believe that there will be a payout down the road."

Looking Forward . . .

The opportunities are endless. The Internet has made the whole world a single community of people. Today, the neighborhood store that sold children's clothes when I was a little girl in Philadelphia, could sell those same clothes to all the people they could entice to visit their website.

The challenge with predicting the future is that it is changing so fast that by the time my fingers hit the keys of my computer, someone like you has invented something new that you can do on the Internet.

So, I encourage you to consider the following:

1. Talk to young people. They are tuned into the newest, the smartest and most exciting innovations all the time. Ask them about their favorite sites, and why they like them. Then visit those places. Use search engines to research things you're interested in, like your hobbies, and then follow the links to see what's out there. Take notes about what you like, and what you don't, so you remember to incorporate those things in your own website and campaigns.

2. After the gold rush of Internet companies came and went from 1995 to 2000, the real companies, the bricks and mortars and companies that had business plans based on solid Direct Marketing

principles, began to emerge. These companies, the successful ones, are working hard to meet the expectations of their customers. What are you doing to exceed your customers' expectations?

3. They say "if you build it, they will come" but the building varies by company. Smaller entrepreneurial companies were going to relatives to set up their sites, larger companies were working on the design elements and ignoring the more important infrastructure and now, more than ever, we are understanding that a highly responsive site needs great planning. You need a reliable technology company to help you to plan, build and oversee the infrastructure of your business . . . so that you can respond to all kinds of demand, and also not outgrow your site, soon after it has been built. That means you have to somehow project what your needs will be, in the future.

4. It is really interesting, especially for direct marketers, that though we have talked for years about relationship marketing, being customer focused, having customers drive the product selection...it never really happened until now. Now the transfer of power from the seller to the buyer is apparent. If you don't like one company's site, you just click over to another's. I can voice my dissatisfaction on the site or in a chat room. Companies who understand this concept will win.

5. Websites in the future will not be operating in the cranky way they often do now, by telling me to "click here for the shopping cart" . . . then sending me to a website with an 800 number available from 9 to 5 Eastern Standard Time. They will be always on. That means there will be real-time customer service people waiting to help me with my questions around the clock.

6. The new businesses will integrate e-commerce into their existing companies, so it will appear beautifully seamless to the customer. So, I may buy something in your bricks and mortar store, and have a question about returning it. I can go to your website and ask the question to a real-time customer care person and get my answer on the spot. Maybe I wanted to return my purchase and they will tell me how to do it. Or, I may buy the item on the website and

return it to the store. Then in a few weeks, I can check the site to see if my account was credited correctly. My purchase history (hopefully) will be on one database, so salespeople can help me by working on a knowledge level. "Oh, yes Ms. Geller you purchased the Royal Doulton Country Garden pattern for your daughter-in-law last year. I'll just put in an order for two more place settings." Wouldn't that be helpful?

7. In the business-to-business environment, there will probably be a host of consolidations and streamlining of processes. There are already huge search engines on the Web that can help manufacturers source parts they need. They can find the part and in some cases insert it into a drawing in minutes . . . a procedure that might have taken hours to do before the Internet.

8. The potential for commerce on the Internet is still not projectable. Consider that less than 5 percent of the world is using it now. The potential is huge. As long as we treat our customers well when they visit us online, they will tell lots of other people just like themselves.

One great advantage of the Internet is that it opens up all kinds of possibilities for direct marketers. We can test on our sites by putting an offer on it for three hours a day then test a completely different offer. We can track our results easily.

We can test different ways to drive people (qualified prospects) to our website. Direct mail, email deployments, banner ads, links. Which ones generate the most profitable customers? Direct marketers love delving into these great pockets of opportunity.

The Internet is a chance for us to get closer to our customers than we ever have before, and to provide them with a level of service that will delight them. Consider the Federal Express site. You can track your package and find out that it is presently in Omaha on the way to Lincoln, Nebraska.

The next great idea may be yours. The Internet gives us the opportunity to create a whole new world. Small companies can act like they're big and no one will ever know. Big companies can create a "human quality" online and bring their brand closer to their customers and prospects.

The opportunities are endless.

Checklist:

BUILDING FUTURE RELATIONSHIPS ONE AT A TIME

- ☑ Servicing and caring for customers
- ☑ Loyalty programs
- ☑ Offer aftermarket selling

THE INTERNET

- ☑ Website basics
- ☑ Keep it simple
- ☑ Online branding
- ☑ Interactivity
- ☑ Developing a great site…over time
- ☑ Caring for customers online
- ☑ Creating traffic
  - √ Search engines
  - √ Direct mail
  - √ Promote URL
  - √ Links
  - √ Content
  - √ Partnership opportunities
  - √ Viral promotions
- ☑ Privacy and security

EMAIL MARKETING

- ☑ Customization
- ☑ Privacy and permission
- ☑ Write for electronic media
- ☑ Track and test
- ☑ Personalization
- ☑ Leveraging email opportunities

15
CHAPTER

Direct Marketing Around the World

irect Marketing is largely an American phenomenon. Although Japan has a long DM history dating back to the beginning of the 20th century, the United States is where the industry started, and this is where its amazing growth has taken place. America has been such fertile ground for this industry because it meets two basic conditions: it has a large population and a relatively high income level. There are enough people here who make enough money to support the huge variety of products and services being offered. Direct Marketing has not been as successful in some less densely populated countries because they don't have a large enough universe of people with the means to buy. Larger countries, like China, Germany, India and even Latin America have a huge universe of potential customers, but in some countries, the percentage of people with the economic ability to buy has been very small.

All that is changing rapidly. Political and technological advances have now made it possible to market to combined populations and economies, expanding the search for prospects worldwide. As many as 93 percent of major companies have websites, and accept international orders. And you can mail to several countries at once, broadening your prospect base. Border restrictions in many parts of Europe have become nonexistent. And new developments in communications technology and software make it possible not only to contact customers around the world, and to establish long-lasting personal relationships with them.

There is also a great demand for U.S. products and services in most international consumer markets. And, when the U.S. economy has a downturn, income from new markets can supplement decreased spending in the United States. Industry insiders have been discussing Direct Marketing in the international arena for many years, but until recently, relatively few companies have ventured into foreign markets, and fewer still have been successful in their efforts. While many Fortune 500 companies now have global DM campaigns underway, too many marketers want to seize the opportunities without spending the necessary time on research and testing. If you think that your product or service is appropriate for overseas marketing, now is the time to study the markets, make exploratory visits, and learn as much as you can about each country's laws and regulations. Foreign markets can be very responsive, although it may take much more time to get results than in the United States. Response rates outside of the United States tend to be higher. Yet in turn, so are the costs.

There are, of course, numerous questions you must ask yourself before you contemplate marketing your product or service overseas, including:

- Does my product have universal appeal? Just because it sells well in the United States, will it have the same appeal elsewhere?
- Do I have a clear strategy?
- In what particular countries will my product sell best? Why? How do I conduct the necessary research to answer this question?
- Are there competitive products or services already established in those countries? If so, have I analyzed them thoroughly so I know how my product might fare against theirs?
- Will my customers in targeted countries be responsive to an offer in English? If not (and this is most likely) how do I go about translating and localizing the offer?

Truly global marketing, where one mailing can be successful anywhere in the world, is not yet a reality, and probably never will be. Direct Marketers have to be sure that their products are suitable for a particular country's needs and culture. Many regions of the world are offering smart marketers an opportunity to become involved in this burgeoning, and potentially lucrative, industry.

Regions of Opportunity: Canada, England, Ireland and Germany

I often advise clients who are looking to move into new markets to begin with Canada, because Canadians and Americans have so many similarities. In fact, 80 percent of Canadians live within a two-hour drive of the United States. That's not too say we're the same, however. The two countries are really quite different. Canadians in general are more responsive to Direct Marketing than Americans. They get 50 percent fewer direct mail pieces than the average American does, which means there is less competition arriving in the mailbox.

TIP Here's some demographic information about Canada:

Population: 30.7 million
Currency: Canadian dollar
Household size: 2.84 people
Median Household income: U.S. $34,387
Internet Use: 50%
Ethnic background: 42.5% of Canada's population is composed of English or French ethnic origins. The Asian population is among the fastest growing of all other ethnic groups.

TIP Use the 10:1 rule in Canada. For every 10 units you sell in the United States, expect to sell one in Canada.

Here are some of the major points to remember when marketing to Canada:

★ Most Canadians speak the same language we do, but still write the King's English. Examples of their spelling include: labour, colour, flavour, and cheque. Canadians can spot an American Direct Marketing package just by noticing the differences in spelling. It makes them stop and focus on the words rather than the message.

More than 23 percent of all Canadians speak French, 81 percent of Canadians living in Quebec speak French. (Figure on a 90 percent English/10 percent French ratio when mailing.) Although this is one of the most responsive markets in Canada, there are stringent regulations that apply to Direct Marketers. One of the most important is that you have to mail in French to French-speaking residents of Quebec (you can rent lists of French-speaking residents from list brokers). The Province of Quebec prohibits Direct Marketers from mailing unsolicited materials to Quebec residents in English unless the resident has requested that he or she be mailed information in that language. Some companies try to get around this by mailing bilingual pieces, but results of these mailings have proven less successful than those composed in French.

Quebec residents currently have the right to have their names removed from a house-list, upon request. List managers must also advise customers that there are files maintained on them. These files include information about where their information is maintained, who has access to their information, and what the information is used for. Consumers can be given access to their files upon request, and they have the right to correct errors. There are heavy fines for companies that do not comply with these regulations.

★ The copy should sound as if you are Canadian. If you are sending a mailing in French, be sure it's Canadian French, and not just a strict translation from American copy. Hire a Canadian to translate or write your copy. Your return address should be in Canada, and your toll-free number accessible from there. You don't have to pretend to be a Canadian company, but you do have to make it easy for Canadians to order from you. You don't want to ask your customers to pay more to mail their order form over the border. Prices should be in Canadian dollars.

★ Copy should be conservative and formal. Canadians (who were under British rule almost 100 years longer than we were) seem to have retained the English sense of reserve in their speech and their behavior. Direct mail copy should be straightforward, using no slang or exaggerated promises. Also, be very polite in your copy, using "please" and "thank you" liberally.

★ Canadians often charge their purchases, as they do in the United States. The majority of orders will be purchased by credit card. They also pay by "cheque."

★ Canadians love American products. According to the Organization for Economic Cooperation and Development, Canadians pay 79 percent more for similar American products in Canada, and choices may be limited. As a result, Canadians often cross into U.S. border towns to buy goods. Also, as in many other countries, there is a certain status to owning American products. They watch American television stations and read American magazines and want to own American products for a number of reasons, including familiarity, variety, quality, and price.

★ Products do not need to be described using metric measurements, although Canadians do use the metric system. Except in rare cases, Canadian clothing and shoe sizes are the same as America's.

TIP   Of course, if you choose to mail to Canada, or any other foreign country, you must familiarize yourself with the culture, the customs, the mail and phone systems, and the laws that apply to Direct Marketing.

Much of the same advice applies to marketing in England and Ireland. Direct Marketing in both those countries is expanding rapidly. In the United Kingdom, the overall volume of direct mail has increased by over 115 percent in the last eleven years, and is growing still. Direct mail expenditure has increased by 142 percent in the last eleven years. In 2001, over 5 billion items were mailed in the U.K. It is one of the most sophisticated countries in terms of Direct Marketing support, especially in their ability to merge/purge and target customers.

In Ireland, with its population of only 3.84 million, Direct Marketing has been used most successfully in the business-to-business market, although consumer marketing is now widespread. Direct Marketing in Ireland is still in its early stages. Yet, the Irish economy has been strong with sustainable growth for the past few years. This is due largely to high-tech industries that have created a young, affluent class of consumers. The Irish government has been very successful in making Ireland a "call center" capital for Europe. Telemarketing and fulfillment infrastructures are in place. Ireland has experienced the most growth in direct and interactive marketing, and in 2001 was the leading country in Europe, with 17 percent annual increase.

Ireland primarily trades with the U.K. Twenty-six percent of Ireland's trade is with the U.K. These two countries share close historical links. Thirty-five percent of its trade is with other countries in the European Union. Customs and cultures in England and Ireland have great similarities as well as great differences from our own—and from each other. There are many language similarities, yet that does not mean these countries will have the best target market for your product.

TIP   Be sure you're familiar with the lifestyles and buying habits of your potential buyers before designing and implementing any program. Make sure that you do proper research on the market to make sure it is a good target, and that is not already saturated. Just because the country may be English-speaking, does not mean there aren't other existing barriers to business. And if you don't have firsthand knowledge to rely on, hire people who do.

Jon Lambert, Chairman of Acton Ltd., a leading Direct Marketing company that specializes in international DM, explains that Germany has the third largest Direct Marketing services expenditure in the world. The German-speaking world encompasses not only Germany, but also Austria and German-speaking Switzerland. This means a marketer who goes to the trouble to translate to German can "get by" in these other two very powerful markets without doing additional translation (there are currency issues, but these are rather easy to overcome). Generally speaking, response rates in Austria are about double those in Germany, and nearly triple in Switzerland—even though the markets are small, they are very productive and make for very nice add-on business. One of the biggest advantages of the German market is the availability of lists which are fairly targeted.

TIP   An easy way to get a view of the international marketplace is to attend an international trade show. One of the big German shows is the DIMA, which is typically held in September. This show is attended by many non-Germans, but you should bring a translator with you to take full advantage of the show.

Europe

Alfred M. Goodloe, is the President of Direct International, a multinational publisher and conference company. In evaluating the Direct Marketing potential of various regions of the world, Goodloe observes that "collectively, the European (West and East) population is almost double that of the United States. You will encounter plenty of local and international competition—much more than in Asia and Latin America—so don't expect the robust responses you can achieve elsewhere."

Douglas Sacks, Senior Vice President of Infocore Inc., and Chair of the U.S. DMA's International Council talks about the economy in Europe, "Economic growth rates vary but many have not been affected by the recent U.S. downturn. Also, the successful introduction of the Euro as a standardized form of currency has added some needed excitement and confidence to the market. It also makes Pan-European Direct Marketing more of a dream and less of a nightmare."

In Europe, the better responding countries will be:

Germany	France	England	Switzerland
Portugal	Ireland	Austria	
Netherlands	Eastern European countries		
	(Poland, Czech Republic, Hungary)		

Goodloe's experience indicates that the small countries can't produce all the products that prospects want to buy, and so are ripe for foreign Direct Marketers. Doug Sacks explains that the downside of this is that the infrastructures needed to support large-scale Direct Marketing often are not in place or fully developed in the smaller countries. Access to data can be a problem. So you have to decide whether to market in a larger or smaller country.

One of the fastest growing areas for Direct Marketers is Eastern Europe. Jiri Matousek, Art Director for ad agency BBDO in Prague, reports that just a few years ago Direct Marketing was unknown in Eastern Europe. The first programs started in Prague around 1993. "Most of the Direct Marketing is in business-to-business, but consumer marketing is growing rapidly," says Matousek. "Banks and financial institutions, who have never before talked to their own customers, are beginning to use Direct Marketing.

"If you do a personalized mailing in Prague, which is something most natives have never seen before, you can experience a 30 percent response rate. However, marketing to Czechs is different than marketing to Americans. Czechs are wary. They've been cheated out of their money too many times, and they don't have consumer protection laws like the ones in America. So Direct Marketing has to concentrate on the credibility of the company—you have to convince consumers that your company will do what you promise, and stand behind the products you sell. Czechs also like to know minute details about the products they're buying. They're more concerned about quality than price."

Matousek has observed that Direct Marketing is growing rapidly in Eastern Europe, and thinks it will continue to grow at a very quick pace.

Japan

In 1995, Japan became one of the hottest catalog markets in the world. Shopping by catalog spread through the country like wildfire. Whole new cultures are being built around it. Japanese women are forming "buying circles" to consolidate their orders and save on freight and ordering charges. Some U.S. retailers in Japan have actually become little more than catalog showrooms. Customers go into the stores, try on merchandise they like, and then order from the catalog, which is usually a less expensive option than buying retail. And catalog clubs are being formed which offer discounted prices and assistance in placing orders to the United States.

Doug Sacks points out that now, seven years later, the factors leading to this have changed...but not completely. In 1995, there was a favorable exchange rate for the yen. This is no longer the case. Also, historically, to make their goods more attractive for export, Japanese companies have lowered their prices in foreign markets. Japanese consumers, of whom as many as 60 percent travel internationally, saw that prices for their own goods at home were higher than in foreign cities. So ordering from catalogs became attractive financially. Creatively, U.S. catalogs, who often devote a full page to an item (depending on the product) were more attractive than in the telephone directory style of many Japanese catalogs.

With a weaker Yen, and a long-running recession, Japan is no longer the dream market for many foreign "consumer" items. Yet there is a huge potential in the business-to-business segment. Many U.S. catalogers and retailers have pulled out of the market.

Doug Sacks also states that, "Japan's desire for and perception of the quality of many foreign goods remains high. But the Japanese consumer is much more particular than his American counterpart. And what's worse, when a Japanese consumer is dissatisfied, they rarely complain, they just disappear. While the continued recession is troubling, and major economic changes will need to be implemented (some of them drastic), Japan is still a very *rich* country. I'm higher on the B2B market in Japan right now for Direct Marketers than I am for consumer items. For consumer marketers, take a close look at the demographics. Japan has a rapidly aging population. Marketers targeting the seniors should be very successful. These people are living longer and are spending money on themselves."

TIP   Here's some demographic information about Japan:
Population: 126.7 million
Currency: yen
Per capita income: U.S. $28,000
DM Sales: U.S. 23.9 billion
Most popular purchases: women's clothing, underwear, men's clothing

---

Here are some of the major points to remember when marketing to Japan:

★ Japanese customers do not usually use personal checks. Most often, they pay by credit card, and sometimes by postal money order.

★ Be sure that your database is modified to handle Japanese addresses, which can run up to seven lines.

★ Sizes must be converted to the metric system.

★ Consumers will get their first impression of your company from the back cover of your catalog, as Japanese books and magazines open the opposite way from ours.

★ Catalog copy can be in English, but you should include detailed ordering instructions in Japanese, including how to contact your company.

★ Be sure to state return policies clearly in Japanese. Most Japanese consumers are not used to returning items. Some stores in Japan do not even accept returns.

★ Consider establishing a call center in Japan. Set up a customer service base where consumers can call and speak in Japanese to order items and ask questions. One such company, Tokyo-based Prestige International, has a computer-telephone system linked directly to its U.S. clients so that Japanese customers can get immediate product and pricing information from the United States. The company has approximately 60 bilingual operators (speaking English and Japanese). Costs are high for this service. There is a large setup fee, depending on the size of the company and the number of products being sold, a monthly management fee, and a $2 to $7 charge per call. If you were considering using such a service, you would have to compare costs of accepting toll-free international calls, hiring an American telemarketing firm, and finding Japanese-speaking operators.

★ Quality is a key issue. The picture of goods must match the delivered product.

★ Contact the Commerce Department's American Catalog House (see "International Services" in Resource Directory). In two locations in Japan, U.S. catalogs are displayed for the public to peruse. Catalogs can then be purchased for a nominal fee. If consumers want to order from the catalogs, they can fax orders to the United States on the spot. The fee for companies to participate is $600. You are required to furnish the Catalog House with 200 catalogs for each location, and to replenish those supplies as necessary.

One of the largest success stories in marketing to Japan has been L.L. Bean, which shipped an average of 9,000 packages a day to Japanese customers. L.L. Bean mails its catalogs, receives orders, and ships its merchandise from the United States, as opposed to establishing a Japanese presence. Most of its customers came from full-page ads, in Japanese, placed in local newspapers, which offered free catalogs. The catalogs are in English, although the order form and ordering instructions are in Japanese. Part of L.L. Bean's cost efficiency comes from the fact that it has no corporate presence in Japan. If it had a corporate presence there, the company would have to use the Japanese domestic postal service, which is more than one and one-half times the U.S. international postal service rates. It would also have to pay a 55 percent corporation tax in Japan, the highest in the world.

Dick Leslie, Vice President/Japan, L.L. Bean, suggests that to be successful in Direct Marketing in Japan you need to do a lot of research. "You need to visit the marketplace, to see what people do, see what's in the stores," he says. "Talk to advertising agencies, and find out about the Japanese lifestyles and the products they buy. You also need to understand the infrastructure, especially the mail and telephone systems. Study the kinds of catalog business and the markets in the country. Do people buy the kinds of products you're offering? Does the clothing you sell fit the Japanese body?" These are the kinds of questions you must answer before you consider testing your products in Japan.

List quality and availability has improved greatly since our last edition. Major compiled and responder files are available for both business-to-consumer and business-to-business applications. Hakuhodo Institute for Life and Living (HILL), a division of Hakuhodo, a leading Japanese and global advertising agency produces a Lifestyle Survey, Seikatsu Teiten, every other year. This tracks present and future lifestyle trends among the Japanese and can be a very useful research tool for the direct marketer. For more information contact info@athill.com.

> TIP   The Japanese Direct Marketing Association (JADMA) is very active. Every other year they publish a very complete survey of the DM industry in Japan. This is available at a very reasonable price directly from JADMA (www.jadma.org).

China

China is a difficult market, yet Direct Marketing is beginning to surface there. Lists from foreign-owned catalog and book club publishers have now come onto the market and they have "selects" available. One problem is the current reluctance of list owners to release their lists for independent merge-purge, but this may soon change.

American magazines are making inroads with Chinese language versions. One product that had been successfully marketed in China is *McCall's* pattern books, which are easily manufactured and have very little text.

Payment is mostly through postal giro (a means of transferring funds directly from a bank account via the post office) and debit card charge, but more and more Direct Marketing merchandisers are successfully using Cash-On-Delivery. The market continues to be very price-sensitive and most products are sourced locally.

James Thornton, Managing Director of MLA Global Lists Specialists, explains that China is not a country for inexperienced marketers—although now would be a good time to begin the necessary research. Direct sellers such as Avon have been successful in China. Now, more and better quality databases are coming onto the market, including email databases. The Chinese post office provides services for direct marketers. But this is still not a country for the faint of heart, or those on a tight budget, or those who need to see a quick return on their investment.

China requires a local presence or local partner. It's difficult to get things done, when you're outside of the country.

Southeast Asia

Countries within this region are easier to reach and penetrate than China. Good regional (and some local) lists are widely available. It is not necessary to have a local presence in any one local market unless and until it has been proven to be particularly responsive.

Indonesia and Thailand respond well, generally. Hong Kong and Singapore perform well for financial and information offers. Response rates in Malaysia are down. Roll-outs in Japan, Taiwan and Indonesia must be in local language, and there are severe restrictions on mailing within Korea due to data protection laws.

Discounted first-class bulk mail rates out of Hong Kong and Singapore and low production costs in Asia are leading many international mailers towards using Asia as a "gateway" into global markets. Both Australia and the Middle East can be reached cost-efficiently from Hong Kong or Singapore.

While Asia offers large populations, only countries with the best economies should be targeted for Direct Marketing. However, response rates and average order values tend to be higher than in Europe.

The same old principle applies. If you have a product that sells through Direct Marketing in any one country—it will sell just as well in other countries—including Asia.

Australia

Vin Jenkins of Clemenger Direct, a Direct Marketing firm in Australia, tells us that there has been substantial growth in the applications of Direct Marketing in Australia over the last 15 to 20 years. Almost all of this growth is related to database marketing, direct mail, telemarketing (inbound and outbound), and direct response advertising. Direct response advertising has proliferated in the print media (mainly magazines), but the adoption of direct response television has been relatively weak. In 2001, total DM spending in Australia was 13.8 billion. The English-speaking population is approaching 20 million.

"Australia is probably about five years behind the U.S. and U.K. in the development of Direct Marketing, not so much in terms of strategic capabilities or even technology, but rather in terms of the scale of operations, industry by industry," says Jenkins. "The list rental business was underdeveloped in Australia. We've had much more success here with two-step programs—enquiry or lead generation in the main media (private list-building), followed up by a multiphase conversion process (usually direct mail and telemarketing)."

One challenge for Direct Marketing in Australia is to convince top corporate management that not all customers are the same, and to show them the benefits that follow personalized mailings and loyalty programs.

Another challenge in Austrailia is the public's concern about privacy. This has limited the growth of e-commerce, and a public relations campaign may be needed to ensure the public that transactions can be safe and secure on the Internet. Special rules apply when a company uses endorsements, testimonials, guarantees, sweepstakes and the use of the words "free" and "new" in Australia. List management actually is not done in Australia—list brokers go to list owners directly. List brokers perform multiple duties; from research to results analysis. List brokers are very up-to-date on the current privacy issues as well.

Although mail order growth had been relatively modest from 1985-1995, there have been a some great successes, including Myer Direct, the mail order subsidiary of Myer Grace Brothers, the largest department store group in Australia. Myer Brothers' mail order business began modestly in April of 1989, with one catalog. They are now mailing 12 catalogs per year, focusing mainly on women's apparel, and are currently the largest mail order business in the country with sales of approximately $100 million Australian dollars.

Latin America and Mexico

Latin America can be a risky area for Direct Marketers, yet it is an area with great potential. Political upheavals and instabilities make this an unpredictable market. According to Ed Nash, former Executive Vice President for Direct Marketing at Bozell Worldwide, countries such as Argentina, Brazil, and Costa Rica, where Direct Marketing is just beginning to surface, require a great deal of creative thinking, Nash told *DM News* (August 21, 1995) that Direct Marketing "is in the same stage down there as the United States was 15 or 20 years ago, but with much more energy."

One of the problems in the region is that you can't necessarily create one direct mail piece that will be effective for the entire country. Argentina, for instance, has a wide variety of demographics, from the most affluent urban societies to the poorest rural areas. Brazil's two largest cities, Sao Paulo and Rio de Janeiro, are both affluent and urban, yet have very different personalities. Direct Marketers mailing to these countries will be best off working with local people who can advise them on the cultural differences.

"Mexico needs to be viewed as distinct from Latin America," says Doug Sacks of Infocore, Inc. "NAFTA (North American Free Trade Agreement) has been a huge help and has served as a bridge for both mutual economic growth and cultural understanding between the United States and Mexico. Mexico has very little economic interplay with South America, relying much more upon the United States and Europe. There has been huge growth in Direct Marketing in Mexico and it is one of our busiest and most lucrative markets. Data quality and availability has improved exponentially and many Fortune 500 companies have had successful DM campaigns there. The growth of the U.S. Latino population (a majority of whom are Mexican) has opened the eyes of many U.S. marketers to this demographic segment. Marketing in the United States in Spanish is now quite common. And taking the next step, which is to market to consumers in Mexico, no longer seems like such a giant leap."

TIP Here's some demographic information about Mexico:
Population: 100 million
Currency: peso
Household size: 5.5 people
Direct mail received: 60 pieces per year

The Mechanics of Overseas Campaigns

Many experts suggest that the future of Direct Marketing is in the overseas markets, and that if you don't jump on the bandwagon soon, you will lose a golden opportunity. What they fail to note is that international Direct Marketing is a highly complicated process, and must be researched carefully. Each country presents unique problems and challenges, and companies who go in without knowing the culture, the rules and regulations, and the mail and telephone systems are in for very rough times.

That said, there is great potential in international Direct Marketing. Here are some suggestions for developing successful campaigns:

Selecting a Product. According to Al Goodloe, roughly 80 percent of all global direct mail is for information products: newspapers, magazines, newsletters, encyclopedias, directories, online products, courses, and seminars. "Information flows easily across national borders," he says. "It's much more complicated, for instance, to mail glassware internationally. There's so much more involved."

Florence Leighton, head of the international list brokerage division of Greenwich, Connecticut-based Direct Media, agrees with this assessment. As she told *Target Marketing* (November 1995), "Books and magazines are easy to fulfill and cross borders without import duties." She cites such successfully marketed publications as *The Economist, BusinessWeek,* and *Time.*

However, many countries around the world are interested in all things American, and as companies such as UPS expanded into previously underdeveloped areas, shipping has become less of a problem.

Lists. Once you have identified a region and culture that is suitable to your product or service, you must locate appropriate lists of prospects.

Selecting lists depends on your product or service. Different lists include consumer, B2B, compiled, mail response, local/national, multinational, and most recently, email. Just a few years ago, international marketers didn't have the abundance of lists that they currently have.

In terms of list planning, some lists have shown to work better than others. Multi-national lists are better than national.

The consumer direct mailer can find major country lifestyle lists (on a per country basis). The global list industry around the world is a major source of revenue, due to the current advances in technology and computers.

With the downturn in the economy, there are few new productive lists becoming available. More recently, there have been shifts to email programs, as the availability of targeted email lists has increased.

The number of available international lists has grown to almost mirror the number in the United States. The same 250 (approx.) represent the best pool. Here is a short overview:

- Institute of International Resarch—a major global seminar company that releases large multi-national lists

World-wide magazine publishers are a good representation of top multinational paid response lists. They include:

- Time Inc.: with *Fortune* and *Time* in all regions of the world
- *Newsweek*
- *Harvard Business Review*
- *The Economist*
- *Financial Times*
- *The International Herald Tribune*
- *BusinessWeek*
- *Scientific American*
- *National Geographic*
- *Wall Street Journal*

Computer lists abound. Currently they are the largest niche market available world-wide, with a multitude of selections.

List costs have risen considerably, although some selectivity within lists is possible (from sophisticated list owners). The average list cost including selects for a program of 500M names, selected from approximately 100 lists worldwide is currently $295/M.

Developed nations are still the most productive, but also the most competitive. And it is necessary to know the language problems that can arise from mailing into different countries. For example, for the Japanese market, there are targeted lists such as Nikkei, but they must be mailed in the local language, Kanji. These lists can also be very expensive. But, with the right product at the right time, companies like Victoria's Secret has made the Japanese market work well for them.

A new list market has just opened in India. Although there is no track record for mailing into India, English is their business language. India represents a great potential area to target for the future.

TIP   Keep in mind that if you choose to market in English instead of the native language you will effectively eliminate 95–98 percent of a country's population. Even those who speak and read English are often more comfortable making "purchasing decisions" in their native language. Take the plunge and go local in the local language.

Writing Copy. If you use multinational lists, you are mailing primarily to people who speak English as a second language. When writing copy for foreign markets, you must use common sense. Be careful with idioms. Foreigners often speak a more formal English than Americans might use in their copy. American copywriters sometimes leave out verbs. For instance, they might say "Great deal!" For international marketing, a better way to say it would be, "We have a great deal for you!" It may not have the same punch, but at least it will be understood.

Try to write using the formula: noun, verb, object. Avoid complicated dependent clauses. Cut adjectives to a minimum and reduce the length of sentences. Simple, short sentences need not be childlike. On the contrary, these sentences can be powerful and will be clearly understood by your prospects. Consider the majesty of this sentence from Genesis: "In the beginning God created the heaven and the earth."

If your company, product, or service is not well known, you need to reassure prospects that they will get what they pay for. Present your credentials, emphasize the quality of your product, and include a strongly worded guarantee.

Mailing. Some companies mail directly from the United States, and others set up mailing centers in individual countries. There does not seem to be a right or wrong way to do this. For instance, L.L. Bean does all its mailing from the U.S., while Lands' End has set up mailing centers in England and Japan.

One point to remember is that if you mail from within a country, you are bound by local laws and regulations. In Germany, for example, you are not allowed to offer free premiums or sell merchandise at a discount. If you send your direct mail from the United States, however, you are not bound by these laws, so your premiums and discounted rates may be very appealing to German consumers.

One way you can save some money mailing overseas is to use a service of the U.S. Postal Service called International Surface Airlift (ISAL). Other postal administrations—Britain, the Netherlands, and Denmark—offer similar and highly competitive services. There are also a number of private remailers and consolidators (see Resource Directory) who provide a variety of international postal options. You would do well to shop around.

ISAL airmails your material to a principal city in approximately 126 countries and delivers by surface thereafter with each country. For a .7 oz. (20 gram) promotion package, of the postage is currently 80 cents to Europe, 80 cents to Latin America, 50 cents to Mexico, 60 cents to Canada, 80 cents to the Pacific Rim, and 80 cents for the rest of Asia, Africa, and the Middle East. Package weight is critical. International mail goes by gram weight, and every gram counts (not like domestic American mail, which costs a certain amount for one ounce and lesser amounts for each ounce thereafter). If you reduce your international weight by even one or two grams, you can garner significant postal savings. International rates fluctuate, so be alert for change.

Collecting Money. When you're marketing internationally, you must decide how you're going to handle payments received from foreign customers. There are three main factors:

Payment Currency (what currency will prices be set in); *Payment Options* (what payment methods will customers be allowed to use); *Payment Clearance* (how will payments be cleared and collected). When considering your options, remember that the choices you make will affect your response rates. As with all other aspects of your mailing, testing will help you to know what pricing and payment options work best for you.

Renee Frappier, Marketing Manager for PacNet Services Inc., has been involved with international payment obstacles for the last five years. She explains that setting prices in the local currency of your target market will lift response rates in most cases. A local-currency price makes your product accessible to more people. Customers will not have to go out of their way to pay for your product, or guess at what the actual price might be after conversion.

On multi-national campaigns consider offering local currency prices in four or five countries that represent the highest percentage of addresses on your list, but offer U.S. dollar options in smaller markets. Once you have decided which prices you will offer, and in which countries, your lettershop can easily print the appropriate prices for the appropriate countries as part of the personalization process. Keep your choice of payment as simple as possible. Check and credit card are easy to offer in U.S. dollars or local currencies, and you won't need to change the copy for each region.

Renee Frappier also explains that currency fluctuations can pose a significant risk in some markets, and there are ways to minimize your exposure. One popular way is to build a cushion into local currency prices. There are a couple of ways to approach this.

If you set your foreign currency prices 5 to 10 percent higher (depending on the market), you will be protected against most currency fluctuations; the expense of clearing your payments will usually be covered; and because the cost of goods is often higher in other countries than in the United States, you will still see a lift in response rates that most international companies (that price in local currencies) experience.

Rather than printing local currency prices, Al Goodloe of Publisher's Multinational Direct sets prices in U.S. dollars. He includes a currency exchange table on the back of his order form. Goodloe sets his rates at 8 to 10 percent higher than the bank rate in order to protect against fluctuations 2 or 3 months in advance.

Despite the global nature of the Internet, a lift in response can be expected for targeted e-commerce campaigns. Andersen Consulting reported in 2000 that 70 percent of online shoppers in Canada prefer to shop at Canadian e-commerce sites. One of the greatest reasons is a preference to pay for goods in Canadian dollars. Offering a local-currency credit card payment option will go a long way toward winning Canadian customers.

A similar preference can be noticed in Europe. More and more Europeans who shop on-line are purchasing from local sites rather than foreign sites. Keep in mind your consumer's preference for local currency pricing, and a local look and feel.

While check and credit card are the most widely used mail order payment options around the world, in some countries people prefer not to use credit or enclose payment with order. Marketers should try to find out which payment options are being offered by local merchants who do what they do. Companies selling to countries such as Germany, Austria, the Netherlands, Norway, Belgium and Japan where the cultural attitude toward payment and credit is different from America need to be aware of important payment methods such as bank giro transfer and direct debit. This is true for direct mail and e-commerce.

According to NUA Internet surveys, from NUA.com (www.nua.ie), of 460,000 Belgians on the Internet, 75 percent will not give their credit card number for online purchases. There are many would-be shoppers around the world who do not want to purchase on credit, or who do not feel safe giving their credit card details online to a merchant they have not met. You can expect these customers to shop once other options like Internet bank transfer and direct debit become available.

A bank / giro transfer is a form of payment where the customer instructs their bank or post office to transfer a sum directly to the company's bank or post-office account. The customer does not send payment directly to your company. This payment method is particularly relevant for payment on invoice e.g., subscription renewals, catalog orders, etc. If you are comfortable with invoicing for goods, the bank transfer payment option will be your most important payment option in Germany, the Netherlands, Belgium, Denmark, Norway, and Sweden and Japan.

Direct Debit, known as ACH in some countries, is becoming more and more familiar to customers in Europe. Rather than enclosing a check with order, customers simply fill in an authorization to debit their bank account directly. This payment option can be used for mail order or for e-commerce campaigns, and has the advantage of an easy offer and easy clearance. Direct debit files can be submitted to the banks for authorization in much the same way as batches of credit card information.

Are you going to deposit the checks in the country to which you're mailing, or back in the United States? You may choose to use a bank in the country in which you're marketing and keep the money available in that country for future promotion costs.

It is important to clear international payments through the appropriate channels. The cost of clearing international payments through a U.S. bank is usually prohibitive. A foreign check can cost as much as $40.00 and take as long as eight weeks to clear through a U.S. bank. It is also better to submit U.S. checks to U.S. banks, instead of foreign banks.

It is not possible to process foreign currency credit card transactions through a U.S. account without a currency conversion shown on the cardholder's statement. This means that the published price and the end price shown on the customer's statement will not be the same, which could result in charge backs.

For companies that are heavily committed to a particular market, have offices and a local staff to service that market, investing time and energy to develop a local banking infrastructure makes a lot of sense. In many countries, banks will require local incorporation, security deposits, and extensive information about the company before they will allow them to have merchant accounts.

Alternatively, multi-currency payments can be cleared conveniently and affordably through an international payment processing company. This will be the best option for companies that are testing new markets, new payment methods, or that are targeting several markets and wish to maintain control over payment receipts. An international payment processing company will have access to a worldwide network of banking contacts for clearance of all major currencies and all popular forms of payment. They're able to establish foreign currency merchant accounts for card processing in their clients' names.

Privacy. Privacy legislation has a major impact on international direct marketing. There is a European Union model that differs from the U.S. self-regulatory model. For example, Germany has outlawed cold call telemarketing and faxing. Theoretically, Italy has outlawed list brokering.

Each country in the European Union can "interpret" this legislation, so some countries are strict and some lenient. In other parts of the world, countries are using the European Union privacy legislation as their model. It is important to research the country's privacy regulations as you develop your marketing strategy. And, there are many privacy websites and resources available on the Internet, such as www.privacy.org and www.privacyexchange.com.

Customs. There are a number of ways to handle customs within the country of destination. Lawrence J. Chaido, Director TransGlobal Consultants (NA) Inc., states that you must keep in mind customs issues refer to the duties (taxes) that are charged by a country of destination on articles of value that you send to recipients within their borders. Each country may assess a duty percentage along their specific guidelines and classifications. Your first order of business is to check with the U.S. Department of Commerce to find out a particular country's rules and regulations, as well as verify if there are any additional taxes relating to the items entering a specific country. In some countries the normal pattern is to say the customs duties are the responsibility of the recipient. This information must be very clear in that when the product is delivered to a country, the recipient will be advised by the customs authority that there is payment due. In some cases payment may be greater than the value of the item ordered, and may cause refusal of the item.

When the product is delivered, the delivery company will collect the customs charges, as well as any additional fees related to the collection of the duty for the items. This is the preferred method if you're mailing to many countries at once, because it would be difficult to calculate a specific duty for each article sent to an international customer. Another method, particularly in Western Europe, is for the mailer to pay customs charges and other fees relating to sending articles in "bulk" commercial shipments to a particular entry point within the European Union. Upon entry and the payment duties, fees and taxes, the items are available to be distributed free of duty fees to customers within a specific region. You export your merchandise to a warehouse in Amsterdam or Britain, for example, and pay the customs duties for the entire shipment.

Maintaining Long-Distance Relationships and Customer Service. Foreign customers are more expensive to obtain than American customers, but their order values are usually much higher, which means that every foreign customer you get is worth a lot to your business.

Once you obtain foreign customers, you should not let them down. Customer service is extremely important. The people you're dealing with are looking for a relationship with you. A quality product, a strong offer, and an attractive price will bring in customers. But it's the relationship that will keep them buying.

Many companies are setting up local calling centers, such as Japan's Prestige International, to handle customer service inquiries. That way, customers can speak to representatives in their own language and receive the help they need quickly and easily. When an order arrives, an acknowledgment should be mailed saying "We have received your order and it will be shipped to you by _____." This is especially true when people pay you by check. In many countries, customers don't get their checks back from the bank the way Americans do. Americans can use their check as a receipt; overseas customers often need verification that their check has been received as proof of payment.

It takes a lot of hard work to make international Direct Marketing a success. Many people will advise you against trying it because it is such a complicated process. However, you might choose to heed the words of Direct Media's Florence Leighton. As she told *Target Marketing*, "What if you're told, 'We've never done anything like that here. It goes against our culture.' Go for it. You'll probably make a fortune."

Checklist

QUESTIONS TO ASK PRIOR TO MARKETING OVERSEAS

☑ Does my product have universal appeal?

☑ In what particular countries will my product sell best?

☑ Are there competitive products or services already established in those countries?

☑ Will my customers in targeted countries be responsive to an offer in English? If not, how can I localize my offer?

REGIONS OF OPPORTUNITY

☑ Canada, England, Ireland and Germany

- ☑ Europe
- ☑ Japan
- ☑ China
- ☑ Southeast Asia
- ☑ Australia
- ☑ Latin America and Mexico

THE MECHANICS OF OVERSEAS CAMPAIGNS

- ☑ Selecting a product
    - √ What shipping services are available for your product in countries to which you are marketing?

- ☑ Lists: Sources for multinational paid response lists include:
    - √ *Financial Times*
    - √ *BusinessWeek*
    - √ *Harvard Business Review*
    - √ *Time*
    - √ *Fortune*
    - √ *Newsweek*
    - √ *National Geographic*
    - √ *The Wall Street Journal*
    - √ *Scientific American*
    - √ *The Economist*

- ☑ Writing copy:
    - √ Beware of idioms
    - √ Use the formula: noun, verb, object
    - √ Use short sentences
    - √ Present your credentials
    - √ Emphasize the quality of your product
    - √ Include a strongly worded guarantee

- ☑ Mailing Options:
    - √ Mail directly from the United States
    - √ Utilize ISAL or overseas postal administrations in Britain, the Netherlands, or Denmark

- √ Utilize private remailers
- √ Be aware of package weight—every gram counts

☑ Collecting Money: There are three options to consider:

- √ Payment currency
- √ Payment options
  - √ Direct Debit (ACH)
  - √ Credit cards
  - √ Check in U.S. dollars
  - √ Check in local currency
  - √ On-line purchases
  - √ Bank/giro transfer
- √ Payment clearance

☑ Privacy:

- √ Make sure you research the privacy legislation and regulations in your target market, as it is constantly changing

☑ Customs options:

- √ In some countries, have the delivery company collect customs duties from the recipient
- √ Ship your merchandise to a central point and pay the customs duties for the entire shipment

☑ Maintain long-distance relationships:

- √ Set up local calling centers to handle customer service inquiries
- √ Acknowledge that customers' orders have been received

16

CHAPTER

The Successful Marketer

Feasting on Direct Marketing Success

Imagine this scenario: It's your wedding anniversary, or the Fourth of July, or your 40th birthday. The doorbell rings. An overnight air delivery service has a special package for you. It's an odd shape and it's kind of heavy and you can't wait to open it. When you do, you find...live lobsters, clams, mussels, corn, new potatoes, onion and sweet Italian sausages, packed in fresh seaweed in their own steamer pot, ready to be prepared and enjoyed in the comfort of your very own home! You're in seafood heaven and it's all due to Clambake Celebrations, a Cape Cod-based company that ships high-quality seafood nationwide.

Clambake Celebrations is definitely a Direct Marketing success story. In 1989, Jo-Von Tucker was an international catalog marketing consultant living in New York City. She was continually traveling, always "hopping on and off" airplanes. But Tucker suffers from emphysema and is constantly on oxygen. Traveling was getting difficult. Her doctors told her to move out of the city and change her lifestyle.

As an established expert in the Direct Marketing field, Tucker began to look for a business that would lend itself to mail order success. She came across a retail operation that packed and sold clambakes for people on Cape Cod. "I got very excited about this company because it was such a unique concept. I didn't need to tamper with the product," says

314

Tucker. "And I thought that marketing this product directly to consumers all over the country could work very well." So Tucker bought the company—and within five years Direct Marketing represented 90 percent of the business.

Tucker started by renting lists from companies with mail order buyers she felt would match the Clambake customer's profile. She tested in lots of 5,000, and when she found a list that worked, she would roll out and go with a larger segment of that list. Clambake Celebrations now has a house list of more than 90,000 names.

Clambake gets many of its new customers through direct response advertising in magazines such as *Saveur* (an upscale gourmet magazine), and *Food & Wine*.

"I've tried small ads and I've tried large ones," says Tucker. "The one that works best for us seems to be a one-sixth-page black and white ad with the headline 'Give the Gift of Exceedingly Good Taste…The Lobster Clambake-to-Go!® Gift Certificate.'

"One issue of *Food & Wine* can generate between 200 and 300 inquiries, which we convert to sales at a rate of about 28 percent," says Tucker. "That's why we stick with this ad—it works."

Figure 16.1 shows the ad, and the toll-free number for prospects to call for a free brochure or to place an order. Once prospects call, they receive a four-panel color brochure (Figure 16.2). The front page of the brochure includes a color photograph of a sumptuous lobster clambake feast. Throughout this "mini-catalog" there are testimonials, including a quote from *Redbook* magazine which features a testimonial from actress Angelica Houston, who received a Clambake dinner as a Christmas gift and said it was "one of the most imaginative presents" she'd ever been given.

The majority of orders are for gift certificates (Figure 16.3). When Clambake Celebrations redeems a gift certificate and ships a seafood dinner, a pre-stamped postcard "Thank You" note (Figure 16.4) accompanies it. The recipient can

Figure 16.1

This one-sixth page, black and white ad proved to be the perfect design to attract customers.

**Give the Gift
Of Exceedingly Good Taste…**

The Lobster Clambake-to-Go!® Gift Certificate.

This is it…the *sure-to-please, destined-to-be-enjoyed* Holiday gift for the most discriminating palate! Your *gift* will be the most memorable one received.

Packed in a steamer pot, shipped live and fresh via FedEx, the famous seafood feast from Cape Cod arrives ready to be steamed, with sweet, succulent lobsters, steamer clams, mussels, corn, potatoes, onion and Italian sausage.

1-877-792-7771
to order or to receive a free brochure.

Clambake Celebrations®
1223 Main St.
Chatham, MA 02633

Figure 16.2

Customers who call, write or inquire about the company through their site, receive a two-side, four-fold brochure. Among the many testimonials, is one from actress Angelica Houston.

Clambake Celebrations®
presents
Clambakes-To-Go!®

Traditional Cape Cod Lobster Clambake feasts,
ready to cook in their own steamer pot,
air expressed overnight to your door.

"We've enjoyed some world-class food in some fine restaurants—but
this meal was right up there with the best, plus it was at our own table,
and NO TROUBLE!"

~ Dr. Wood, Menlo Park, CA

"For the past 5 years we've enjoyed your Clambake with our visiting relatives from Quebec. It has become a tradition for our family. The seafood
is extraordinary, and your company never misses a detail! On-time delivery, and very friendly customer service, too. Keep up the good work!"

~ The Kiszka Family, Methuen, MA

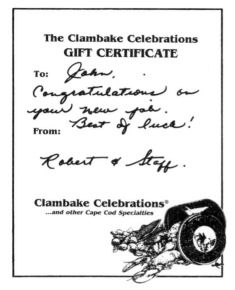

Figure 16.3
Clambake Celebrations highly recommends sending their exclusive Gift Certificate for a specific dinner, because this way the recipient can choose the day they want to have their fresh seafood feast-in-a-steamer pot to arrive!

Figure 16.4
The pre-stamped Thank You card makes it easy for recipients to acknowledge the gift and it lets the sender know that the gift has been received.

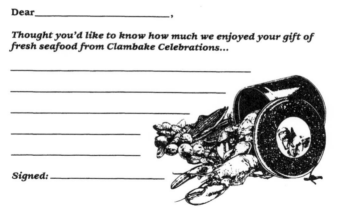

fill out the postcard and send it to whoever got them the gift. This is an important selling point of Clambakes as gifts, particularly for business/corporate accounts. People who give a gift like to know that it's been received, appreciated and enjoyed!

Along with every clambake or lobster order shipped, Clambake Celebrations provides a ride-along, stamped survey card (Figure 16.5) offering "A Penny for Your Thoughts." This allows customers to express

Figure 16.5

Survey cards, offering "A Penny for Your Thoughts" allows customers an opportunity to express their opinion on the clambake experience.

Clambake Celebrations®
1223 Main Street
Chatham (Cape Cod), MA 02633

         ...A penny for your thoughts

Clambake Celebrations®
... and other Cape Cod Specialties
Toll Free: 1-877-792-7771
ENJOY YOUR FEAST!

Order # _____ Order Taken by _____ Prepared by _____ Packaged by _____

Your opinion is important to us! We'd love to hear your thoughts on customer service, delivery, cooking instructions, ease of preparation and quality of food _____
_____
_____
_____

Anything else you'd like to see us offer? ❑ Other Seafood items, ❑ Desserts, ❑ Cooking accessories, ❑ Serving pieces ❑ Cape Cod arts/crafts. ❑ _____
Send us your favorite seafood recipe or suggestions for Clambake leftovers.
Please send brochure to:
Name _____
Address _____
City _____ State _____ Zip _____
Thank you for your comments. **We appreciate your business!**

their opinion of the entire clambake experience . . . on-time delivery, customer service, ease of preparation, quality of food, etc. If there was a problem (which is very rare), Jo-Von can then follow up with the customer.

Clambake has about a 64 percent reorder factor. Tucker feels that her background in Direct Marketing helped make the company a success, but there's another, even more important, factor. "It's our exceptional customer service," she says. "We do back flips for our customers and go out of our way to serve them however we can." One customer, an elderly woman who had moved to California from her native New England, called Tucker with an unusual request. She wanted to make cranberry sauce for her family, and couldn't get the fresh berries she wanted. She asked if Tucker could get some for her. "I personally got in my car, drove to the next town, bought the cranberries at the market, and shipped them to her. We did that for several years until she passed away.

"My philosophy about direct mail is that it is an extremely experiential transaction for a customer," says Tucker. "Everything about that experience has to be positive and reinforcing and pleasurable. So we knock ourselves out to make sure that happens. We ship a product that's one of the most perishable things we could have chosen. But we track delivery of our orders by computer from the time they leave Cape Cod until they arrive at the customer's door. We always follow up with a phone call to ask 'Did you receive your package safely?' and to find out if the customer has any questions about preparation. We constantly get thank you notes from customers saying how much they appreciated the call and the service."

The staff of four at Clambake Celebrations take turns doing whatever needs to be done. Tucker, who is chairman of the company, often personally applies labels to mailings as large as 10,000. For larger mailings of 25,000 to 100,000, she uses a local lettershop.

The company also has their name as a URL, **www.clambake celebrations.com** as well as a website, www.clambake-to-go.com. The company's online presence has become an increasingly important factor in their success. Orders now come via their sites from established customers, reflecting the growing trend of traditional catalog users to shop over the Internet. The sites have also proved to be a good source for new business by generating qualified leads and new orders.

Tucker did meet some challenges along the way to her success. "We were undercapitalized to begin with," she says, "and it is almost impossible to raise money for working capital with banks. If you're a mail order company, they don't want to talk to you. Plus I've got two other strikes against me—I'm a woman and I have emphysema. But we've managed to hang in there on our own.

"Direct mail is a wonderful business for people who have special challenges. It's a friendly business for people with disabilities. It's the kind of business you can accomplish from any vantage point as long as you have a computer to maintain your database and track your orders and can oversee the quality of your operation. Yes, I have emphysema. Yes, I'm on oxygen. But my customers don't know that even when I'm speaking to them on the phone. I work very hard every single day at making this a successful business."

Characteristics of Success

Jo-Von Tucker is a perfect example of the kind of person who is successful in Direct Marketing. So are the other people we've profiled in this book, people like Dr. Jan Teitelbaum of Smith-Teitelbaum Chiropractic, Steve and Lori Leveen of Levenger, Carole Ziter of Sweet Energy, and Geoff and Lynn Wolf of Back in the Saddle. I see the success of Direct Marketing growing every day. On the hot and muggy July afternoon I came into my office to work on this chapter, I took a few minutes to look through my mail . . .

There was a catalog from Dell Computer. Michael Dell is one of the best representatives of a successful Direct Marketer in our industry today. He bought his first computer at the age of 15. As a freshman in college in 1983, Dell began buying surplus computers at cost and adding features such as more memory or disk drives. He then took out tiny, one-column ads in the local newspaper offering the computers at 10 to 15 percent off the retail price. By spring break, he was selling nearly $50,000 per month worth of PCs out of the trunk of his car. In 1995, his company's sales rose to $3.5 billion, and by 2001 sales were over $31.8 billion. Michael Dell's motto is, "If you think you have a good idea, *try it!*"

Even in high school, Dell was using Direct Marketing to earn extra money. Hired by the *Houston Post* to sell subscriptions, Dell thought that newlyweds would be good prospects. So he hired friends to go down to city hall and copy names and addresses from marriage licenses. He entered these into his computer, and sent personalized letters offering the newlyweds a free two-week subscription. Dell made $18,000 and bought himself a BMW at the age of 17.

When Dell started his computer business, he used customer service as his point of difference. Unlike other computer manufacturers, Dell offered a money-back guarantee, as well as next-day on-site service for his products. He also introduced a 24-hour toll-free hotline so that customers could speak directly to Dell technical experts. He used that hotline as a close connection to his customers—technicians would not only solve problems, they would find out what customers liked and didn't like about various products. As Dell told *Reader's Digest* in March of 1994, "My competitors were developing products and then telling customers what they should want, instead of finding out what the market really wanted and then developing products."

It is this kind of thinking that makes for successful Direct Marketers and keeps our industry developing and thriving. As I continued looking through my mail, I found a catalog from Lillian Vernon with a cover headline that shouts, "Summer Sale! 153 new items!" There was a mailing from Charles Schwab that explained international investing (and asked me to call their toll-free number for any questions I might have); a mailing from *American Health* magazine that said I had a chance at winning $5 million in their sweepstakes; a Home Shopping Club magazine; a flyer from a local restaurant telling me they had a special $19.95 dinner menu; a co-op mailing with many different business offers in a postcard package—and the list goes on.

Every day I receive a fat pile of mail like this, and it always puts a smile on my face. Why? Because all of this mail means that our industry is expanding. In every batch I receive there is always a new catalog, a new direct mail package or self-mailer. Some are from major companies, some are from Mom-and-Pop operations just beginning.

The interesting part of this business is that you can't tell from the look of the package or the size of the company who will be successful and who will not. I have seen major companies foray into Direct Marketing and then walk away after not achieving the success levels they want. And I have seen entrepreneurs who have little time and money make huge fortunes in this exciting industry.

So I have taken some time to examine hundreds of case studies to see if I can outline for you what the real secrets are to success in Direct Marketing. Many of these characteristics would make a person successful in any business. I have seen it happen time and again. People who attend my courses at New York University and at corporations and do really well at learning the principles are not always the ones who excel when they finish the course. Those who succeed have a quest for knowledge combined with an entrepreneurial spirit.

There was a young woman who recently took my course who seemingly had everything she needed to be a successful Direct Marketer. She did well in the course. She had a good product concept. She had the financing she needed. But she didn't have the spirit; she couldn't make the leap of faith one needs to take plans on paper and move them into reality. That same semester, I taught a construction worker, a high school dropout who didn't excel in class, but who took the knowledge he gained about Direct Marketing, applied it to the business he knew, and is doing phenomenally well.

After studying hundreds of success stories, my experience shows that people who end up with growing businesses of their own, or who move rapidly up the corporate ladder, have several common characteristics:

★ *Successful Direct Marketers remain committed.* Direct Marketing has always had a get-rich-quick reputation. You see ads every day that make you think you can make a million dollars in two weeks selling key chains for $1.98. But the only way to make Direct Marketing work is to have a plan and stick to it. This is not a business for anyone with a short attention span. This is a business built on trial and error; if you're not willing to start again when one idea doesn't pan out, you might as well quit before you begin. People who make a long-term commitment to selling their goods or services through Direct Marketing almost always succeed.

The media always focuses on overnight sensations such as Victoria Jackson, who has sold millions of dollars' worth of her cosmetics through infomercials and QVC. The truth is that she had many years of experience in her field before she ever went into Direct Marketing, which gave her a strong foundation for her business. Her product—makeup—is not unique, but it has a "point of difference": it is sold as the "no makeup" makeup. Jackson pioneered her first commercials on the air in 1989, yet every time you see her on TV she is testing something new—a new creative, a new color club (with automatic shipments every three months), or an alliance with Spiegel's catalog. In 1995, she made approximately $500,000 to $600,000 in one hour on QVC alone! The important part of her success is that she is committed. Dolly Parton, Estee Lauder, and others have tried infomercials with little success. Victoria Jackson is in the Direct Marketing business for the long term and it has paid off for her handsomely.

Of course, there are people who do get rich quick using Direct Marketing. A few years ago, someone invented a simple plastic device to help women style their hair in attractive ponytails and upsweeps. Hundreds of thousands of these were sold through Direct Marketing. This was the one-shot quick hit we all hear about. But the product was a fad; there was no plan for the long term development and growth of the business. Once the fad faded, there was no more source of income.

There are hundreds of stories like that one. The reason I have not included these in the book is that I feel these "make a million dollars in one year through direct mail" tales attract get-rich-quick kinds of people, who have little patience if their mailboxes aren't immediately filled with orders. In fact, such people come and go in and out of every industry trying to find the easy money.

For most of us, there is no easy money (unless you're lucky enough to have inherited it from a rich uncle). And in this industry, the people who succeed are committed to their company, or their products, or to making a business of their own grow to major proportions. It takes a great deal of patience to do this, because Direct Marketing can be a tricky business. One-month response rates may go through the roof, while the very next mailing is a dismal failure. You can't be discouraged by such ups and downs—you have to be willing and able to analyze the successes and learn from the failures so that the next program will be more uniformly successful and have the results you want.

Direct Marketing is a step-by-step business with myriad details to track. You simply must have a long-term commitment to succeed. You have to stick to your plan. Even if your first results are less than exciting, look for the pockets of opportunity—find the one list that pulled a good response, test some more enticing offers next time, add some color to your next piece, and you will see that it will pay off for you in the end.

★ *Successful Direct Marketers are budget-conscious.* I think Direct Marketing is fun. It's exciting to do a beautiful mailing piece, an eye-popping ad, or a catchy headline. But Direct Marketing is also an exacting science. I speak at Career Night every year at New York University. Recently, a woman in the audience raised her hand and asked if it was possible for her, a Wall Street CPA, to change her field and succeed in Direct Marketing. The answer is a resounding "YES!" People with accounting backgrounds, who know how to track money and make sure the finances are in line with promotion costs and profits, are the kind of people who do really well in this business.

If you're not this kind of person, you need to work with someone who is, because you have to watch every dollar and how it's working for you. Start by writing out your objectives, your strategies, and your tactics. Create a marketing plan as if you were going to show it to someone considering investing in your company. Itemize each step of the process and estimate costs before you begin. Realize that you won't get rich quick—in fact, you may even lose money at the beginning in order to make it back in the end.

★ *Successful Direct Marketers have something unique to sell.* When I mention this in the course I teach, I look out into the room at a sea of frightened faces. If you have one of those faces right now, bear with me. Many of the companies I consult with feel the same way. They tell me (with an air of defeat) that their product is much the same as their competitor's. I tell them, "That's okay. It only means you have to do some creative marketing."

Your product has to be unique even if it is virtually the same as someone else's. How is that possible? Think of the telephone companies who are all vying to sell you their services. The service is essentially the same—a long-distance call is a long-distance call. But look how smart these companies have been in differentiating themselves from one another. MCI created the concept of "Friends and Family" where you listed your calling circles and got a discount whenever you called those people. This brilliant strategy also meant that the consumer had to recruit the people in that circle. Sprint used the strategy of discounting all calls and developed a loyalty program whereby you saved your points for radios, movie tickets, and other products. AT&T offered True Savings, whereby you got larger and larger discounts depending on how much you spent in long-distance calls. They also positioned themselves as the carrier you can rely on, the one with the "true voice."

So what kind of product is unique? A product is unique when it fills the need or want of a particular target market. A while ago I went to visit the media buying agency Stephen L. Geller, Inc. We were talking about a product that was hitting the roof, a collapsible golf club. It was doing very well for a particular audience: someone who was a novice golfer and wanted to practice his or her swing in the office or at home. A seasoned golfer wouldn't be interested in such a product. It had a particular niche, and was doing very well in it.

If your product doesn't fill a need, it may have exclusive features. Lillian Vernon's catalog doesn't really contain many unique products. You can find the same items in other catalogs, or in local retail stores—with one BIG exception. Vernon learned early on that personalizing products—making it possible for people to put their names or initials on them—boosted their sales. The terry cloth robe she offers may be similar to one I can find in a dozen other places. However, put my initials on it—a big LKG—and you've got yourself a sale. I have bought all kinds of gifts from her over the years for that reason, everything from personalized pencils for my son to a cloth attaché case with initials on it for my friends and clients at holiday time. Lillian Vernon is an expert at taking a ho-hum product and adding an exclusive feature. Look for these kinds of features when you are deciding on a Direct Marketing product.

Where do you find a new product if you don't already have one to sell? Usually, people start with a product in mind they wish to market. But that's not always the case. Some people decide first that they want to go into Direct Marketing and then begin looking for a product to offer. There are many places to find products, beginning with the Yellow Pages of your phone directory. Look under "Merchandise," "Wholesalers," or "Product Importers."

There is a section in *The New York Times* called "Merchandise Offering." There, companies advertise everything from odd lot merchandise to imported goods at wholesale prices. Most large papers have similar sections. It would be a good idea to call a number of these suppliers to see what they are offering. You can also go to the library and use *Thomas' Register of Manufacturers*. You might find a company there that makes something you would like to offer in the mail.

Attend trade shows, such as the Merchandise Show and the Premium and Incentive Shows in New York (call your local branch of the Direct Marketing Association to find out when these types of shows will be in your area). If you don't find a product there that catches your eye, at least you'll walk away with dozens of inspirational ideas.

Another alternative is to develop your own product. Perhaps you have expertise in a craft, or are a terrific public speaker, or collect particular kinds of model railroad trains. You can put your expertise to work by making your own instructional audio—or videotapes, with the help of production professionals (whom you may be able to find at your local radio or television station). You can also share your expertise in a book or pamphlet. Starting small can help you test the waters for your first mail order venture.

Find a product that lends itself to repeat business or line extensions. It doesn't make financial sense to offer only one product and hope you will make a long-term profit from it. Once people have purchased from you, you have established a database. Don't waste it by having nothing else to offer.

★ *Successful Direct Marketers believe in their product.* It's very important that the product you select is one that you think is terrific. It's much easier to market a product you like than one you don't. Show your product to friends, relatives, and colleagues, and see if they endorse it too. This informal focus group will reinforce all the product's benefits (and alert you to its weaknesses) and help you market it correctly.

Believing in your product also helps you stick with your program when the initial test results are not good. This is exactly what happened at Boardroom, a Connecticut-based company that publishes newsletters and books.

One of the greatest copywriters in the business, Mel Martin, was asked to write a direct mail package to sell *The Book of Checklists*, a volume filled with ideas for the smart consumer, for the skilled traveler, and for getting the most out of your leisure time. Martin wrote a great package, but it didn't pull the results Boardroom was expecting. When Martin analyzed the package, he realized that the title of the book was not as good as it could be. The word "checklist" implied a chore for readers—some people might think this was a type of workbook. So Boardroom changed the title (keeping all the contents the same) to *The Great Book of Inside Knowledge*, a title that implies readers are receiving valuable information (which they are).

That lifted response somewhat, but not enough to carry the book long-term. So they changed the title again. This time Boardroom made the information included seem even more valuable by calling it *The Book of Secrets* (Figure 16.6) and it was a success. Mel Martin, taking advantage of the airfare wars that were going on at the time, created the winning copy line for the book's mailing piece: "How to get refund on non-refundable airline ticket. Page 105" (Figure 16.7). This headline was followed by other teasers, such as "Stop a headache by pressing a secret spot on your wrist. Page 204," and "Vitamin E is good for your sex life, right? *Wrong*. Page 188." The title change and the enticing fascinations made this an irresistible offer.

If Martin and the marketing people at Boardroom had walked away from the product in the beginning they would have lost out on a big success. The moral of the story is "Don't give up on a product you believe in." Examine all facets of a program when evaluating it. Try a new creative, a new offer, or a teaser on the envelope. When you've improved the creative, look at the product again. Perhaps there are minor adjustments you can make—as small as the title of a book—that can turn a failure into a success. If you believe in it enough, you can make it work.

When I worked for the Meredith Corporation, we marketed a product call the *Better Homes and Gardens* Recipe Cards. We included free sample cards in the direct mail package. At first, we featured a card that had recipes for an entire meal, thinking it

Figure 16.6
The two books contain the same information. When the title was changed from
The Great Book of Inside Knowledge to *The Book of Secrets*, sales increased dramatically.

gave prospects the most value. But it wasn't until we changed the
package and featured the card with a recipe for strawberry shortcake
that we produced a real winner!

★ *Successful Direct Marketers are abnormal.* Do something special. Be
more than creative; people who have succeeded in Direct Marketing have made it with innovative thinking, with the unusual, the
weird, the extraordinary. Your product doesn't have to be the only
one of its kind, but your marketing ideas must be unique. Find a
niche for your company and your ideas. Turn your brain inside out
and find a way to make your company extraordinary too.

Figure 16.7

The great copywriter Mel Martin created "fascinations"—teasers that make customers so curious they almost have to buy the product.

★ *Successful Direct Marketers are cockeyed optimists.* The only way Direct Marketing will work is if you truly believe in what you're selling. If you're the kind of person who gives in and gives up, Direct Marketing is not for you. You must believe that through the process of testing and retesting you'll find the formula that will make your product sell. That means caring enough about what you're doing to make sure that the product is the best it can be, that the packaging reflects well on you and your company, and that you treat your customers with care and respect.

You Are Not Alone...

I hope you could tell while reading this book that I love Direct Marketing. My goal is not only to impart the nuts and bolts of the business to you, but to get you as excited about this industry as I am. However, I realize that if you're just starting out, whether you're in a large company or going out on your own, it can be a pretty scary prospect. I want you to use this book as a reference guide. I also want you to know that I am here for you. If you need more information, write to me and if I can't supply the answers, I'll help you find them. If you're starting a new program and you want some feedback, put it in writing and I'll be glad to make comments. Cut out the last page of this book, send it in with your questions, or fax it, and I will respond as quickly as I can. For my quickest response, email me at loisgeller@loisgeller.com

I believe in this business, and I believe that you can be successful if you are willing to make that commitment, to take that chance, to work hard and get excited about what you do. I want this industry to flourish, and I want you to flourish with it! Good luck!

Glossary

Active Buyer. A buyer who has purchased something from a mail order company in the last year.

Address Correction Requested. When this phrase is been printed on the upper left-hand corner of the direct mail envelope, it is telling the post office to provide a new address if the person no longer lives at the address indicated. There is a charge for this service, and it is a good way to update your mailing list.

Back End Costs. Costs connected with doing all the jobs necessary after an order is received (fulfillment, shipping, postage, etc.).

Banner Ad. This is an advertisement placed on a website either above, below or on the sides of the Web site's main content and is linked to the advertiser's own Web site.

Benefits. All the reasons a person should buy a product so it will enhance his or her personal life, career, well-being.

Bind-in card. A card that is bound into a publication (usually a magazine) with a reply card or order form. It is usually perforated for easy removal. Bind-in cards are designed to adhere to post office standards of size, so they can be mailed.

Bleed. This term refers to reproducing an illustration or photograph so that it covers the entire page, leaving no margin. An ad that runs off one, two, three, or four sides of the page is called a bleed ad, and most publications charge more for its use, as the ad is larger than if it had a margin around it.

Bookmark. This allows an Internet user to mark a document or a specific place in a document for later retrieval. Most Web browsers include a bookmarking feature that lets you save the address (URL) of a Web page so that you can easily go back to the page at a later date.

Bounce-back. A second promotion included in a shipment that offers the buyer a chance to buy another product from the same company. A bounce-back can be a single offer or an entire catalog.

Broadside. A very large brochure that is folded many times to fit into a direct mail envelope. It is used when the product offered needs large photographs and type to convey the message. You might use a broadside, for instance, to show twenty volumes of an encyclopedia set and a beautiful photograph of each volume.

Brochure. A flyer, broadside, or bound printed piece included in your direct mail package. This piece usually highlights a product and offer, and should include all the benefits of the product.

Bulk Mail. Large quantities of direct mail (packages, catalogs, self-mailers) that are sorted before going to the post office. Bulk mail allows the mailer to qualify for discounts.

Call-Out. A word, phrase, or sentence that calls attention to or explains a particular part of an illustration or photograph. It points, via a straight line, to the feature it is describing.

Cheshire Label. A mailing label that is imprinted by the computer and cut (by a Cheshire machine) into individual labels on a long sheet. They are then glued to the direct mail packages by machine at the lettershop. Cheshire labels are less expensive than pressure-sensitive labels, which you can peel off and stick onto envelopes.

Cleaning. List cleaning refers to keeping the list as up to date as possible by eliminating duplicate names and incorporating changes of address.

Click. The action of a user pressing the mouse button, generally to cause an action on a computer.

Clickstream. This is a record of a user's activity on the Internet, including every website and every page of every website that the user visits, how long the user was on a page or site, in what order the pages were visited, any newsgroups that the user participates in and even the email addresses of mail that the user sends and receives.

Compiled List. A list of names and addresses that are created specifically to be used by Direct Marketers. The names are usually taken from directories, census information, and registration files. Compiled lists have specific target markets—for instance, all pediatricians, school principals, or car owners.

Comp Layout. This phrase is short for comprehensive layout. A comprehensive layout can be done for a whole direct mail package, a catalog, or an advertisement. It shows the placement of the photographs and type, in correct proportions, and allows changes to be made before costly separations and plates are made.

Computer Service Bureau. A service that provides a variety of mailing services such as list maintenance, merge/purge, list rental, subscription fulfillment, and database manipulation. Since this is the only type of work computer service bureaus do, they can usually do it more economically than a company could do in-house.

Continuity Program. A continuity program is one where similar items are sold to a customer over time. Sometimes, a series of books are sold this way, or recipe cards, or a collection of porcelain thimbles. A negative option continuity program means customers will continue to receive the products until they say they don't want to continue the program. A positive option continuity means customers send in a card when they want the next shipment. Negative option continuities usually keep customers in a program longer than positive option continuities.

Cookie. A "Cookie" refers to small data files written to your hard drive by some websites when you view them in your browser. The main purpose of cookies is to identify users and possibly prepare customized Web pages for them.

Cost Per Inquiry. Some two-step campaigns require prospects to inquire about a product first, and then be converted to a sale. Once you add up total costs and divide by the number of inquiries received, you then need to figure out how many inquiries actually converted to sales. You need to know the cost per inquiry so that you can compare costs among the various media you may be using.

Cost Per Order. The sum of all the production costs (creative, printing, lettershop, postage, and so on) divided by the total number of orders received. This ratio enables a marketer to evaluate how profitable a promotion is by comparing the cost per order for various marketing efforts.

Creative. Sometimes a shortened form of "creative strategy," creative refers to the comprehensive layout of an advertisement, direct mail campaign, or catalog.

Creative Brief. The creative brief is the input given to the creative team to help them develop the creative for a particular target market. A brief usually includes the background of the product, its features and benefits, a description of the target market, and the objectives of the campaign. It can also include the competition, budget parameters, and anything else that is important for the creative team to know.

Database. A database is a collection of information, stored in a computer, which can be readily accessed as needed. The type of information you might want to retrieve (besides basic name and address) includes your most recent customers, customers who have bought from you most frequently, customers who have children, customers who own homes, etc.

Data Mining. This term pertains to the process of determining hidden patterns in data. For example, data mining software can help retail companies find customers with common interests. True data mining software actually uncovers previously unknown relationships among the data.

Decoy. A name and address that is placed on a list by its owners to make sure that the rented list is used only once, by the correct mailer, and with the approved direct mail package.

Demographics. Statistics about customers that refer to external life patterns—such as age, sex, income level, education, size of family.

Dummy. A dummy is a rough layout that can consist of blank pages that show the printer how the finished product is to be constructed, folded, perforated.

Dupe. The shortened form of duplicate, which in Direct Marketing also refers to a name repeated on a list.

E-commerce. Transaction-based online interaction. Examples of E-commerce include: online stores, business-to-business trading websites and online auctions.

Email. This stands for "electronic mail." Email is the exchange of text and HTML messages over the Internet.

Email address. A name that identifies an electronic post office box on a network where email can be sent. On the Internet, all email addresses have the form: <name>@<domain name>. For example, loisgeller@masongeller.com

Envelope Stuffer. An additional offer that is enclosed in the monthly billing statement. It can be a direct mail insert with an order form, or it can be informative literature or an announcement of some kind. Sometimes it is called a "bounce-back."

Features.   The particular factual attributes of a product that make it interesting to prospects such as size, color, shape.

Frequency.   The average number of times an advertisement is run or a commercial is viewed by a person or household during a specific period of time (usually a few weeks). Frequency, together with reach (the number of different households exposed to your message), determines what percentage of people are being reached and how often they are seeing the message. Frequency can also refer to the number of times a particular customer orders from your company.

Friend of a Friend.   Also known as member get a member, this is a technique that offers current customers an incentive to refer new customers to a company, product, or service.

Front End Costs.   These are costs that are incurred at the beginning of a promotion, which would include direct mail costs, advertising, promotion and creation of a commercial.

FSI.   Free-standing Insert, or an advertisement, booklet, catalog or a brochure that is inserted in a newspaper (usually the Sunday edition). The newspaper charges a fee for inserting an FSI, usually a cost per thousand.

Fulfillment.   Fulfillment is the back end of a Direct Marketing campaign, or all the activities that go on once the customer's order is received: opening orders, entering the information for that order into the computer, preparing a label or invoice (or both), processing payments, selecting appropriate merchandise to fill the order, and reporting the necessary information to analyze the program.

Hit.   The retrieval of any item, like a page or a graphic, from a Web site. For example, when a visitor calls up a Web page with two graphics, that's three hits, one for the page and two for the graphics. For this reason, hits often aren't a good indication of Web traffic. See page view.

Hotline Buyers.   Customers who have recently purchased something or inquired about a service, usually in the last three months.

House File.   An internal list that includes customer information. It can be formatted as a marketing database or a simple list of customers and transactions.

HTML.   This stands for *Hypertext Markup Language*. It is the formatting codes that are used to layout a page to be published on the World Wide Web.

HTTP.   This stands for Hypertext Transfer Protocol, the underlying protocol used by the World Wide Web. The other main standard that controls how the World Wide Web works is HTML, which covers how Web pages are formatted and displayed.

Hyperlink.   An underlined element of a document or page that, when clicked, will take you to another screen or page. Hyperlinks contain HTML-coded references that point to other Web pages.

Indicia.   An indication on a direct mail piece that postage has been paid by the mailer. It is used instead of a postage stamp or meter strip. It includes a permit number, the permit holder's company name, and the class of mail, and is usually imprinted on the upper right-hand corner of the mailing piece.

Inquiry.   Usually a request for information, it is sometimes a way for Direct Marketers to generate names of prospects they can then convert to buyers. These inquiries then become leads for follow-up mailings or sales calls.

Involvement Device.   Sometimes called an action device, the recipient is asked to check off "yes," "no," or "maybe" on the order form, or to peel off a stamp or sticker and move it from the mailing piece to the order form. It is a device used in Direct Marketing to get the prospect actively involved with a mailing.

Johnson Box.   A graphic device used to highlight a particular message or offer in a sales letter of a direct mail package. It is placed above the salutation, and it used to be made of asterisks forming the box. Now it is sometimes printed to look as if it were handwritten.

JPEG.   This stands for *Joint Photographic Experts Group* and it refers to an image file format commonly used for online graphics and ad banners.

Key Code.   See Source Code.

Layout.   A sketch of what a marketing piece will look like after it is printed. It shows where the copy will be and where photographs or illustrations will appear, as well as the typefaces that will be used. Layouts can be shown at various phases of a particular job. A writer's roughs or the rough layout is usually a sketch of how the creative team envisions the piece. A finished layout is more detailed and may even include some photography in place. A comprehensive layout shows exactly how the finished piece will look. Sometimes layouts are produced on computer and sometimes they are rendered by hand.

Lettershop.   Sometimes called a mailing house, this facility does all the preparation necessary to get direct mail into the post office and into the homes (or businesses) of recipients, including list and label preparation, personalization, as well as stuffing, addressing, collating and sorting envelopes.

Lift Letter.   Once called the publisher's letter, this component of a direct mail package is meant to lift response by capturing those prospects who might need a little more encouragement to purchase a product. It usually stresses one major selling point. The piece is (usually) folded and on the outside it may say, "Open this letter if you have decided not to order." It is usually a cost-effective piece in a mailing, as it is relatively inexpensive to include and often does lift the response of a mailing.

List.   Names and addresses of individuals and businesses having a specific interest or purchase history. There are three kinds of lists: in-house, direct response, and compiled.

List Broker.   A specialist who researches appropriate lists for mailing, recommends lists to the mailer, gets the lists to the lettershop on time for the mailing, and following the mailing does an evaluation of the lists' performance.

List Cleaning.   See Cleaning.

List Manager.   A person or company who works for the list owner and is responsible for marketing the list to list users and list brokers. The manager is also responsible for the maintenance of the list, all clearances necessary before the mail date, record keeping, and billing. The list manager may also be the broker.

List Rental.   An agreement, frequently handled by a broker, between a list owner and a list user whereby the owner provides names and addresses to the mailer on a one-time basis. The mailer pays the owner at an agreed-upon rate per thousand names. Most lists are delivered to the mailer's lettershop on disk or Cheshire labels.

Loyalty Program.   A program designed to make customers want to patronize a particular company more frequently than they may have. One of the most familiar loyalty programs is the frequent flyer plan.

Mailing House.   See Lettershop.

Mail Order Buyer.   One who purchases a product or service in the mail. That product may be purchased as a result of a direct response commercial, print advertisement, direct mail package (email solicitation or online offer).

Mail Preference Service.   A service provided by the Direct Marketing Association for consumers who wish to have their names deleted from mailing lists. This file is available as a purge file, on a subscription basis.

Merge/Purge.   A computer process that combines two or more lists to eliminate duplicates and undesirable names in order to provide the best list for a promotion.

Model.   A computer system comprised of mathematical formulas to help Direct Marketers locate their best prospects or forecast sales. Sometimes programmers examine a company's best customers, define criteria, and then construct a model to find outside lists similar to that house file.

Multiple Buyer.   A person on your house list who has purchased from you two or more times.

Negative Option.   See Continuity Program.

Nixie.   Undeliverable mailing pieces returned to the sender because they have incorrect or incomplete names or addresses.

Nth Name Selection.   A process to select a representative portion of a large list that ensures a renter won't be limited to names from one or part of the alphabet, or from certain zip codes. It selects, for instance, every tenth name in the file, or every twentieth name.

Offer.   A unique promotion put to the consumer prior to the consumer's consent to buy. A newspaper offer might be five daily issues for $2 ($1 off the newsstand price). The offer becomes a contract when the completed order form is returned to the vendor.

Offer Card.   A response device, soliciting purchases through the mail, which customers fill out and mail to order merchandise or to receive information.

Offer Test.   A test in a Direct Marketing promotion that varies a price or offer element. It is important in a Direct Marketing test to change only one portion of a package, so that any differences in the response rate of the test package can be measured against the control.

Opt-in Email.   Email communication which only happens if the recipient has specifically requested it from the particular source.

Opt-out.   An option to unsubscribe from receiving email solicitations from an online marketer, online magazine or any other source. This area is becoming increasingly regulated and providing an opt-out hyperlink (see hyperlink) in any Direct Marketing email has become standard practice.

Order Form.   A document containing all pertinent information required to complete the purchasing transaction. The order form is usually precoded for tracking the source of the order.

Package.   The sum of all components in a direct mail promotion (outer envelope, business reply envelope, letter, inserts, order form, lift letter, etc.)

Package Insert.   See Bounce-back.

Page Impression. This refers to the exact number of times a specific website has been accessed or viewed by a user. A page impression acts as a counter for Web pages, informing site owners how many times their sites were visited. Page impressions are also referred to as hits.

Per Inquiry Ad. An arrangement made with a magazine or newspaper whereby you pay them an agreed-upon amount per inquiry you receive in response to that ad.

Permission email. Email which is only sent to users who select to receive them or opt-in. See Opt-in.

Per Order Inquiry. An arrangement made with a magazine or newspaper whereby you pay them an agreed-upon amount per order you receive in response to that ad.

Personalization. The method of printing an individual's name and/or address or other personal information about that customer or prospect on the direct mail package. This can include any component of the package, from the order form to the letter to user-specific information within a catalog.

Polybag. Clear polyethylene wrap covering some direct mail packages, magazines or card decks.

Positive Option. See Continuity Program.

Premium. An award given away or sold at a nominal price to the consumer to promote the sale of merchandise. Premiums are often items which complement the product offered for sale, e.g., bookends to promote the sale of books.

Prime Time. Broadcast periods which command high advertising rates because of the large viewing or listening audience. Prime time for television is 8:00 P.M. to 11:00 P.M., Monday through Saturday.

Projection. Taking data from a test sample and extending it to a total population or universe.

Promotion Partners. Two or more companies who get together to promote themselves with a unique offer.

Public Television. Programming without advertising that is broadcast through the support of government and corporate funding and direct donations from the pubic.

Publisher's Letter. See Lift Letter.

Purchase History. A record of all the purchases a customer has made over a period of time.

Purge. The process by which a computer eliminates duplicates or unwanted names and addresses among several lists.

Psychographics. Particular personality characteristics and attitudes that affect a person's overall lifestyle and purchasing behavior.

Qualified Prospect. A prospect who has met some criteria to demonstrate that he or she is likely to become a customer in the future. The prospect may have shown interest in the product or service (by responding to an advertisement or a direct mail campaign), have the income level necessary to pay for the product, or have the authority to make the purchasing decision.

Rate Card. A brochure or single sheet of paper that tells the cost of advertising in a particular medium. A magazine rate card, for instance, will give you the cost of various size ads, black and white versus color, closing dates for publication, special issues, and discount plans.

Renewal Series.   A series of letters encouraging customers to renew their subscriptions.

Response Rate.   The gross responses received from a Direct Marketing program as a percentage of the total number of direct mail pieces sent or contacts that were made with readers or television viewers. A response can be either an order or an inquiry which can be coverted to an order.

Roll Out.   The mailing to a full list after a portion of that list has tested well.

Seasonality.   A pattern in a marketing program in which response shows variation with the changes of season. Every product should be tested to see if there are certain months which will outperform others.

Second Class.   In the postal rate system, this is the level of mail service that covers magazines and newspapers published at specific intervals of times (monthly, bimonthly, quarterly) and on a regular basis.

Sectional Center.   Sometimes referred to as SCF (Sectional Center Facility), this is a U.S. Postal Service mail-handling distribution unit that serves a group of post offices whose zip codes all begin with the same first three digits.

Self-mailer.   A self-contained direct mail piece, usually including a reply form, that is mailed without an envelope.

Sheet-Fed.   A printing process in which the paper is fed into the press in single sheets instead of paper rolls, usually used when there are low-volume print runs.

Shopping Cart.   A shopping cart is the online interface that allows consumers to select merchandise; review what they have selected; make necessary modifications or additions; and purchase the merchandise.

SIC Codes.   Standard Industrial Classification is the U.S. government's four-digit code for categorizing various industries. SIC Codes are used by Direct Marketing companies to identify particular industrial prospects.

Solo Mailing.   A mailing to promote a single product or service, which usually consists of a letter, a brochure, and a reply device enclosed in an outer envelope.

Source Code.   A series of numbers or an alphanumeric code placed on an order form, coupon, or other response mechanism. Each offer has its own code so that marketers can determine and compare the responses.

Space Ad.   An advertisement in a print medium such as a newspaper or magazine. This space is sold to advertisers on the basis of the size of the ad, the position of the ad, and the circulation of the publication.

SPAM.   Email which is unsolicited and sent for a commercial purpose.

Splash Page.   The page of a website that the user sees first before being given the option to continue to the main content of the site. Splash pages are used to promote a company, service or product, or are used to inform the user of what kind of software or browser is necessary in order to view the rest of the site's pages. Often a splash page will consist of animated graphics and sounds that entice the user into exploring the rest of the website.

Split Run.   A technique used to test the effectiveness of two creatives for the same product by placing the creatives in different copies of the same publication. Not all publications offer split runs to their advertisers.

Spread.   An ad that appears on two facing pages in a magazine or newspaper. The direct response order form usually appears on the bottom of the right-hand page, or as a bind-in response card between the two pages.

Standby Rate.   A discounted rate for placing an advertisement in a publication on a standby basis. As soon as there is space available (within an agreed-upon prescribed time limit), the magazine or newspaper will run the ad.

Statement Stuffer.   A direct response piece, enclosed with a customer's account statement, that usually offers a single product and includes an order form.

Teaser.   An advertisement or promotion that is planned to build excitement or curiosity about a product that will be offered in a later campaign. Also copy in a direct mail program, often used on the outer envelope, to entice the prospect to open the envelope and read the package.

Telemarketing.   Use of the telephone as an interactive medium for promoting a product (outbound telemarketing) or promotion response (inbound telemarketing).

Test.   The evaluation phase of a program where one or more elements of a program are introduced to a relatively small audience. All facets of a program are then evaluated and the most successful are rolled out to a larger audience. In a direct mail test, the elements usually tested are product, offer, list, and creative.

Testimonial.   Often used in Direct Marketing copy to add credibility to your promotion, a testimonial is a statement made by a customer who is satisfied with a product or service. This statement may be made by a public figure or any satisfied customer.

Test Panel.   A sample group taken from a full list of people to test out a specific creative approach or a new offer.

Third Class.   The U.S. Postal Service's designation for bulk mail, including direct mail packages and catalogs that weigh less than one pound. Special discounted rates are permitted if mailings meet certain presort requirements and quantity levels. A third-class permit is required.

Tie-in Mailing.   A cooperative mailing done by two or more partners, connected by a particular theme.

Tip-on.   A product sample, reply form, or coupon that is glued to a printed piece.

Toll-Free Number.   Telephone service that is billed directly to the receiver with no costs incurred by the caller.

Typeface.   A particular style of alphabetical letters, numbers, and symbols used in the design of advertising and Direct Marketing packages.

Unique Visitor.   This refers to a person who visits a Web site more than once within a specified period of time. Software that tracks and counts Web site traffic can distinguish between visitors who only visit the site once and *unique visitors* who return to the site.

Universe.   The total population or market for a particular product. In Direct Marketing, the universe is the total number of names on all the lists available for that product.

Web Press.   A press that prints on a continuous roll of paper, rather than individual sheets. Web paper is less expensive, and these presses are suitable for large-volume, high-speed printing.

Website.   A series of linked pages which might function in a variety of ways, such as an online store, an association with online resources, a service organization or a family website.

White Mail.   Incoming unsolicited mail that is not on the form sent out by the Direct Marketer, and is usually in the customer's own envelope, which contains complaints, address changes, inquiries, or special order instructions.

Window Envelope.   An envelope with one or more openings through which the name and address of the recipient shows, plus perhaps parts of the creative.

Wrapper.   A cover, wrapped around a catalog or magazine, that is used to personalize a message to a particular group of customers.

Zip Code.   ZIP is an abbreviation for Zoning Improvement Plan, and is a way for the U.S. Postal Service to identify where a particular piece of mail is going. It was designed for easier sorting and dispatching, and was expanded from the original five-digit code to Zip +4, or nine digits in total.

Zip Code Analysis.   A way of analyzing how many orders come from particular zip codes so that Direct Marketers can track their best and worst prospects geographically.

Direct Marketing
Resource Directory

Industry Publications

Catalog Age
P.O. Box 10757
Riverton, NJ 08076-0757
(800) 441-0294 or
(888) 892-3613
www.primedediabusiness.com

Direct
P.O. Box 10756
Riverton, NJ 08076-0756
(888) 892-3613 or
(888) 892-361
www.primediabusiness.com

DM News
PO Box 2037
Skokie, IL 60076
(847) 588-0675
www.dmnews.com

1-to-1 Magazine
Merritt on the River
20 Glover Ave.
Norwalk, CT 06850
(203) 642-5121
www.1to1.com

Target Marketing
North American Publishing Co
401 N. Broad Street
Philadelphia, PA 19108
(800) 777-8074
www.targetonline.com

Other industry publications available for a fee include:

Advertising Age
Crain Communications
711 Third Avenue
New York, NY 10017-4036
(212) 210-0100
www.adage.com

Mail Order Digest
National Mail Order
  Association, LLC
2807 Polk St. NE
Minneapolis MN 55418-2954
(612) 788-1673
www.mailorderdigest.com

Potentials Magazine
VNU Business Media
50 S. Ninth St.
Minneapolis, MN 55402
(800) 328-4329
www.potentialsmag.com

Response
Division of Advanstar
  Communications
201 Sandpointe Ave.,
  Suite 600
Santa Ana, CA 92707-5761
(800) 854-3112 or
(714) 513-8400
www.responsemag.com

Who's Mailing What!
North American Publishing Co
401 N. Broad Street
Philadelphia, PA 19108
(800) 777-8074
www.napco.com/
  dmcenter.html

Directories

Direct Marketing Market
  Place
National Register Publishing
121 Chanlon Road
New Providence, NJ 07974
(800) 473-7020
www.nationalregisterpub.com

Shop At Home/Belcaro Group
7100 East Belleview Avenue,
#305
Greenwood Village, CO 80111
(303) 843-0302
www.shopathome.com

BestCatalogStores.com
c/o Publisher Inquiry Services,
Inc.
951 Broken Sound Parkway
NW
P.O. Box 3099
Boca Raton, FL 33431-0999
(800) 555-4053
www.bestcatalogstores.com

Direct Marketing Association

Another essential resource is
the Direct Marketing
Association. You might want
to consider membership, as it
offers informative workshops,
and can help direct you to
vendors you may need. The
DMA library also houses all
the ECHO Award winners. In
it you can examine some of
the most successful Direct
Marketing programs that have
been created over the years.

Direct Marketing Association,
Inc.
1120 Avenue of the Americas
New York, NY 10036-6700
(212) 768-7277
www.the-dma.org

Note: The following resource
lists have been compiled from
various sources. We have tried
to include companies from
each state whenever possible.
The inclusion of companies
on these lists does not imply
endorsement, since I have not
personally dealt with all of
them. Be sure to ask to ask to
see samples and check
references before you do
business with any company for
the first time.

List Brokers

Arizona
A.A.A. BEST Mailing List Inc.
7505 East Tanque Verde Road
Tuscon, AZ 85715
(800) 692-2378
www.bestmailing.com
Full-service mailing list specialist

Arkansas
Acxiom Corp.
301 Industrial Blvd.
Conway, AK 72032
(501) 342-6318
www.axciom.com
Business and consumer lists

California
Names in the News California
Inc.
1300 Clay Street, 11th Floor
Oakland, CA 94612
(415) 777-1171
www.nincal.com
*Mail list brokers, managers, and
consultants*

Experian
475 Anton Blvd.
Costa Mesa, CA 92626
(714) 385-7000
www.experian.com
*List rental, merge/purge, and
business credit reports*

Colorado
Mailgraphics
1668 Valtec Lane, Suite F
Boulder, CO 80301
(303) 449-4053
www.mailgraphics.com

R.J. Persson Enterprises, Inc.
401 Main Street North
Entrance
P.O. Box 2069
Montrose CO 81402
(970) 249-6000
www.rjperrson.com
*Specializes in building databases
of work-at-home job seekers*

Connecticut
Direct Media Group
200 Pemberwick Road
Greenwich, CT 06830
(203) 532-1000
www.directmedia.com
*Mail order and subscription lists
in all markets; full-service
Direct Marketing, list brokers,
and managers*

Donnelly Marketing
One American Lane
Greenwich, CT 06831
(203) 552-6400
(800) 711-4913
www.donnellymarketing.com
*Database marketing services,
consumer databases,
enhancement services*

District of Columbia
Columbia Books
1212 New York Ave. NW,
Suite 330
Washington, DC 20005
(888) 800-2800
www.columbiabooks.com
*Provides mail lists and
directories*

List America Inc.
1202 Potomac Street, NW
Washington, DC 20007
(202) 298-9206
www.marketdevelopment.org
*List brokerage, management and
compilation*

Florida
Professional Direct Marketing
& Mailing Lists Incorporated
2600 N Military Trail,
Suite 205
Boca Raton, FL 33431
(561) 241-4414
www.professional-direct.com
*List compilers specializing in
executive, professional, affluent
markets*

Georgia
Alpha List Marketing
P.O. Box 921293
Norcross, GA 30010
(800) 822-2902

Illinois
Alan Drey Companies
333 N. Michigan Ave.
Chicago IL 60601
(312) 346-7453
www.alendrey.com
*List brokerage firm specializing
in analytical services in addition
to the traditional services
supplied by list professionals*

Rubin Response
111 Plaza Drive
Schaumberg, IL 60173
(847) 619-9800
www.rubinresponse.com
*List broker and manager
specializing in direct response,
consumer and business-to-
business lists*

Indiana
Harris Marketing
   Incorporated Office
6100 N Keystone Ave.
Indianapolis, IN 46220
(317) 251-9729
www.listsandmail.com
Database of mailing lists

Kentucky
Gannett Direct Marketing
   Service
3400 Robards Ct.
Louisville, KY. 40218
(502) 454-6660
*Business-to-business and
residential lists*

Louisiana
Impact Mail & Printing
3720 Hessmer Avenue
Metarie, LA 70002
(504) 455-3364

Massachusetts
Direct Marketing Mailing Lists
Quinlan Publishing group
23 Drydock Avenue
Boston, MA 02210
(617) 542-0048
www.quinlan.com
*Personnel, labor, real estate,
legal and safety lists*

Harvard Professional Lists Inc.
955 Massachusetts Avenue,
   #306
Cambridge, MA 02139
(617) 661-0617
List owners and brokers

PCS List & Information
   Technologies
39 Cross St.
Peabody, MA 01960-1628
(800) 532-5478
www.pclist.com
*Full-service list compiler, broker,
and manager of business-to-
business, consumer, accounting,
banking, legal, medical, and
publishing lists*

Michigan
R.L. Polk & Co.
26955 Northwestern Hwy.
Southfield, MI 48034
(248) 728-7000
www.polk.com
*Consumer list database of over
90 million households*

Minnesota
L90 Direct
7616 Currell Blvd., Suite 200
Woodbury, MN 55125
(651) 264-3053
www.L90.com

Nebraska
ACTON International Ltd.
3401 NW 39th St
Lincoln, NE 68524
(402) 470-2909
www.acton.com
List management

Lortz Direct Marketing Inc.
13936 Gold Circle
Omaha NE 68144-2359
(800) 366-7686
www.lortzdirect.com
*Direct response list brokers,
agency and consultants*

William Neil Associates
1 Cabela Drive
Suite 2114
Sidney, NE 69160
(800) 860-2547
www.william-neil.com

New Hampshire
Millard Group Inc.
Ten Vose Farm Road
P.O. Box 890
Peterborough, NH 03458
(603) 924-9262
www.millard.com
*Mailing list broker, manager and
consultant*

New Jersey
American List Counsel, Inc.
4300 US Hwy. 1
Princeton NJ 08543
(609) 580-2500
www.amlist.com
*Compiler, broker and manager
of business and consumer lists*

Database America Lists
470 Chestnut Ridge Rd.
Woodcliff Lake, NJ 07677
(201) 476-2300
www.infousa.com
*Consumer and business list
compiler*

Dun & Bradstreet
   Information Services,
   North America
One Diamond Hill Road
Murray Hill, NJ 07974
(908) 665-5100
www.dnb.com

New York
Hugo Dunhill Mailing Lists, Inc.
30 E. 33rd St.
New York, NY 10016-5337
(800) 223-6454
www.hdml.com
Compiling of mailing lists

Leon Henry, Inc.
455 Central Ave.
Scarsdale, NY 10583
(914) 723-3176
www.leonhenryinc.com
Mail list brokerage

List Technology Systems
Group
1001 Avenue of the Americas
New York, NY 10018
(212) 719-1875
www.ltsg.com
*List management and list
brokerage*

Rickard List Marketing
88 Duryea Road, Suite 204
Mellville, NY 11747
(631) 249-8710
www.rickardlist.com
*List management and list
brokerage*

Walter Karl
1 Bluehill Plaza
Pearl River, NY 10965
(845) 620-0700
www.walterkarl.com
*List management and list
brokerage*

North Carolina
NC Direct Marketing
1304 Broad Street
Durham, NC 27705
(919) 382-9383

Ohio
Matt Brown & Associates, Inc.
2769 Orchard Run Road
Dayton, OH 45449
(937) 434-3949
www.mbalists.com
*List brokerage and management,
merge/purge, list enhancement
consulting*

Oklahoma
Zed Marketing Group
416 Autumnwood Ct.
Edmond OK 73003
(405) 348-8145
www.zedmarketinggroup.com
*List management and brokerage
services, specializing in catalogs
and package inserts*

Pennsylvania
North American Publishing Co.
401 North Broad Street
Philadelphia, PA 19108
(215) 238-5300
www.napco.com
*Business-to-business consumer
lists*

South Carolina
Evergreen Marketing
100 Watersedge
Shelter Cove Marina
Hiltonhead Island, SC 29928
(843) 686-2244
Mail list broker

Texas
Allmedia Incorporated
17060 Dallas Pkwy.
Dallas, TX 75248
(972) 818-4060
www.allmediainc.com
*Broker and manager for mailing
lists, alternate media, and
computer services worldwide*

Virginia
Affinity Marketing Group
9663 Main St., Suite C
Fairfax, VA 22031
(703) 978-4927
*List brokerage and marketing
services*

Wisconsin
JHL Mail Marketing Inc.
3100 Borham Avenue
Stevens Point, WI 54481
(715) 341-0581
www.jhl.com
*Full-service lettershop and data-
processing services, list broker
and management service*

Canada
WATTS List Brokerage Ltd.
455 Horner Avenue
Toronto, Ontario M8W 4W9
(416) 503-4000
www.wattsgroup.com
Mailing list broker

Computer Service Bureaus

Arizona
American Computer Group
420 S Smith Rd.
Tempe, AZ. 85281
(480) 858-9000
www.mailorder.com or
www.whitehat.com
*Computer service and data
processing*

Axciom
301 Industrial Blvd.
P.O. Box 2000
Conway, AZ 72033
(501) 342-3600
www.axciom.com
*Consumer and business data
enhancement, consumer and
business prospect names, and
telephone and address matching*

California
Infomat
2360 Plaza Del Amo Suite105
Torrance, CA 90501
(310) 212-5944
www.directmarketingcenter.net
*Mailing list brokerage and
management firm*

Direct List Technology
Incorporated
1950 W Corporate Way
Anaheim, CA 92801
(714) 772-3282
www.directlist.com
*Computer services, data
processing, list & subscription
fulfillment companies*

Connecticut
Blumenfield Marketing
Incorporated
30 Academy St.
Norwalk, CT 06850
(203) 854-6737
*Computer services, data
processing, list & subscription
fulfillment companies*

Walter Karl
One American Lane
Greenwich, CT 06831
(203) 552-6800
www.walterkarl.com
*Merge/purge, list maintenance,
list rental fulfillment, zip
verification, nixie processing*

Colorado
EDS
833 W. South Boulder Road
Louisville, CO 80027
(303) 666-7000
www.eds.com
*Provider of integrated Direct
Marketing services including
merge/purge, inbound and
outbound telemarketing and
database management*

Florida
Time Customer Service
    Incorporated
1 N Dale Mabry Hwy,
    Suite 150
Tampa, FL 33609
(813) 878-6100
*Subscription fulfillment for
magazines*

Georgia
Experian
5909 Peachtree Dunwoody Rd.
Atlanta, GA 30328
(678) 731-1000
www.experian.com
Marketing analysis

Gates Marketing
3080 McCall Dr.
Atlanta, GA. 30340
(770) 455-9662
www.gatesmarketing.com
*Mail services, data processing
and printing*

Illinois
Creative Automation
    Company
220 Fenci Lane
Hillside, IL 60162-2098
(708) 449-2800
www.cauto.com
*List processing and
personalization services,
marketing database design,
building, and maintenance*

Iowa
Communications Data Services
2005 Lakewood Dr.
Boone, IA 50036
(515) 433-5000
www.cdsfulfillment.com
*Magazine and product
fulfillment, database
management, merge/purge, and
list maintenance*

Maryland
Group 1 Software Inc.
4200 Parliament Place,
    Suite 600
Lanham, MD 20706-1844
(800) 368-5806
www.g1.com
*Provider of database marketing,
demographic/geographic,
document production, and
address verification software*

Massachusetts
W.A. Wilde Co.
200 Sumner Street, Box 5838
Holliston, MA 01746
(508) 429-5515
www.wilde.com
*Database and list management
and specialized mailing services*

New Jersey
Automated Resources Group
    Inc.
135 Chestnut Ridge Road
Montvale, NJ 07645
(201) 391-1500
www.callargi.com
*List processing, merge/purge, list
maintenance, list rental,
subscription fulfillment*

New York
Hyaid Group
Six Commercial Street
Hicksville, NY 11801
(516) 433-3800
www.thehyaidgroup.com
*Direct mail consulting and
complete order processing for
continuity, one-shot credit card
charge systems, negative option
newsletter, and magazine agent
servicing systems.*

Direct Access Marketing
    Systems, Inc.
33 Queens Street
Syosset, NY 11791
(516) 364-2777
www.daxcess.com
Database service bureau

Pennsylvania
CC3
1044 Pulinski Road
Ivyland, PA 18974
(215) 675-2000
www.cc3.com
*Computer service bureau for
Direct Marketing companies*

D.A. Lewis Associates
3805 Old Easton Road
Doylestown, PA 18901
(215) 340-6800
www.dalewis.com
*Computer and mailing services
to the direct mail industry*

Texas
Affiliated Computer Services
    Inc.
2828 North Haskell Avenue
Dallas, TX 75204
(214) 841-6111
www.acs.com
*Data processing and transaction
services*

Dynamic Marketing Services
5884 Point West Drive
Houston, TX 77036
(713) 995-2200
www.kbm1.com
*Advanced data processing
technology in merge/purge, list
enhancement, marketing
database development, list rental
fulfillment*

Printers

Alabama
The Brown Printing Company
2734 Gunter Park Drive West
Montgomery, AL 36109
(800) 489-4700
www.1brownprintingco.com
*Specializes in long-run and
process color work*

California
Wallace Inc.
6811 Walker St.
La Palma, CA. 90623
(562) 926-7832
www.wallace.com
*Full-color direct mail advertising
pieces*

Connecticut
Allied Printing Services
  Incorporated
1 Allied Way
Manchester, CT. 06040
(860) 643-1101
www.alliedprinting.com
Large commercial printer

Banta Direct Marketing Group
Prindle Lane
Danbury, CT 06811
(203) 792-5500
*High-volume multi-color
commercial printer*

Florida
Modern Graphic Arts
1527 102nd Ave N.
Saint Petersburg, FL. 33716
(727) 579-1527
Commercial web printing

Georgia
Williams Printing Co.
1240 Spring Street NW
Atlanta, GA 30309
(404) 875-6611
*Complete design and production
services*

Idaho
Selkirk Press
1714 Industrial Drive
P.O. Box 875
Sandpoint, ID 83864
(208) 263-7523
Printing and related services

Illinois
R.R. Donnelley & Sons
  Company
77 West Wacker Drive
Chicago, IL 60601-1696
(312) 326-8000
www.rrdonnelly.com
*Full service printing and
computer service bureau*

Schawk
1600 East Sherwin Avenue
Des Plaines, IL 60018
(800) 621-1909
www.schawk.com
*Complete prepress services for
catalogs and direct mail*

Indiana
Newcomb Printing Services
605 East Ninth Street, Box A
Michigan City IN 46360
(219) 874-3201
www.newcombcreative.com
Business to business direct mail

Iowa
The Fisher Group
1250 North Center Point Road
Hiawatha, IA 52233
(319) 393-5405
www.fishergroup.com
*Catalogs, magazines, brochures,
self-mailers, letters, and bind-in
cards*

Kansas
Intelimail
14601 West 99th Street
Kansas City, KS 66215
(800) 255-6496
*Full-service printing, plus
person..ization and full mailing/
lettershop services*

Kentucky
Fetter Printing Co.
P.O. Box 33128
Louisville, KY 40232
(800) 234-4771
www.fetterprinting.com
*All services, from color
separations to binding*

Louisiana
Harvey Press Inc.
246 Harbor Circle
New Orleans, LA 70126
(504) 246-8474
www.harveypress.com
Commercial printing

Maine
The Maine Connection
903 Pendelton Point Road,
Box 285
Isleboro, ME 04848
(207) 734-6742
*Complete direct response
promotional mailings, from data
processing, printing, and mailing
all materials*

Maryland
McArdle Printing Co.
800 Commerce Drive
Upper Marlboro, MD 20774
(301) 390-8500
www.mcardleprinting.com
*Bindery and mailing services for
direct marketing, newsletters,
booklets and publications*

Que-Net Media
4414 Lottsford Vista Rd.
Lanham, MD 20706
(800) 683-5266
*Quality color separations and
desktop publishing interface*

Michigan
Inland Press
2001 West Lafayette
Detroit, MI 48216
(313) 961-6000
www.inlandpress.com
Commercial printing

Minnesota
Nahan Printing
7000 Saukview Drive
St. Cloud, MN 56302
(320) 251-7611
*Web, sheetfed, full service direct
mailer*

Missouri
Felco Printing and Mailing
1910 Walnut, Box 411667
Kansas City, MO 64108-1810
(816) 421-5164
*Typesetting, printing, and
mailing services*

Sayers Communications Group
9600 Manchester Road
St. Louis, MO 63119
(314) 968-5400
Full service direct mail printer

Nebraska
The Omaha Printing Co.
4700 "F" Street
Omaha, NE 68117
(402) 734-4400
www.omahaprint.com
*Printing and office product
supply*

New Hampshire
Concord Litho Company Inc.
92 Old Turnpike Road
Concord, NH 03301
(603) 225-3328
www.concordlitho.com
*Consumer package goods direct
response programs*

New Jersey
Applied Printer
77 Moonachie Avenue
Moonachie, NJ 07074
(201) 933-9600
www.appliedprinting.com
Full service direct mail printer

New York
Castlereagh, Inc
320 Buffalo Ave.
Freeport, NY 1152
(212) 926-1066
Sheet fed, full service printer

Georgian Press
175 Varick Street
New York, NY 10014
(212) 924-1763
*Full-spectrum direct mail web
and sheet-fed printing; state-of-
the-art digital imaging*

Precision Marketing
   Concepts, Inc.
469 President Street
Brooklyn, NY 11215
(718) 875-7300
Lettershop

Ohio
Champion Printing Inc.
3250 Spring Grove
Cincinnati, OH 45225
(513) 541-1100
www.championprintinginc.com
Total-service printer and mailer

Oregon
Graphics Arts Center
2000 NW Wilson Street
Portland, OR 97209
(503) 224-7777
www.gacnw.com
Full-service direct mail printer

Pennsylvania
MACORP Business Forms &
   Systems
Union Hill & New Dehaven
   Street
Conshohocken, PA 19428
(610) 941-6000
www.4macorp.com
*Direct mail, computer
fulfillment, and lettershop
services*

Schiff Printers
Box 95175, 300 Poplar Street
Pittsburgh, PA 15223
(412) 441-5760
www.schiffprinting.com
*One-to-six color books,
brochures, and direct mail pieces*

Texas
Focus Direct
9707 Broadway
San Antonio, TX 78217
(800) 299-9185
www.focusdirect.com
*Printing, lasering, lettershop,
data processing*

Lone Star Web Inc.
6730 Oakbrook Blvd.
Dallas, TX 75235
(214) 638-4946
www.lonestarweb.com
Direct mail printers

Williamson Printing
6700 Denton Drive
Dallas, TX 75235-9827
(214) 352-1122
www.wpcnet.com
*Business-to business direct mail
printer*

Utah
Banta Book Group
2600 North Mail Street
Spanish Fork, UT 84660
(801) 798-0880
www.spanish.banta.com
Commercial printer and bindery

Vermont
The Offset House
89 Sand Hill Road
Essex, VT 05451
(802) 878-4440
www.offsethouse.com
Prepress, printing, and mailing

Virginia
Balmar Printing & Graphics
   Virginia
2818 Fallfax Dr.
Falls Church, VA 22042
(703) 289-9000
www.balmar.com
*Offset printing, prepress and
binding*

Wisconsin
Arandell Schmidt Division of
   Arandell Corporation
N82 West 13118 Leon Rd.
Menomonee Falls, WI 53051
(262) 255-4400
www.arandell.com
*Offset printing, prepress and
binding*

Direct Marketing Training

Direct Marketing Boot Camp
Lois Geller
80 Park Avenue, Suite 16J
New York, NY 10017
(212) 697-4477
loisgeller@masongeller.com

New Media

Bigfoot Interactive
263 Ninth Ave., 10th Fl.
New York, NY ,10001
(212) 295-3000
www.bigfootinteractive.com
Email marketing services.

DoubleClick, Inc.
450 W. 33rd St.
New York, NY , 10010
(212) 271-2542
www.doubleclick.com
*Email marketing, Internet
advertising syndicate,
clickstream analysis*

NetGenesis
1 Alewife Center
Cambridge, MA 02140
(800) 982-6351
www.netgen.com
Online response analytics

NetCreations
379 West Broadway
Suite 202
New York, NY 10012
(212) 625-1370
www.netcreations.com
*Opt-in email marketing, list
services.*

International Services

ACTON International Ltd.
3401 NW 39th St
Lincoln, NE 68524
Phone: (402) 470-2909
Fax: (402) 470-2673
www.acton.com
International lists

Alexander Hamilton Institute
70 Hilltop Road
Ramsey, NJ 07446-1119
(201) 825-3377
International lists

Direct Media Inc.
200 Pemberwick Road
P.O. Box 4565
Greenwich, CT 06830
(203) 532-1000
www.directmedia.com
International lists

Infocore, Inc.,
285 N. El Camino Real,
   Suite 204,
Encinitas, CA 92024
(760) 634-5064
www.infocore.com
International lists and consulting

Mardev
2 Rector Street, 26th Floor
New York, NY 10006
(800) 545-8517
www.mardev.com
International lists

Worldwide Media Group Ltd.
Collins House
68-72 High Street
Burnham, Buckinghamshire
SL 17JT England
tel #: +44 (0) (208) 987-4405
International lists

MLA Ltd.
6/F, Sea Bird House
28 Wyndham Street
Central Hong Kong
tel #: 0086 852 2526 1208
www.mlalists.com
International lists

PacNet Services, Ltd.
Box 24
405-595 Howe Street
Vancouver, BC V6C 2T5
Canada
Tel: +1 604 689 0399
www.pacnetservices.com
International payment services

Catalog

US Department of Commerce
International Trade
   Administration
Attn. Direct Marketing
   Specialists
Washington, DC 20230
(202) 482-2000
www.doc.gov

Direct Marketing Associations

DMA National Office
1120 Avenue of the Americas
New York, NY 10036-6700
Phone (800) 273-8703
Fax (212) 768-4546
www.the-dma.org
chapters@the-dma.org

Australia
Australian Direct Marketing
   Association
PO Box 464
Kings Cross, New South
   Wales 1340
Australia
Phone: +61 2 936 8 0366
Fax: +61 2 936 8 0866
www.adma.com.au

Belgium
Direct Marketing Association
Buro Design Center
Esplanade Heysel Bte. 46
1020 Brussels
Belgium
Phone: +32 2 477 1797
Fax: +32 2 479 0679
www.bdma.be or
www.marketing.be

Brazil
Associacao Brasileira de
Marketing Direto (ABEMD)
Av. Sao Luis, 50 - Edificio
Italia - 13 andar - CJ 132B
01046-926 Sao Paulo
Brazil
Phone: +55 11 3129 3001
Fax: +55 11 3129 4300
www.abemd.org.br

Canada
Canadian Marketing
Association (The CMA)
1 Concorde Gate, 607
Don Mills, ON M3C 3N6
Canada
Phone: +1 416 391 2362
Fax: +1 416 441 4062
www.the-cma.org

Chile
Publimail
Vicuna Mackenna 2598
Santiago
Chile
Phone: +56 2 290 2600
Fax: +56 2 290 2601
www.publimail.com

Colombia
Asociacion Colombiana de
Mercadeo Directo (AMD)
Calle 35 No. 6-40
Santa Fe de Bogota
Colombia
Phone: +57 1 288 2688
Fax: +57 1 323 0007

France
Union Francaise du
Marketing Direct
Federation des Entreprises de
Vente a Distance (FEVAD)
60, Rue La Boetie
75008 Paris
France
Phone: +33 1 42 56 38 86
Fax: +33 1 45 63 91 95
www.fevad.com

Germany
Deutscher Direktmarketing
Verband (DDV) e.v.
Hasengartenstrasse 14
D-65189 Wiesbaden
Germany
Phone: +49 611 9779 310
Fax: +49 611 9779 399
E-mail: info@ddv.de
www.ddv.de

Hong Kong
The Hong Kong Direct
Marketing Association
Godfrey Rooke Associates
6th Floor, Sinoi Plaza
256 Gloucester Road
Causeway Bay
Hong Kong
Phone: +852 2850 5829
Fax: +852 2851 0227

Japan
Japan Direct Marketing
Association (JADMA)
32, Mori Building
3-4-30 Shiba Koen
Minato-ku, Tokyo, 105-0011
Japan
Phone: +81 3 3434 4700
Fax: +81 3 3434 4518
www.jadma.org

Mexico
Asociacion Mexicana de
Mercadotecnia Directa
(AMMD)
World Trade Center
Montecito 38, Piso 23,
Oficina 14
Col. Napoles
03810 Mexico, D.F.
Mexico
Phone: +52 5 488 3163
Fax: +52 5 488 3165

Pan European (FEDMA)
Federation of European Direct
Marketing (FEDMA)
439 Avenue de Tervueren
B-1150 Brussels
Belgium
Phone: +32 2 779 4268
Fax: +32 2 779 4269
www.fedma.org

Russia
Russian Direct Marketing
Association
Derbenevskaya 10/1 building 3
113 114 Moscow
Russia
Phone: +7 95 956 3148
Fax: +7 95 956 3592

Singapore
Direct Marketing Association
of Singapore (DMAS)
257 Selegie Road
11-283 Selegie Complex
188350
Singapore
Phone: +65 334 5860
Fax: +65 334 4980
www.dmas.org.sg

South Africa
Direct Marketing Association
of South Africa
2 Clamart Road
Richmond, Johannesburg
2006
South Africa
Phone:+ 27 11 482 6440
Fax: +27 11 482 1200
www.dma.org.za

Spain
Federación de Comercio
  Electrónico y Marketing
  Directo
Avenida Diagonal 437 5
08036 Barcelona
Spain
Phone: +34 3 240 4070
Fax: +34 3 240 3134
www.fecemd.org

Sweden
Stationsgatan 3
SE-931 31 Skelleftea
Sweden
Phone: +46 910 776 699
Fax: +46 910 777 296

Switzerland
Swiss Direct Marketing
  Association
b.a.s. AG, Digitalmarketing
  Service
Postfach
Switzerland
Phone: +41 62 839 11 11
Fax: +41 62 839 11 00
www.fedma.org

Taiwan
Taiwan Direct Marketing
  (TDMA)
3/F, No. 2 Min Sheng E. Road
Sec. 5
Taipei 105
Taiwan
Phone: +886 2 2746-1510
Fax: +886 2 2762-8187

United Kingdom
The Direct Marketing
  Association (UK)
70 Margaret Street
London W1W 8SS
United Kingdom
Phone: +44 207 321 2525
www.dma.org.uk

Index

I'd Like to Hear From You

Dear Lois,

I've just read the Revised and Expanded Edition of RESPONSE: *The Complete Guide to Profitable Direct Marketing.*

Can you direct me to the following resources in my area (computer service bureau, lettershop, etc.)

_____

_____

Can you send me more information about

_____

_____

I'd like some feedback on a Direct Marketing campaign I'm planning. My plans include

_____

_____

_____

(If you need more space, attach a separate sheet)

Please add me to your mailing list for all your free communications.

Name _____

Title _____

Company _____

Street _____

City_____State_____Zip_____

Email _____

Email: loisgeller@loisgeller.com

Or complete this form online when you visit us at www.loisgeller.com